THE
MAKING OF AMERICA
SERIES

YORK AND WESTERN YORK COUNTY

THE STORY OF A SOUTHERN EDEN

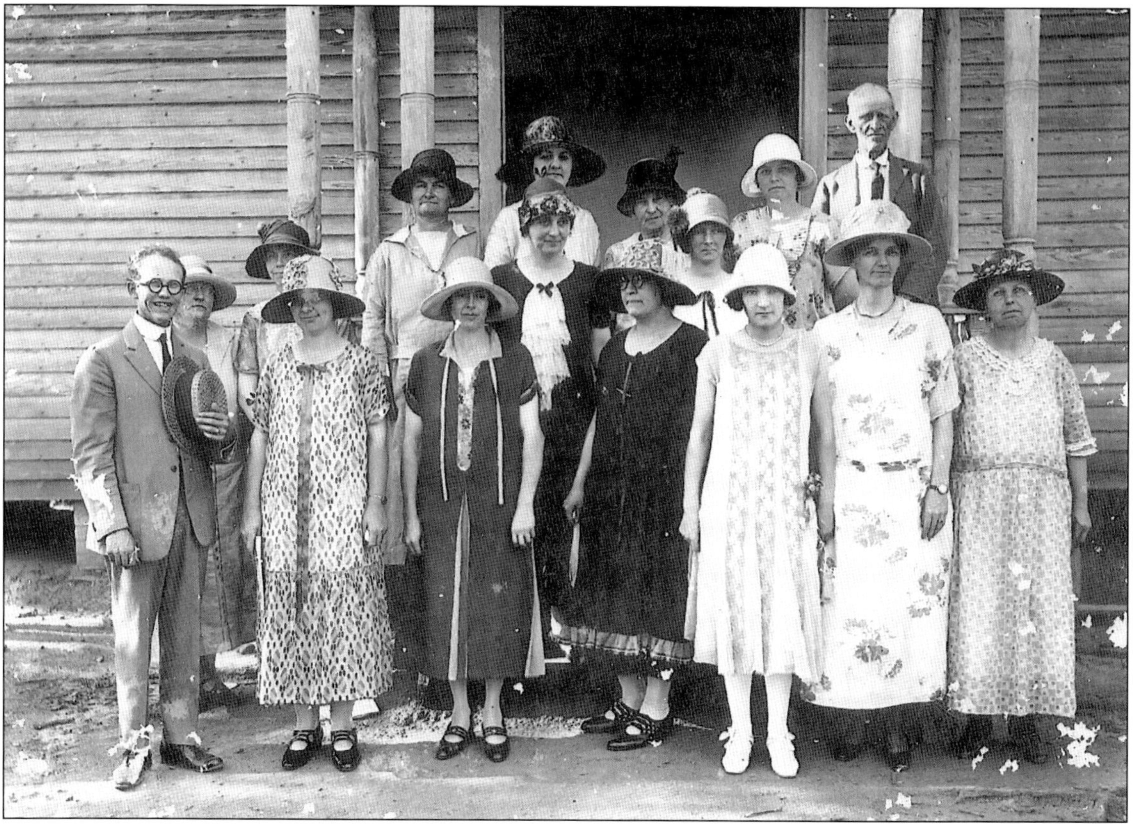

A second Baptist congregation was established in Hickory Grove c. *1890 and continued for a little more than 50 years. This photograph shows one of the early Sunday school classes.*

Cover: Civil defense was on everyone's mind during the Cold War years. Here at McConnells Fire Department, several men from Western York County have gathered to test new equipment for radiation detection.

THE

MAKING OF AMERICA

SERIES

YORK AND WESTERN YORK COUNTY

THE STORY OF A SOUTHERN EDEN

J. EDWARD LEE AND JERRY L. WEST

ARCADIA PUBLISHING

ISBN 978-0-7385-2358-3

Published by Arcadia Publishing
Charleston, South Carolina

Printed in the United States of America

Library of Congress Catalog Card Number: 2001089849

For all general information contact Arcadia Publishing at:
Telephone 843-853-2070
Fax 843-853-0044
E-Mail sales@arcadiapublishing.com
For customer service and orders:
Toll-Free 1-888-313-2665

Visit us on the Internet at www.arcadiapublishing.com

Dedication

For Ola Bankhead Lee, Ann Lee, Elizabeth Lee,
and the Bankheads of Bullock's Creek.
—J. Edward Lee

For my wife, Dianne Moss West,
daughters Renee W. Wickey and Crystal W. Gardner,
and grandchildren Elizabeth Wickey, John Wickey, James Wickey,
Allen Gardner, and Hanson Gardner.
—Jerry L. West

Contents

ACKNOWLEDGMENTS

The authors would like to thank the following for their support and guidance for this project: Jane Hood Adkins, Billy Alexander, Charles and Mary S. Bankhead, Ned Burgess, Bill Caldwell, Bobby Canupp, Midge Chambers, Rebecca T. Chambers, Ron Chepesiuk, Barbara S. Cranford, Tommy Cranford, Ann Evans, Charles Fant, Frances L. Faulkner, Lynn Faulkner, Phillip Faulkner, Sam and Gay Feemster, Jane Gilfillan, Annie Laura Hamrick, Jean Hill, Margaret Hood, Carl Hope, Joe Howe, Mickey Howe, Melvin Howell, John Ingram, Cindy Jonas, Helen Kennedy, Annette Langford, Jim Love, Robert "Bobby" Mendenhall, John W. Plexico, Joe Rainey, John Stringer Rainey, Thomas Ray, Faye Comer Russell, Michael Scoggins, Sharon Town Council, Jean Sherer, Heather South, Joy Sparrow, William Strain, Doris M. Thomas, Robert "Bobby" Walker, Harold Walker, Dianne M. West, Gina Price White, Erline B. Wilkerson, Winthrop University, *Yorkville Enquirer*, and Bill and Doris Youngblood.

Introduction

The drama *Little Foxes* was on national tour in 1941. One of the stopovers for the cast was Rock Hill, South Carolina's Winthrop College. The play's star was none other than 38-year-old Tallulah Bankhead, a sultry, dark-haired Alabaman who was nearing the pinnacle of her career. Bankhead, the daughter of Speaker of the United States House of Representatives William Brockman Bankhead, had stormed Hollywood and was destined to captivate American audiences in the 1944 film *Lifeboat*. Based on World War II, that movie starred Tallulah Bankhead as a steamy female survivor.

At Winthrop's newly constructed Byrnes Auditorium that spring, however, Tallulah dominated *Little Foxes*; her seductive Southern drawl was an instant hit in South Carolina. After her performance, the audience gave her a standing ovation as she bowed repeatedly for her fans. Then, as a reporter asked the Hollywood actress about her fast-paced life in California, Bankhead, in her trademark husky voice, reminded the journalist, "Dahling, I'm from Bullock's Creek!" The large crowd roared its approval when she cast off her Hollywood glamour and proudly disclosed she was one of them. At that moment, it would seem that Hollywood was not very far from the Western York County hamlet of Bullock's Creek.

Tallulah's great-great-grandfather, George Bankhead, had left South Carolina in the 1830s for a new land and a new start in Alabama. And her grandfather, John Hollis Bankhead, had served as an officer in the Confederate army before winning a United States Senate seat while his two sons, William Brockman (Tallulah's father) and John Hollis II, had succeeded their father in the United States Congress, John in the Senate and William in the House. Still, the Bankheads of Alabama were people whose roots were planted in the fertile soil of Bullock's Creek. According to Tallulah's own declaration, it would seem that she and her family had never, really, left Western York County. That fact is what everyone in the Winthrop auditorium in 1941 knew; they were family with the flamboyant actress—she was a daughter of the red hills of Western York County.

Western York County is like that. People may physically move away—for whatever reason—but they, in a sense, never spiritually leave the region. Here, blood and soil mingle, and it can never be separated. So many return to this area, seeking their roots along the waterways of the Broad River, Bullock's Creek,

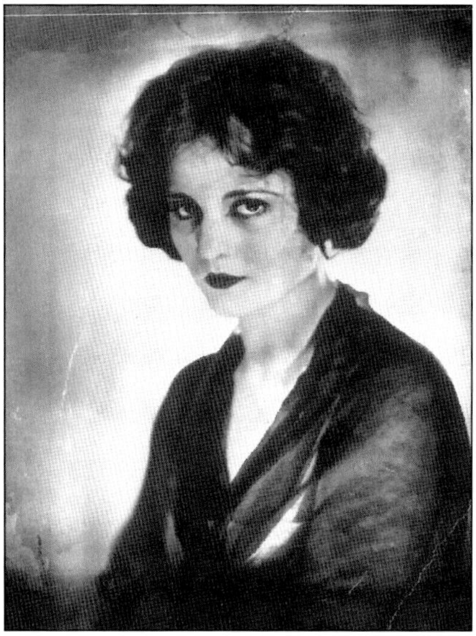

Sultry movie star Tallulah Bankhead was well aware that her heritage and family roots connected her to the waters of Bullock's Creek and the red hills of Western York County.

Kings Creek, and Clarks Fork. They roam the countryside like lemmings under a passionate spirit and up the waterways like salmon seeking the waters of their origin. For hours, they pour over volumes of old records seeking that initial attachment to the land and its people.

As someone once said about the people of the South Carolina piedmont, "they spent their time thinning the soil and thickening the blood." Steeped in the Bible, they use religious metaphors to describe the land and its children: "God's Country," "the Promised Land," "the Chosen People."

Where cotton was once king, the blood continues to run thick with a fierce Jeffersonian independence. And sometimes, during political seasons, that crimson flow may boil, but after elections, the sun parts the clouds, the people reunite in the harmonious qualities of "the Promised Land."

The communities of Western York County are sprinkled across the map like so many jewels: Sharon, Hickory Grove, Smyrna, Hopewell, Bullock's Creek, Hoodtown, Blairsville, and the county seat of York. Although each of them may sparkle with its own distinctive qualities of independence and competitiveness, they never forget the fact that they are cousins in every sense. Mississippi writer Eudora Welty speaks of "a sense of place." She might as well be describing this Carolina paradise. In Western York County, there is a strong sense that a potent concoction is created by the red soil, church pews, cemeteries filled with heroes, laughing children, summers filled with rigorous athletic competition, covered-dish suppers, the bounty of farmers, and the dreams of bold entrepreneurs. For thousands of years, from the time brave Catawba Indians hunted the forests and fished in the streams, this "sense of place" has enriched the people of Western York County and beyond. Thus, Tallulah Bankhead, and countless others, before and afterward, have felt the beckoning call of this Southern Eden.

1. Land as Red as Blood

The history of Western York County, South Carolina, begins with the Catawba Indians, the ancient "people of the river" who have had a presence here since the area was covered by a canopy of green. It appears they ventured southward between 12,000 and 10,000 years ago following the big game of North Carolina's Yadkin River Valley. While the Catawbas are most often linked to the river that bears their name and the present site of the Catawba Indian Nation, these Native Americans also hunted, fished, and camped in the western section of York County. Thus, they can be considered the "people of the Broad River" as well as the Catawba—the Broad being the eastern boundary of the Cherokee Nation. For hundreds of years, prior to the arrival of white Europeans, the Catawbas enjoyed the bounty of Western York County. Early on, they hunted deer and bison and raised gourds and squash. Later, as part of the Woodland Culture, they raised corn and shaped beautiful clay pottery, an artistic and practical creation that still is distinctive of the Catawba people.

By the Archaic Period (10,000–3,000 years ago), the descendants of the early hunters lived in forests and near lakes and rivers that had been produced by the end of the Ice Age. While permanent Catawba villages lined the upper and lower Catawba River, these people hunted and trekked across the region that we call Western York County, the geographical area which stretches from the present city of York westward to South Carolina's Broad River.

During the Woodland Period (3,000 to 1,000 years ago), other Native Americans moved into the Carolinas from the west. These Indians spoke a language known as Siouian, and they are related to the Sioux of the Great Plains. It was these people that European colonists first encountered in the 1500s. About 100 years earlier, sometime in the 1400s, other Indians, this time from the Mississippi River, flowed across the southern piedmont. These Mississippians built large earthen mounds that served as temples and insisted that the other Indians adopt their religious practices. The earlier people, however, resisted the Mississippians—defending their independence while refining their pottery skills. Although these mound-builders have long ago faded into history, evidence of their presence remains in several sites along the Broad River in Western York County.

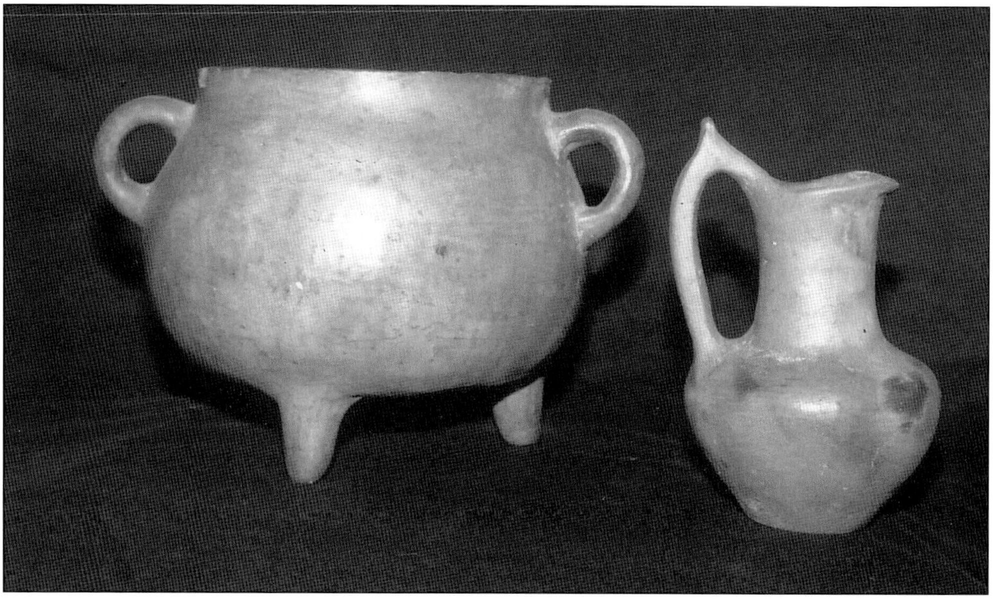

This fine clay pot and sculpted pitcher are examples of typical pottery craftsmanship of the Catawba Indian Nation.

The arrival of European explorers, searching for gold, changed the dynamics of the southern piedmont. In the spring of 1540, Spain's Hernando de Soto traveled through the Catawba Nation. Seeking cities of gold, these Spaniards did not hesitate to kidnap or kill Native Americans in order to persuade them to divulge the whereabouts of gold deposits. Twenty-six years later, another Spaniard, Juan Pardo, followed de Soto's trail. Pardo was in no hurry; his soldiers built forts and stayed among the Catawbas. By the early 1570s, Indian warriors expelled Pardo's troops, and the natives once again controlled their Southern Eden.

For another century, until the 1670 founding of Charles Town by loyal supporters of England's monarch King Charles II, the Catawbas dominated Western York County. The new European arrivals, while not obsessed with gold, sensed the natural richness of the region. They ventured more than 250 miles inland from Charles Town to trade with the Catawbas.

The southern piedmont, which Englishman John Lawson saw in 1700, was indeed a paradise. For two months, he canoed and walked 500 miles through the heart of Catawba country. The soil was rich and the oak trees were so enormous that turkeys roosted in their upper branches, out of range of Lawson's gun. He marveled at "Panthers, Tygers, Wolves, and other Beasts of Prey." Ducks and pigeons blocked the sunlight when they flew overhead. The land, Lawson commented, was "as red as blood."

The collision of cultures changed both ethnic groups, Indian and white. Despite Catawba leader King Hagler's 1754 pledge of "Brotherly love and peace," the natives endured unbrotherly greed from land grabbers and diseases brought by the white man. South Carolina Governor James Glen revealed in 1747 that the Catawbas "are the bravest Fellows on the Continent of North America" but they could not resist smallpox, rum, and the fast talk of land speculators. Thus, by the 1763 assassination of King Hagler by marauding Indians, the Catawba Indian Nation entered a period of decline. Despite guarantees from whites, the Catawbas saw their once enormous empire carved into smaller and smaller slices, whittled away until the Catawbas became ghosts of their former selves. This injustice would not be corrected until 1993, when, under threat of lawsuits, a settlement restored some of the Catawba land and gave these first people of Western York County economic and political security.

The only record of an Indian attack in Western York County occurred in 1754 on Buffalo Creek in what is now Cherokee County. This account is recorded in volume II of Logan's *History of South Carolina*, as related to S.B. Latham of Chester County in 1870. On October 7, 1754, Captain James Frances wrote the following to Governor Glen of South Carolina reporting the particulars of a savage attack on settlers by a party of "French Indians":

> May it please your excellency, I should have written sooner concerning this cruel murder, perpetrated, as I suppose by a camp of French Indians . . . On a stream called Buffalo creek, supposed by some to be in North Carolina, and by others, in the southern province, at the house of a

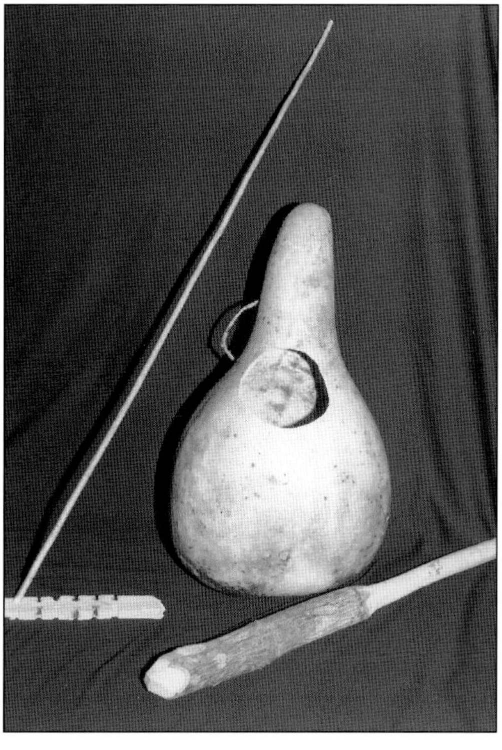

These tools, replicated by Thomas C. Ray of Rock Hill, are similar to those used by the early Catawba Indians; they are, from left to right, as follows: a throwing stick, a gourd for carrying water, and a fire-making implement.

Mr. Outtery, a sociable, hospitable man, and of good resolution, where several families, traveling from the north, had put up; at the same unfortunate time a family from the neighborhood had also come in to wait the return of a young couple, who had gone some forty or more miles to a Justice of the Peace to be married. In the meantime a party of sixty Indians came upon these unhappy people, twenty-one in all, and murdered sixteen of them on the spot. Their bodies were found scattered around in a circumference of some two or three hundred yards, the remaining five were either carried off or killed at a distance from the place where they were attacked. They had not yet been heard from; among them are a woman and three children-—of the fifth one I could get no account.

This sir, is the exact story of this unhappy affair, as far as it relates to the murdered people. Immediately after dispatching these, the savages killed all the hogs, fowls and cattle about the premises and heaped their carcasses upon the dead bodies of the men and women. Twenty head of horses, some of them very valuable, that belonged to the travelers were driven off.

But a single one of the butchered people fell by a gunshot; the rest were all killed by means of arrows and tomahawks, many of which were found sticking in their bodies. The first who discovered the bloody deed were the newly married couple, who returned soon after it was all over, and the Indians just gone. They were completely panic stricken but staid long enough to bury the dead, by throwing them hurriedly into a well, which was near the house.

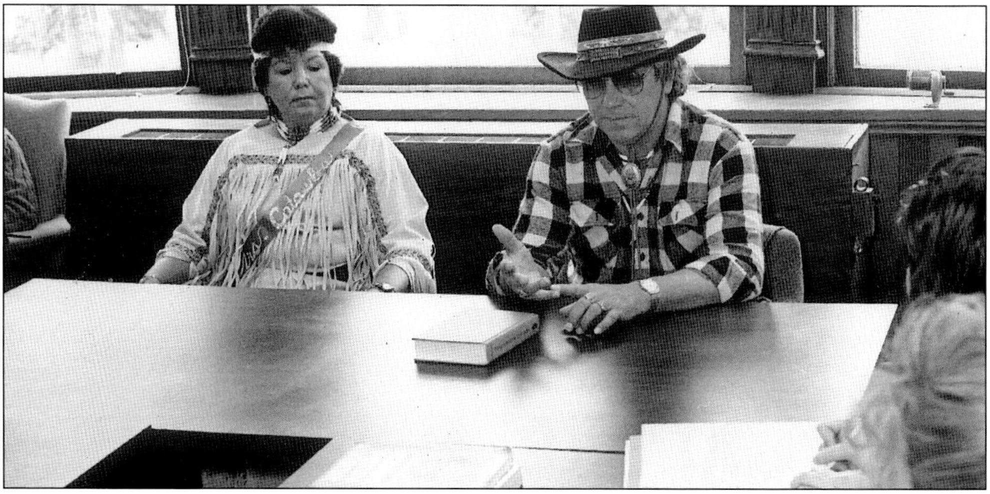

Chief Gilbert Blue is the present leader of the Catawba Indian Nation, and he has served in that capacity since his election to that esteemed position in 1975. Chief Blue's grandfather Samuel Taylor Blue had led the nation before him.

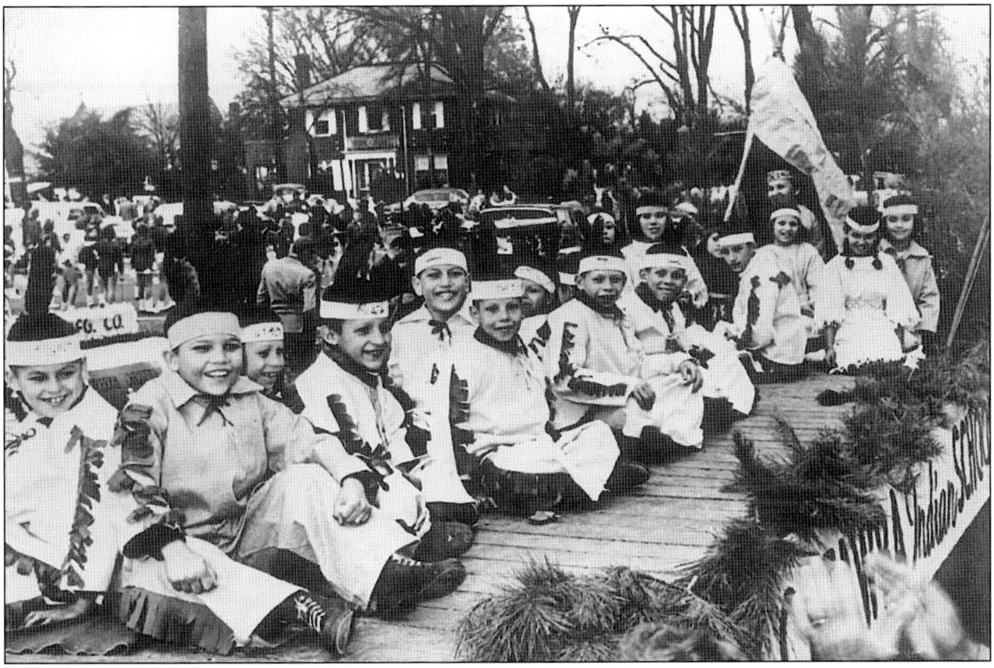

These children from the Catawba Indian School are seen on a Christmas parade float in Rock Hill. (Courtesy Winthrop University Archives.)

> Buffalo Creek is about five miles from where the path crosses the Broad River, that leads from the Cherokees to the Catawbas and Guttery's plantation some twenty miles from that ford which is one hundred miles from the Saluda settlement.

The governor made serious efforts to recover the captured children. A year later he wrote to one of the traders in the Nation to rescue from a party of Savannahs a little white child that was supposed to be one of the kidnapped. A short time later the governor received a letter from John Elliott informing him that a party of Savannahs came to his place and had two white children with them. They claimed that they had obtained them from the Indians who had committed the Buffalo Creek massacre. Elliott made a desperate attempt to get the children from the party, but was unsuccessful and the children were never heard of after that.

The relationship between whites and people of color has sometimes been tense, but long before Western York County took shape, successful efforts were made to clarify boundaries and prevent disputes over questions of land ownership. Treaties were made by Colonial Governor James Glen of South Carolina with the Cherokee and Catawba Nations to live in peace and share the bounty of this Southern Eden. This cooperative spirit, in a "land as red as blood," stands in stark contrast with other regions where whites and Native Americans clashed in a sea of greed.

2. Mastering the River

The native people of Western York County were determined to master the Broad River, an ancient waterway that serves as the present boundary with neighboring Union County and the eastern portion of Cherokee County. In prehistoric times, the Broad River was an invaluable source of fish and game for the Indians. They fearlessly sailed up and down this waterway and its tributaries in search of food such as salmon and trout.

Members of DeSoto's expedition recorded that the Native Americans used dugout canoes to navigate the artery. As a means of transportation, the dugout has been traced to 5,000 years ago in Florida. By the time the Spaniards trekked through Carolina in search of gold, the largest canoes were reported to have a capacity of 75 to 80 people, with 25 oarsmen on each side and room for perhaps 30 warriors. The procedure for constructing such vessels was precise. French accounts of the process stated, "To make these they kept a fire burning at the foot of a tree called cypress until the fire burned through the truck and the tree fell; next they put fire on top of the fallen tree at the length they wished to make their boat." The natives scraped the tree and cleaned with water and smoothed it out in preparation for its voyage. The French observers concluded, "With these they go hunting and fishing with their families and go to war or wherever they want to go."

The natives built smaller boats, occasionally adapting technology used by the white settlers. The French *pirogue* was hewn from cypress or cottonwood and measured from 10 to 50 feet in length. Its hull was thinner than the native vessels and could be used in the more shallow areas of the Broad River because of its light weight. Another period vessel, the *bateau*, was European in origin, also. This boat was small and flat-bottomed. *Bateaux* ranged in length from 12 to 80 feet, averaging between 20 or 40 feet in length. Its pilots used oars, settling poles, or square sails to move up and down the Broad River. This type of boat lacked ribs and keel. It could carry up to 40 tons of cargo.

As the Native American cultures and white setters collided in Western York County in the late eighteenth century, others types of water craft appeared. Often referred to as flats, family boats, arks, Kentucky Boats, or tobacco boats, flatboats were used to transport settlers, household goods, and livestock down river to

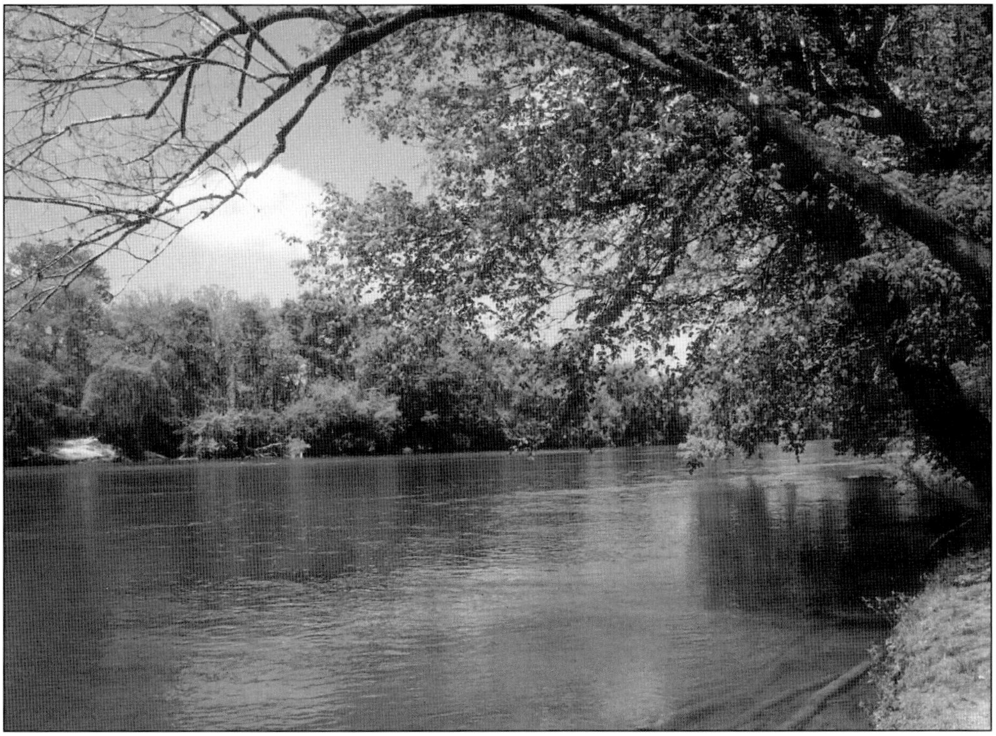

The Broad River flows placidly and majestically by Smith's Ford as it has for eons. The history of Western York County has ebbed and flowed along these waters.

market. Additionally, flatboats carried flour, bacon, cider, pottery, whiskey, tobacco, meat, butter, iron, hemp, and slaves. These vessels sometimes served as mobile country stores, stopping at landings as they drifted down the waterway to sell goods to people who were building a new life in the New World. The flatboats were difficult to propel up river so, after they were emptied of their occupants and cargo, they were sold for lumber, helping lay the foundation for this Southern Eden.

The Broad River, with its bounty, attracted settlers from Europe, men and women who, thirsting for a second chance at prosperity, converged in the New World from several directions. By the mid-eighteenth century, these people were making their way down the Great Wagon Road from William Penn's "Holy Experiment" Pennsylvania, through Virginia's picturesque Shenandoah Valley, past North Carolina villages Salisbury and Charlotte, and establishing themselves along the Broad River. Other immigrants advanced inland from Charleston, following the footsteps John Lawson took in 1700. By 1763, Great Britain had triumphed over France in the Seven Years' War, a conflict to decide the fate of North America, and the influx of English-speaking people (some of whom were not so sure about their love of the Mother County) into the Carolina back country accelerated.

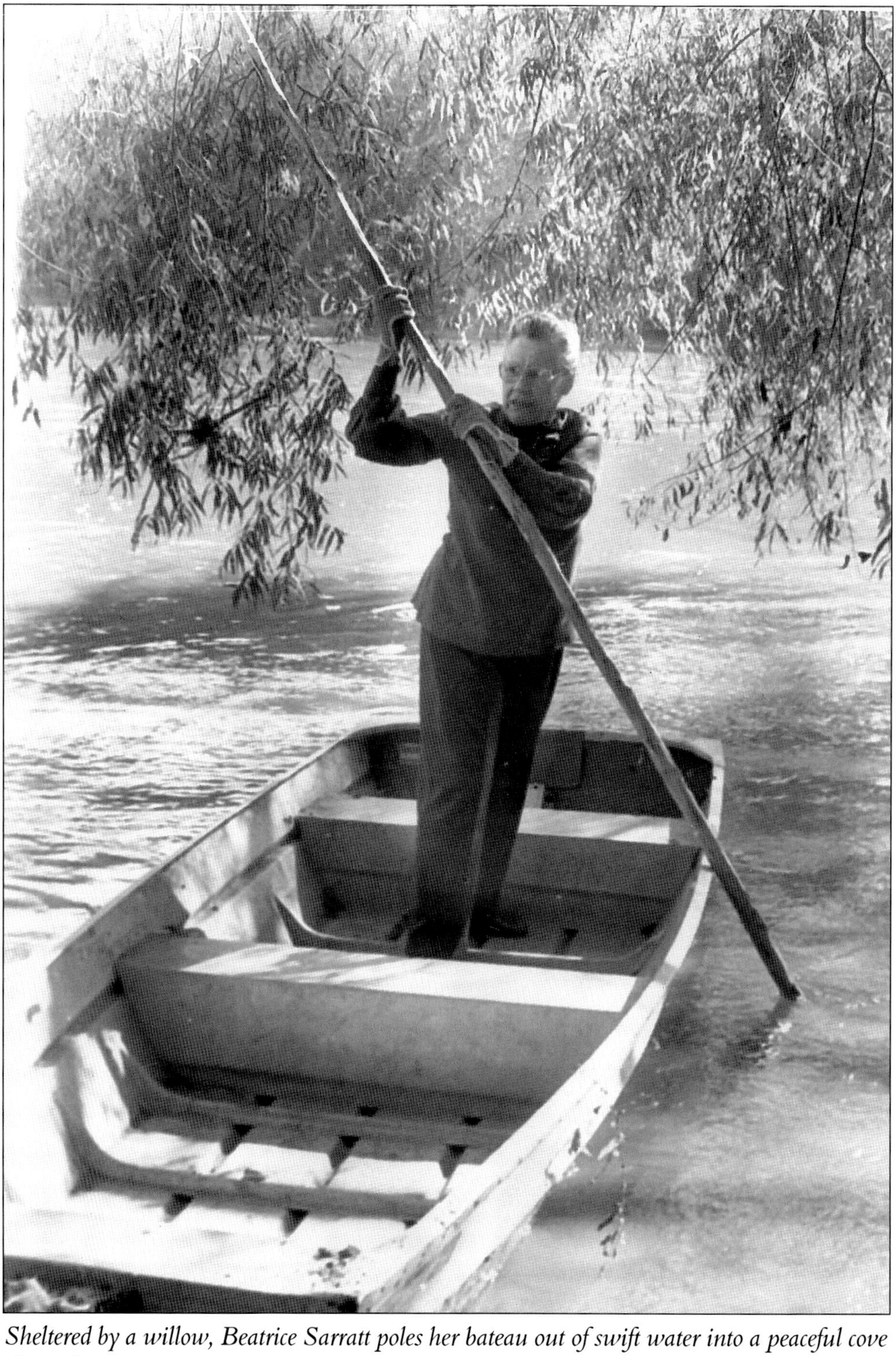

Sheltered by a willow, Beatrice Sarratt poles her bateau out of swift water into a peaceful cove along the river.

Connecting Western York County to settlements on the west bank of the Broad River were several natural fords that had been used for hundreds, and perhaps thousands, of years by American Indians. Near the mouth of Kings Creek was the Cherokee Ford, farther south was Smith's Ford, then Hamilton's Ford, and into what is now Chester County was Love's Ford, often used by folks in the extreme southwest corner of York County.

When whites came into the area they immediately took advantage of these natural fords, connecting them to settlements and markets by a network of ridge roads. Most of these fords were safe to travel; however, Love's Ford was often avoided prior to the Revolution, as it was a favorite hangout for unsavory people. The area was covered with dense canebrakes and the surrounding hills were a tangle of reeds and pea vines nearly to the summit. This provided an ideal landscape for highwaymen to lie in wait to do their dirty work.

Smith's Ford was well used by those traveling from Union and York Counties. By the mid-1770s, the Provisional Congress had established a magazine on the York side to store provisions for refugees from Indian attacks in the Fairforest district of Union County. On June 8, 1775, the Congress at Charleston ordered 100 barrels of flour, each weighing 100 pounds, to be placed at the site. Captain Samuel Watson, a Congressional representative from the New Acquisition, was on hand to receive and oversee the shipment.

During the Revolution, the magazine became a Patriot's camp. While camped here in August 1780, Colonel McDowell learned that nearly 500 Tories were encamped at Musgrove's Mill and Colonels Williams, Shelby, and Clarke were detached and launched a surprise attack resulting in a victory.

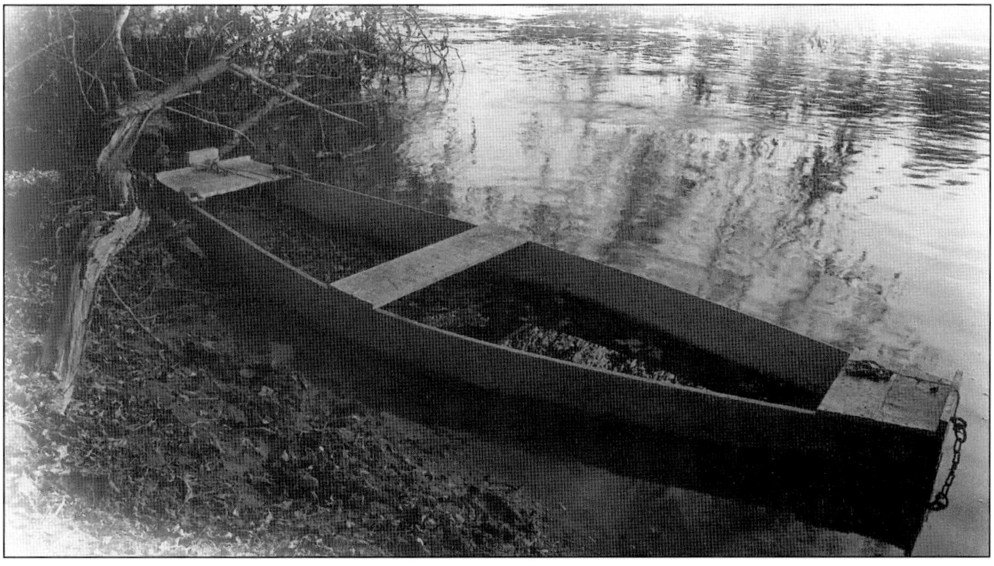

Flat-bottom boats like this bateau, built by Anon Patterson, was a common working craft seen in bygone days of the Broad River.

It was at Hamilton's Ford where British Colonel Banastre Tarleton camped on the evening of January 17, 1780, to lick his wounds from defeat at Cowpens by General Daniel Morgan. From there he moved eastward about 10 miles to Cornwallis's camp near the Bullock's Creek Meeting House, and delivered the details of his defeat to the Earl.

The Broad River with its rich bottom lands was an important feature to the landscape of Western York County. The river itself provided a natural highway to the markets farther south, while the bottoms produced abundant corn crops and the surrounding red hill supported the reign of King Cotton.

In 1785, the South Carolina Senate passed an ordinance for improving the navigation of the Broad. That ordinance required the cost of the operation to be paid by residents living within 10 miles of the river. However, four years later, 75 men from York County sent a petition to the legislature requesting that the limits be extended to 20 miles on the York side and 15 miles on the Union County side. Although the names of those on the petition are not inclusive of all Western York County families, they are representative of those in the area:

James Bale
James Bankhead
Moses Beatty
James Beuford
LeRoy Beuford
Linsford Beuford
Philemon Beuford
Thadberd Beuford
Warren Beuford
George Black
Jacob Black
John Black
Robert Black
Andrew Brown
John Brown
Stewart Brown
Edward Byers
William Byers
William Byers Jr.
Robert Crenshaw
Stephen Crenshaw
John Davis
Simon Davis
David Dickey
James Dickey
William Dickey
Allen Dowdle
Robert Elliott
Drury Goins
John Good
Thomas Gordon
William Hall
William Hall Jr.
Alexander Hamilton
David Hamilton
John Hamilton
William Hamilton
William Hendley
Philip Hinton
William Johnsly
Charles Johnson
John Kennedy
George King Sr.
Samuel King
Stephen Kirk
Francis Kirkpatrick
David Leach
James Lindsay
John Love
Kennedy McCann
William McCluney
Ephraim McLean
Adam Meek
James Meek
Thomas Mitchell
William Philbeck
George Plexico
Joseph Robison
Matthew Rogers
Robert Rutherford Jr.
Hezikiah Salmar
Benjamin Savage
James Sims Jr.
David Smith
Nickles Tessinger
William Thomas
Edward Tilman, Captain
Alex Tomb
David Tomb
J.E.Totler
Thomas Williamson
William Williamson
Hugh Wilson
Thomas Wood

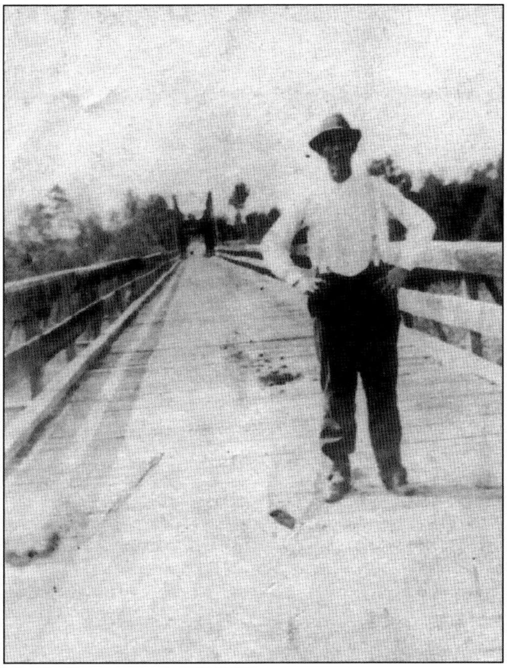

Grover Robinson is seen here in 1915 posing on the two-year-old Irene Bridge. This "new" bridge replaced Howell's Ferry, which had been used since the mid-eighteenth century.

Three years later, in 1788, the General Assembly granted a charter to a company in Union County to keep the Broad River clear as far north as Ninety-Nine Islands and Grindal's Shoals on the Pacolet River. Although the company headed by Colonel Thomas Brandon was authorized to build locks, dams, and canals and to charge tolls, they probably did little more than dredge the streams and clear rocks and debris from the channels. Bandon's company folded in 1801, and at that time the state appropriated $10,000 to clear and improve the two waterways.

Beginning with the nineteenth century, the Broad River basin reached a stable economy that integrated into larger trading systems through exportation of its crops. Western York County's main export crop was cotton, followed by pig iron produced in its several iron furnaces along the river, flour, bacon, whiskey, cider, tobacco, hemp, and slaves. While overland transportation of bailed cotton was expensive and time consuming, a distance of only a few miles from the Broad made it preferable, as it was the handiest.

The only major obstruction on the Broad between Columbia and Ninety-Nine Islands was the upper and lower Lockhart Shoals. The river traveler would experience nearly a 46-foot drop in 1.5 miles and combined with the adjoining rapids, 51 feet in 2 miles. In summer, or dry weather, the lack of water often caused boats to end up on the rocks, while in wet weather, or high water, the boatman would have difficulty in controlling his craft.

After various measures to improve passage over the shoals, in 1819, the General Assembly, launched an expensive program ($1.9 million) to improve river travel. The following year, a canal was begun around both shoals at Lockhart on the

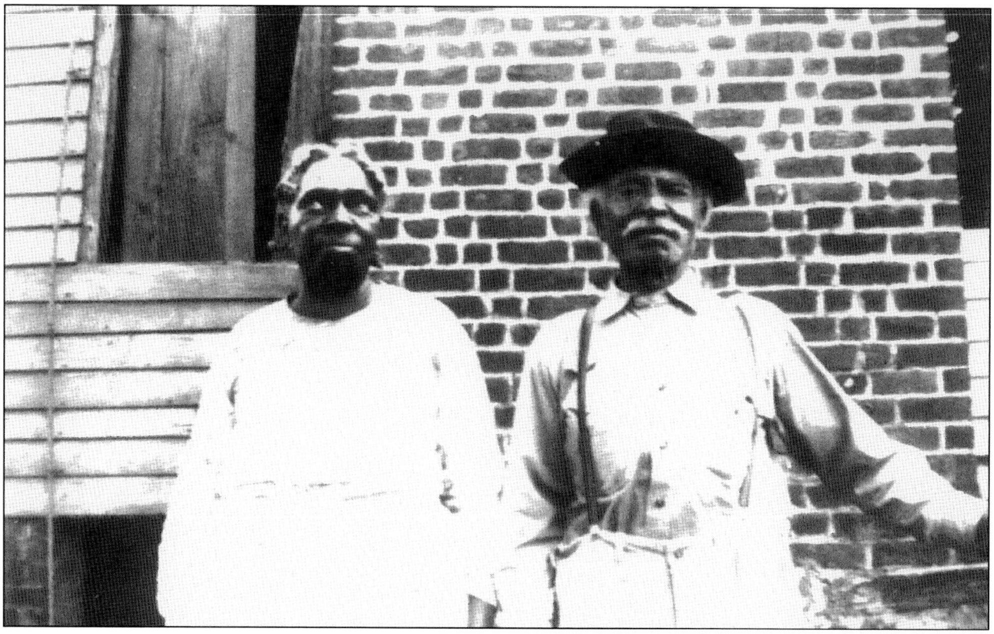

This rare photograph of former slaves of the Whisonant family shows "Aunt Adeline" and "Uncle Abe" Smith. The image was taken at the couple's home at Smith's Ford on the Broad River.

Union County side. Although hampered by floods and freshets, the canal was completed by 1823, but was not opened until January 1826 because of disputes with contractors. Robert Mills, in his atlas work of the sate, described the canal with its seven locks and granite walls as suitable "for boats containing sixty bales of cotton." New locks were installed in 1844 and again in 1851, but the canal was abandoned during the 1850s. But as late as 1889, J.C. Farr, who lived near Pinckneyville, shipped over 200 bales to Charleston "on those old cotton boats . . . on Broad River."

Better roads and the advent of the railroad to the upper Piedmont effectively precluded river travel. Although its construction in 1915 was too late to blame obstruction to river travel, the Lockhart Dam certainly hindered any future plans. By 1922, the water was being diverted to produce electric power to the mills located on the Union side.

Praise of the Broad River as a waterway—real or envisioned—was still being sung in 1883 when "Ramble" took an excursion down the river from Gaffney. Near Cherokee Ford, he spoke of the remnants of old iron works that went defunct after the Civil War. At the time of his river excursion, it was projected that a 50,000-spindle cotton mill was going to be built near the point because of the immense waterpower that was available there. Two miles farther south, he reached the site of the old Kings Mountain Rolling Mill, one of the first of its kind in the United States. Near this point, on the York side of the river, was the

Cherokee Cotton Mill's village and mill, which had been in operation for only 18 months at the time. "Ramble" remarked, "A neat village has sprung up, with church and school privileges, on the ruins of the old ironworks." A mile or so below the mill, he saw a number of flour and corn mills, also on the York side, and remarked the following about the swift water and it potential power:

> From Cherokee Ford to Smith's Ford, a distance of several miles, the great river pitches down over shoal after shoal, and sites for factories are found . . . on both banks. Between Smith's Ford and Cherokee Ford, there are ninety-nine islands, varying in size, and elevation above the water. Many of these islands contain fine locations for summer residences and hotels; and on these islands will stand, someday, a series of summer resorts—a city in the river, communication with the different adjacent islands being carried on by bridges spanning the section of the river between the islands, or by ferry boats.

After the Revolution, the site of Pinckneyville was established in 1791 as a judicial center for a four-county area encompassing the counties of Chester, Spartanburg, Union, and York. Located at the confluence of the Broad and Pacolet Rivers, hopes were that the town would develop as a governmental and commercial center with the growth of river traffic. This, however, would never materialize. Within a few years, the same General Assembly that created the

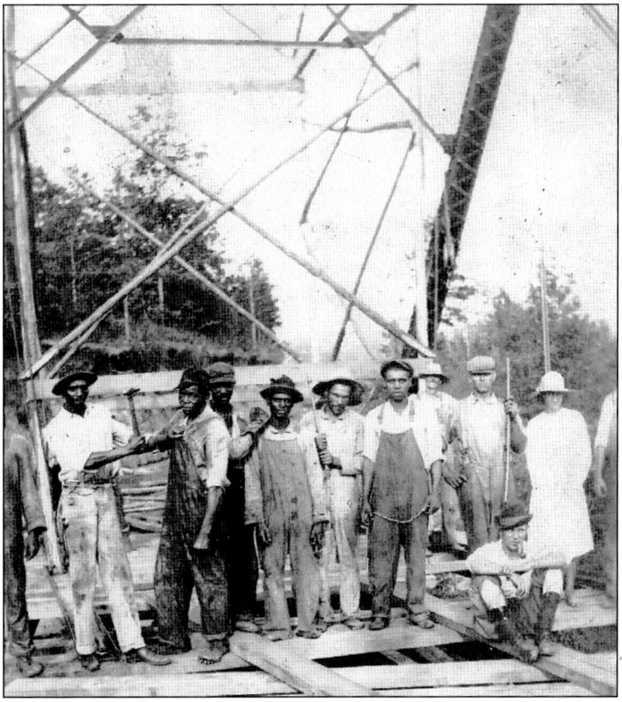

In 1916, torrential rains resulted in a county-wide flood that destroyed many bridges as well as much personal property, crops, and livestock. Shortly after that flood, a work crew paused from their work for this photograph on the Irene Bridge.

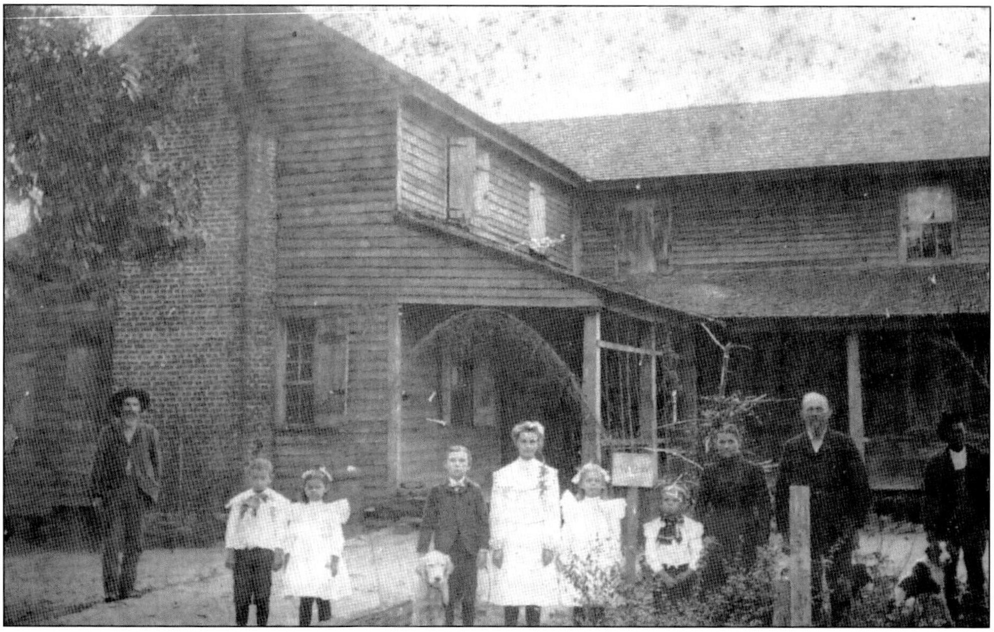

The family of John Jefferson Robinson made their home in the Whitley-Mitchell House near Howell's Ferry in 1915. The families in this area depended on the river for both commerce and recreation.

courthouse town passed an act that created further judicial changes and the town of Pinckneyville gradually faded out of existence. Other towns, Yorkville and Chesterville, for example, eclipsed Pinckneyville.

Another failed attempt at establishing a town on the west bank of Broad River occurred at approximately the same time. Englishman Joseph Reid established the town of Reidsville between Pinckneyville and Lockhart Shoals on the model of an English village. Eventually, several businesses located themselves in Reidsville and the town had the distinction of having the first brick houses in Union County. Tradition has it that the town was deserted because of a monster that lived in the deep waters of the river and would unnerve the residents with its nighttime roars.

In 1809, William D. Martin recorded his travels as he passed through York County. His reflections on the countryside and its people, though not always complimentary, gives a sense of how the Broad River Basin area was developing in the post Revolutionary years. After leaving the courthouse town of Union, he passed through Pinckneyville and traveled up the river to Smith's Ford. Crossing the ford and the home of Judge William Smith, he journeyed several miles into York County before stopping to "breakfast at a miserable Irish hovel seven miles from York." This would have put him just north of the town of Sharon. Martin was not impressed with the lack of cleanliness, which he claimed was a national trait of the Scots-Irish. His hostess was homely, poorly dressed, and prepared her guest's breakfast with a child slung on one hip. She was assisted by an "overgrown girl, very ugly, in a petticoat and wrapper, the original color of which could not without difficulty be ascertained, in consequence of the dirt." He described the scene of his meal as being visited with half-naked children and dogs and cats that continually argued over some position near the fireplace. The house was so wretched that it would "deprive anyone of an appetite," so he settled for a biscuit and "some colored water, intended . . . for coffee."

As soon as the people of Western York County had settled their disputes with Great Britain, mastered the river, and had their farms up and running, they began concerning themselves with their children's education. Throughout the area, men of some education rose to meet the people's demand for schools. At Bullock's Creek, Reverend Joseph Alexander established one of the Upcountry's first classical schools as a college preparatory experience for young men. While this school was exceptional, most schools in the area were teaching grammar and high school levels.

One of Western York County's earliest schoolteachers was Robert Love Jr. A contract to conduct his school, between Love and a number men of the same general community, serves as an example:

> Twelve months after date, we the undernamed co-promise to pay or cause to be paid unto Robert Love, Jun. On order the several sums annex'd to our names to be discharged, Good merchandisable produce, Good pork, Good ground Dry corn, Good Beef Cattle or a Milk Cow or cows or any good Country produce, the corn to be rated at three bushels for a Dollar. Then Love is to Discharge the Duty of a English Schoolmaster, faithfully here amongst us for the Term and Share of one whole year to the best of his skill & ability in English learning in spelling, Reading, writing & arithmetic & we the undernamed is to make the s'd Love a School of twenty scholars with the privilege of a Open School. We also agree that if any Lawful fault by either Employers or master & s'd fault not amended there are to be clear of each other at the end of six months with paying s'd mater full half of s'd salary, we are also to give four Dollars each scholar.

The contract was signed by the following: Asahel Enloe, James Templeton, John Love, Edward Moorehead, William Watson, Hugh Allison, Samuel Turner, James Venables, Isaac Enloe, Joseph Hopkins, James Watson, Andrew Love, Robert Love, and John Venables.

Another early school was located in Blairsville. On August 3, 1818, 18-year-old Robert Young Russell submitted a set of articles for establishing a school at the home of his stepfather, James Hogg. Having completed his high school equivalent education, he conducted Blairsville's first school in a reclaimed corn crib for one year. Returning to his studies, he attended Hopewell Academy one or two sessions and then became its teacher for a short time. By 1830, the Blairsville

Academy was permanently established by Reverend Aaron Williams, the pastor of Salem and Bullock's Creek Presbyterian Churches. This school was located only 1 mile from where Russell had established his school on the Hogg Farm. When Russell became pastor of the Bullock's Creek Independent Presbyterian Church, he became the headmaster of the Blairsville Academy, remaining in that capacity until his death in the late 1850s.

Like many other locations throughout Western York County, the school at Blairsville went through numerous stages until it became part of the public school system. In the early 1920s, during an early period of consolidation, the Blairsville School and others went out of existence, as they were absorbed into larger local schools.

The Broad River, winding its way into South Carolina from Cleveland and Rutherford Counties, North Carolina, has been an economic, social, and political lifeline since the arrival of Native Americans. It is *the river* of Western York County, bringing commerce and water, as well as a natural boundary between counties in the two Carolinas.

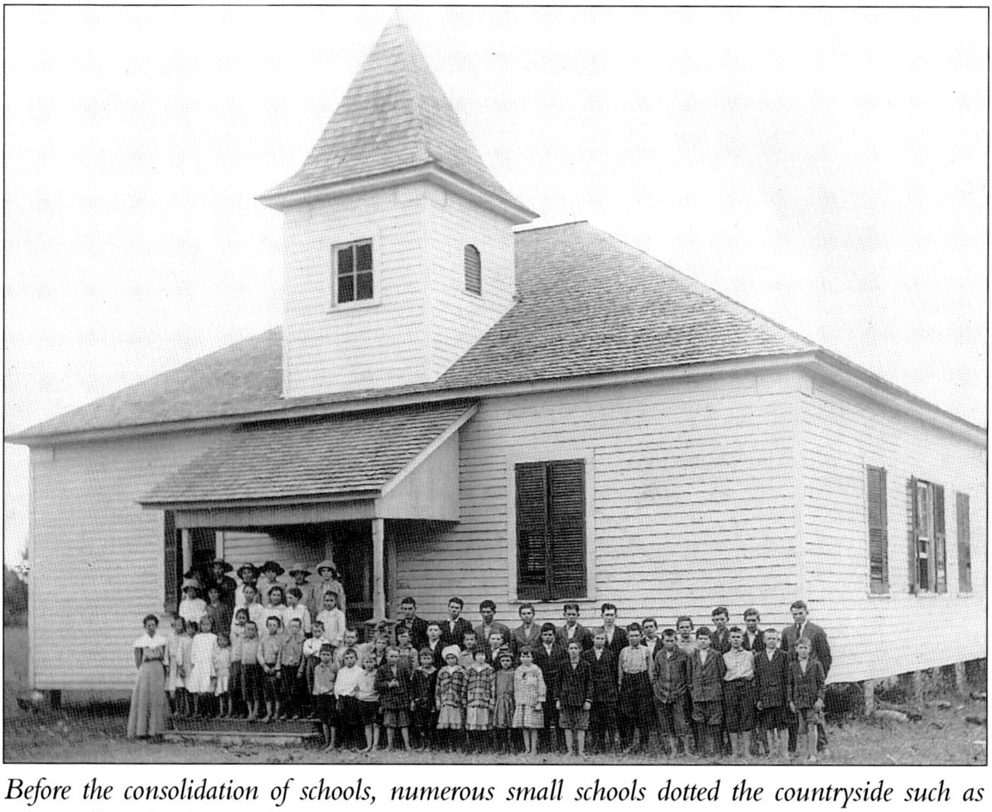

Before the consolidation of schools, numerous small schools dotted the countryside such as Blairsville School, seen here in 1915. This schoolhouse was moved to the campus of the Hickory Grove–Sharon Elementary School. In 1996, under the direction of teachers Lynn Faulkner and Beth Ramsey, it was restored.

3. A Revolutionary People

America was, it should be remembered, founded by people under duress. In the mist of prehistory, the Native Americans walked across the Asian land bridge in search of food as ice blanketed the Northern Hemisphere. When the ice melted, these Indians had drifted far to the south, to the piedmont Carolinas where they mastered waterways such as the Broad River and tracked big game such as deer and bear. By the 1700s, they were no longer hungry but they had come, originally, to Western York County under pressure to feed their families.

The white colonists also came to the New World under duress—seeking liberties and freedoms we now take for granted. Some were "second sons" robbed of their inheritance by the legalities of primogeniture, which favored the firstborn male. Others were dislocated refugees, just out of debtor's prison, or unfortunate in the economic battles of the Old World. Some may have been losers in political brawls, or landless dreamers who wanted a fresh start in a new place. Each of these people, however, brought a hunger for freedom—a desire for political liberty, which they otherwise would not have had in the Old World because of religious, political, or social restrictions.

By the mid-1760s, many of these spirited people had made their way down the Eastern Seaboard, arriving in Western York County, seeking land where they might raise crops and live in peace. Few of the earliest arrivals came with a purse bulging with British sterling; most arrived with little more than their strength, wits, and a determination to carve a home out of the wilderness.

One of the more fortunate ones was William Hill, who had been born in Northern Ireland in 1741 and had some knowledge of iron working. He purchased land on Allison's Creek and set up a "bloomery," where iron ore was smelted and refined into large lumps, or blooms. At the outbreak of the Revolution, Governor John Rutledge convinced Hill to add a furnace to his bloomery for the purpose of supplying South Carolina with cannonballs. The South Carolina Legislature lent him 7,000 pounds and took a mortgage on his property. In the siege of Charleston in 1776, it was Hill's Iron Works that almost wholly supplied cannonballs and other necessary iron implements in the glorious and gallant defense of the capital city. Hill, like other Scots-Irish Presbyterians in York County, early in the conflict with the mother county, threw his allegiance

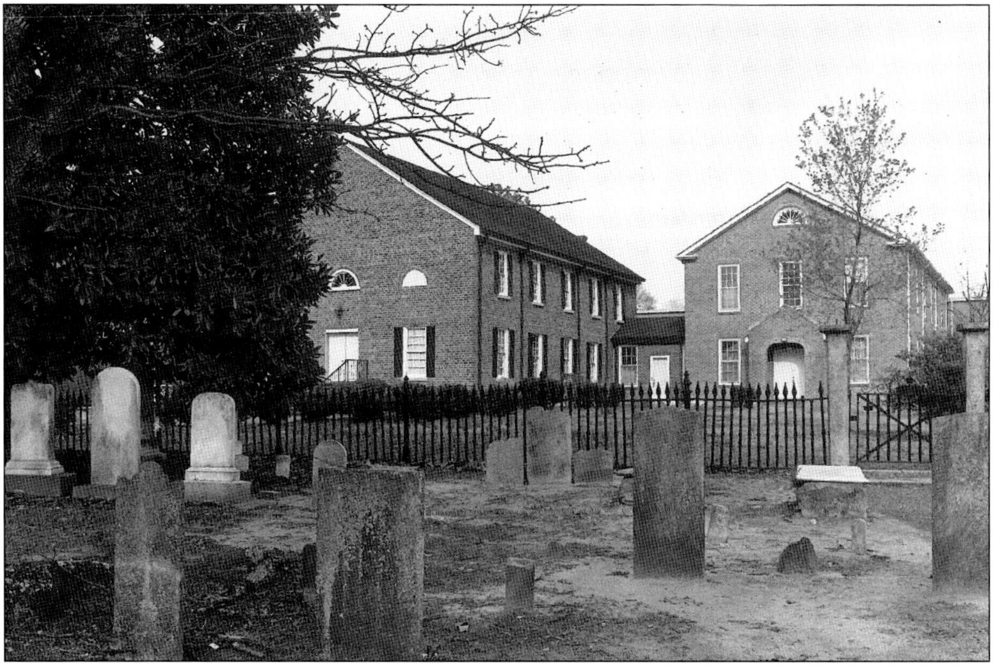

One of York County's oldest churches and one of the "Four Bs," Bethesda Presbyterian Church was established in 1765 and has one of the oldest sanctuaries in the county.

to the cause of liberty. And, like others, he early raised the American flag in defiance of all tyrants who would dare crush what would be later called "the American spirit."

On the eastern boundary of Western York County rose Colonel William Bratton. On the south was Colonel Edward Lacey from West Chester County, who, about 1780, would construct a kind of fort on Turkey Creek in York County. From this vantage point, known as "Liberty Hill," the Patriots watched the movements of the British and Tories up the road from Camden, as well as any movements on Love's and Hamilton's Fords on the Broad River. Farther up the Broad, Colonel Charles McDowell set up a camp at Smith's Ford, where Tory movements from their stronghold in Union County could be observed.

After Charleston fell to the Loyalists in the second assault in May 1780, the breast of the state was exposed to British war machinery. Within a month, Lord General Charles Cornwallis began to execute his plan to push his conquest until all the territory south of the Potomac lay prostrate at the feet of the British lion. And the state's citizens were completely demoralized. With renewed vigor, the Tories and Loyalists fell upon the Patriots and their families with the worst kind of cruelty and oppression. South Carolina Whigs were totally demoralized.

Several Patriot leaders of the New Acquisition Regiment assembled the ranks at Bullock's Creek Presbyterian Church to consider their future options. Colonels

Bratton and Watson, and perhaps others, believed that further resistance would be futile and advised it was every man for himself. Captain James Jamieson, however, was not one to give up so easily and was extremely frustrated over how the so-called "council of war" was going. Rising to his feet, he declared the meeting to be a council of surrender and he wanted no part in the decision. He continued, "There are men who are contending for liberty, and all who will join me in a continuation to the last for liberty, let them meet me tomorrow morning at sunrise and retreat to the north till we meet with a force sufficiently strong to enable us to make a stand." The following morning, 11 men joined Captain Jamieson, and they marched into North Carolina in search of General Thomas Sumter. The rest of the men broke camp with orders to meet the following week at Hill's Ironworks for further discussion.

Hearing of the meeting, Lieutenant Colonel Lord Frances Rawdon sent an emissary to the ironworks saying that Congress and the Continental forces had abandoned the Carolinas. Hill vehemently denied that a surrender was imminent—that it was "damn lies"—and sent the emissary packing. Still, the people remained unsure of which course to follow.

The country was full of prowling Tories who kept Whig settlers in constant terror. To inspire these Tories with courage and incite them into more daring cruelty, the British stationed numbers of soldiers throughout the Upcountry. Although the fire within the spirit of the Scots-Irish Presbyterian seemed to have burned out, it was about to burst into full fury. When news reached their ears that British Colonel Banastre Tarleton had hacked to pieces Colonel William Buford's Patriot force after it had surrendered, this ungentlemanly act of brutality kindled a roaring flame of patriotism throughout the region.

Doubtless, incensed over the treatment of their emissary, Captain Christian Huck was ordered in June to lead a force of British and Tory cavalrymen "to push the rebels as far as they might deem convenient," and burn Hill's Iron Works. These ironworks were regarded by the British as a deterrent to their conquest of South Carolina, and when destroyed, the people regarded it as a great calamity. York County had become, according to historian Robert M. Weir, immersed in "an increasingly ugly war."

Regarding the destruction of Hill's furnace and home on Nanny's Mountain, Governor John Rutledge said, "The enemy seems determined, as they can to break every man's spirit, and if they can't, to ruin him." The spirit of the Upcountry Presbyterians, however, was not easily broken. After the burning of Hill's Iron Works, they acutely saw the American Revolution as an assault on their religious and political liberties.

Early on, Captain Christian Huck had made himself extremely repugnant to the Presbyterians of York County. Not only had he insulted their ministers and on several occasions burned their homes and sought to imprison them, he had been known to burn Bibles and Psalm books, and had made certain blasphemous remarks regarding the deity. On the morning of July 12, 1780, at Williamson Plantation near the home of Colonel William Bratton, the rebels attacked

Huck and a sleeping force of about 150 men. With a somewhat larger force, the several colonels of the New Acquisition Regiment surrounded and destroyed the British and Tories. Huck, still dressed in his nightshirt, was killed by two bullets to his head.

Huck's defeat at the Battle of Williamson's Plantation was an inspiring event. Previously disillusioned, Patriots then began to rally to the cause, and the ranks of the local regiment, under General Sumter, swelled to capacity. Several American victories were won later in the summer.

The turning point of the Revolution occurred at Kings Mountain in what is now the northern portion of York County. On October 7, 1780, the Americans engaged the sizable force of Colonel Patrick Ferguson. At three o'clock in the afternoon, the Patriot army overpowered the Loyalists, killing Ferguson as he frantically rode about on horseback trying to rally his troops.

After the victory, some of the revolutionaries, including Colonels Lacey and Hill, retired to Lacey's Fort on Turkey Creek. Midway, they camped in "the high hills of Bullock's Creek" near the present-day town of Sharon. Here, several British or Tory soldiers were buried (whether they were hanged or died of wounds, one cannot say) before proceeding on to Turkey Creek.

Lacey remained at his fort, sometimes known as "Liberty Hill," until about December 25, when he was ordered to join Colonel Washington. From that time, until the Battle of Cowpens, Lacey was under the command of General Daniel Morgan. Lord Cornwallis, who had been wanting to advance northward from Camden, saw his opportunity and on January 16, arrived at the site, within a few miles of the Bullock's Creek Presbyterian Church. It was here that the British

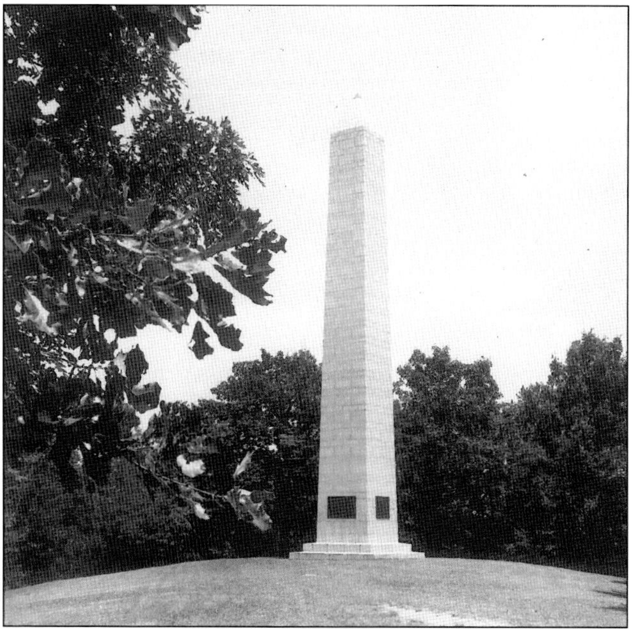

This obelisk was erected by the United States government at the Kings Mountain Battleground in 1909. (Courtesy Winthrop University Archives.)

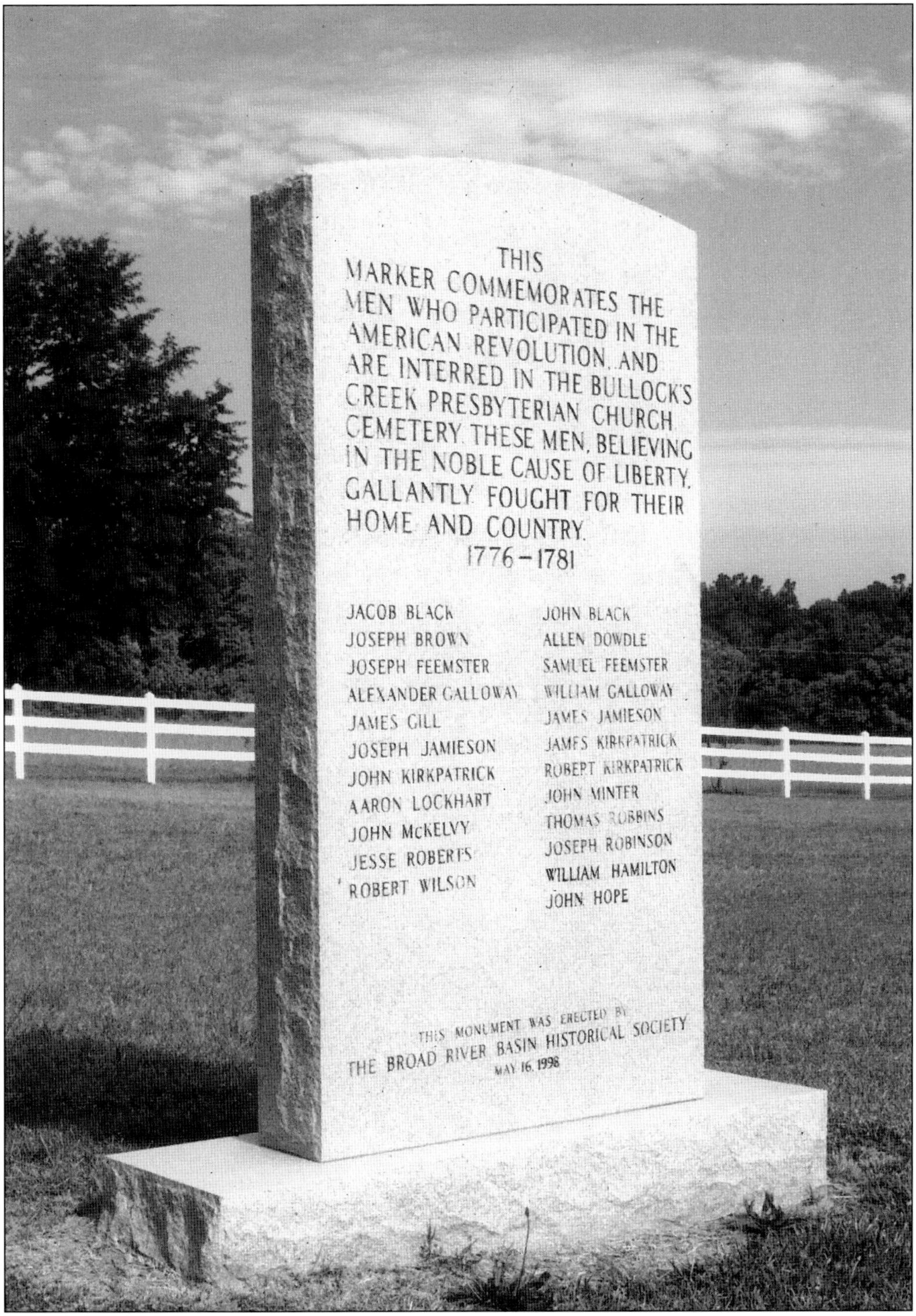

This monument commemorates the more than 20 Revolutionary War Patriots buried in Bullock's Creek Presbyterian Church Cemetery. It was erected in 1998 by the Broad River Basin Historical Society.

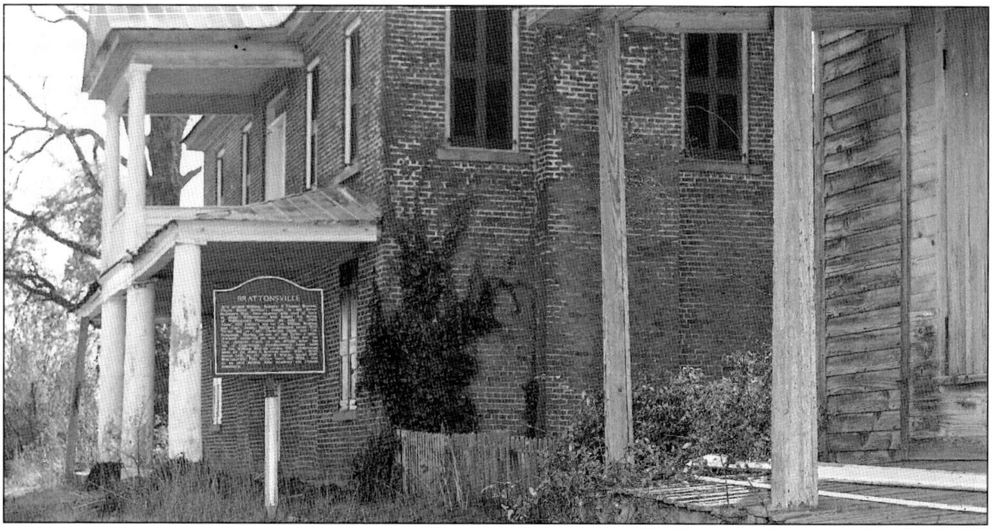

Brattonsville was the site of one of the significant Revolutionary War conflicts in York County. This 1843 brick house was later used as a female academy prior to the Civil War. (Courtesy Winthrop University Archives.)

general received word that Tarleton had been thoroughly defeated by Daniel Morgan at Cowpens the day before. On the morning of January 19, Cornwallis broke camp and with a combined force of about 3,200 men, began his march into North Carolina. Before the end of the month, the illustrious Brit would leave York County and South Carolina, never to return.

During the War of Independence, there were many bright, shining moments. Certainly, the 1777 victory at Saratoga, New York, which persuaded France to increase its assistance to the American Patriots was one of those moments. The winter of 1777–1778 at Valley Forge, Pennsylvania, was another. There, in blood-stained snow, an undaunted spirit was forged in the Continental army that ultimately led George Washington to his triumph over Lord Charles Cornwallis at Yorktown in 1781.

In Western York County, as we have also seen, the land was sprinkled with the blood of Patriots. William Hill of Nanny's Mountain rallied his neighbors to the cause of liberty. At Williamson's Plantation, near Brattonsville, John and Martha Bratton stood tall for resistance to the mother country's marauding troops, led by Captain Christian Huck. The roll of Patriots from Western York County is a long one, with names like Meek, Robinson, McDowell, Moss, Jamieson, Kirkpatrick, Hope, Feemster, Black, and other men and women who cheered independence at places like Bullock's Creek and Kings Mountain. Indeed, these were "a revolutionary people" who changed the world by clinging tenaciously to values such as "life, liberty, and the pursuit of happiness." Today, their descendants live and honor those same values that were shaped by the sacrifices of their ancestors atop hills and in bottom lands in every community of Western York County.

4. The Cotton Kingdom

The soil of Western York County is a farmer's paradise. In the late 1700s, after the American Revolution, Patriot Samuel Watson, who had served in the 1775 Second Provincial Congress, was a "receiver of rice." In the Smith's Ford area along the Broad River, Watson was experimenting with rice production, a crop usually associated with South Carolina's Lowcountry.

Other agricultural products were more successful in Western York County. According to Robert Mills's 1826 research, the region was chiefly a cotton kingdom with other major crops including wheat, corn, rye, and some tobacco. The average acre would produce 150 pounds of cotton, 12 bushels of wheat, 20 bushels of corn, or 12 bushels of rye. The crop prices in the mid-1820s were $1.00 a bushel for wheat, 50¢ a bushel of corn, and 10¢ per cotton pound. These crops were then transported to the nearest market.

Gradually, cotton came to dominate the economy. As a labor-intensive crop, cotton required huge numbers of workers to harvest the fields. While most South Carolina whites did not own slaves, a significant number (43%) did and this factor planted the seeds for disunion—as did the state's racial dynamics. South Carolina had been, since Eli Whitney's cotton gin made the crop easier to strip of its seeds, a majority African-American state. Tremendous fortunes could be made off cotton, but a large pool of laborers was essential for the cultivation of the crop. Thus, by the 1840s, a national debate was occurring among people who cherished the Union and, on the other hand, cotton farmers who felt persecuted by an anti-slavery movement, which criticized the "peculiar institution" of the South, an institution that brought financial success.

Nearly from the formation of the nation, the South was on a collision course with the North; this was especially so in South Carolina, where a particular political arrogance was forever leading its people to extremism. The 1820s and 1830s were a particularly troubling period eventually leading to a serious consideration of secession. In the late 1840s, a number of South Carolinians began a call for secession as the only solution to end political clashes with the North—clashes that seemed to constantly hinge on slavery. This call, intensified by the proposal of the Wilmot Proviso, spread rapidly over the state and citizens began choosing sides.

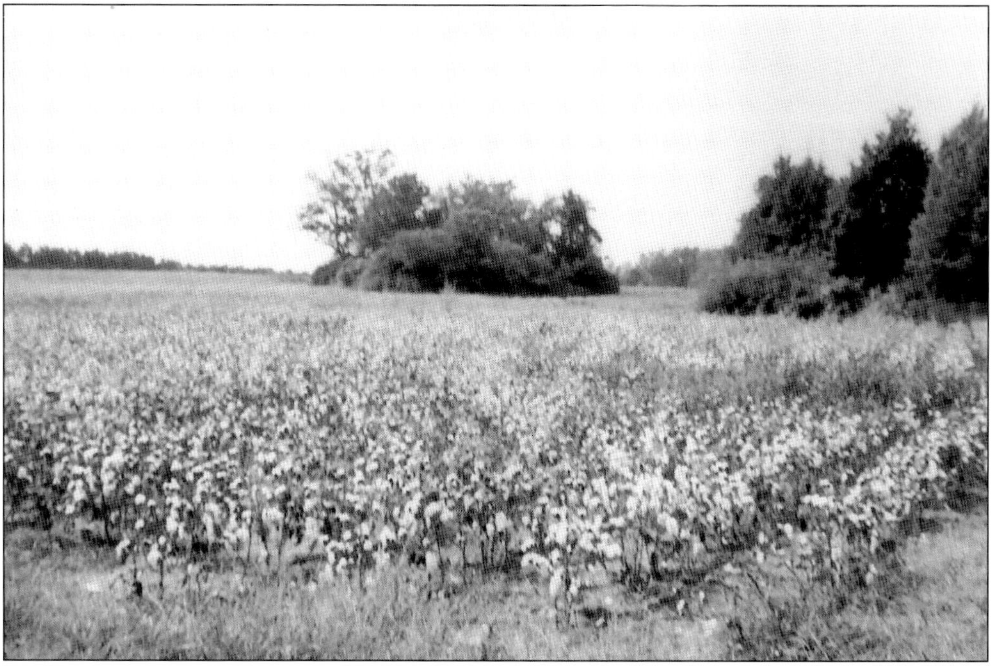

Scenes like this cotton field near McConnells must have inspired the song, "Them Old Cotton Fields Back Home." These pastoral scenes are quickly vanishing from the landscape of Western York County.

The 1846 Wilmot Proviso, proposed by a young Pennsylvania Democrat before the United States Congress, acted as a catalyst that touched off a serious secession crisis in South Carolina. In response to President Polk's request to use public money to purchase Mexican territory during peace negotiations between the two nations, Congress agreed so long as the territory would be a free state with a prohibition of slavery. South Carolina had another of its nervous fits when 14 of the 15 Northern states passed resolutions supporting the proviso, noting a new rise in abolition. The amendment was passed by the House, but was killed in the Senate. Death of the bill would lead one to believe that the proviso was a moot subject, but it ignited a long and heated controversy in the South which centered in South Carolina.

While South Carolina had no ambitions of its own to expand the institution of slavery into an empire, its politicians and wealthy planters could not resist snatching up the gauntlet of "free soil" thrown down by the Wilmot Proviso. South Carolina's old warrior, John C. Calhoun, advised citizens it was always best to "meet danger on the frontier, in politics or in war." Waddy Thompson, planter-lawyer of Spartanburg County, who owned land in Western York County, urged "resistance at all hazards and to every possible extremity to this insulting, degrading and fatal measure." Thompson saw the proviso as a sign the North ultimately wanted to turn the South into a "black province" surrounded by free states and territories, which would limit where slaves would be allowed to be worked and sold, thereby crippling the economy of the South.

The death of the Wilmot Proviso had no effect on the nervous disposition of South Carolina. Across the state, skillful politicians used negrophobia in their public addresses to stir the masses toward secession, but the South was not solid on the question of secession. The other Southern states were not as eager as the sandlappers, and discussion arose whether South Carolina should leave the Union alone or not. Certain particularities of South Carolina's politics were forever bringing it to a crisis. One was a persistent heritage from the Revolution era: an acute love of independence and a strong paranoia about power and government. The second laid in the fact that South Carolina had never developed a two-party system in its politics, and did not have the luxury of balance. While the Democratic Party in South Carolina had minor differences among its members, they agreed in all major "republican" ideology. This republicanism, which consumed all the Upcountry and much of the midlands, had the tenants of state's rights, minimal government, low taxes, and opposed any sign of aristocracy.

On October 20, 1848, William D. Henley of Columbia, Tennessee, wrote to his kinsman John D. Smarr, who lived at Red Hills Plantation in Union County,

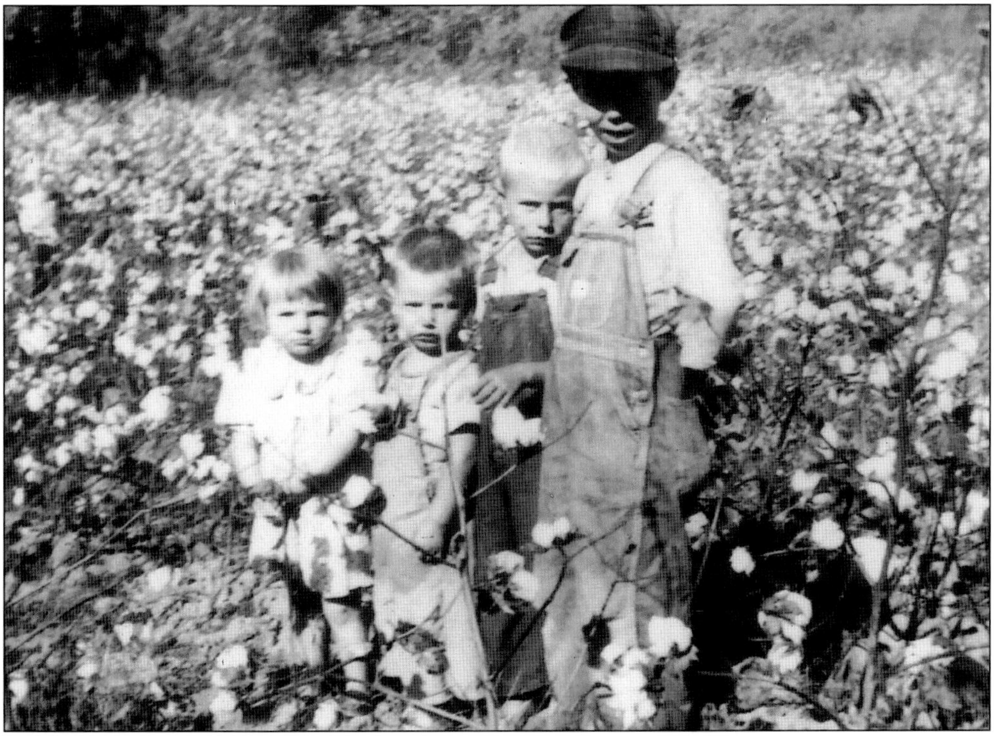

Cotton has served as an important cash crop for Western York County for years. Seen here in 1949, these children, Ann Traylor, Jimmy Moss, Ronald Moss, and Jesse Moss Jr., pause from their play in one of the cotton fields of Western York County.

South Carolina. Mr. Henley was concerned over his kinsman's politics as well as his marital state:

> I am sorry that we disagree both in matrimony and politics and I hope the next time I hear from you I may hear that you have got a wife and that your area is far from seeking the union dissolved as you would be from being willing to be dissolved from your dear and beloved wife.

By the summer of 1849, every district in the Upcountry of South Carolina had established Vigilance and Safety Committees. Each committee was to be part of a statewide network to keep a vigil against roving abolitionists. While there is little evidence of their apprehending abolitionists, there is much evidence of their paranoia. While these committees were originally non-partisan, they later fell under the control of rabid, fire-eating Secessionists. While one may hear the argument that the Civil War was not over slavery, but over states' rights, slavery was one of the institutions the Southern states considered to be their right to decide upon and not the business of Northern states or the federal government. The strength of the states' rights argument was augmented by the fact that the

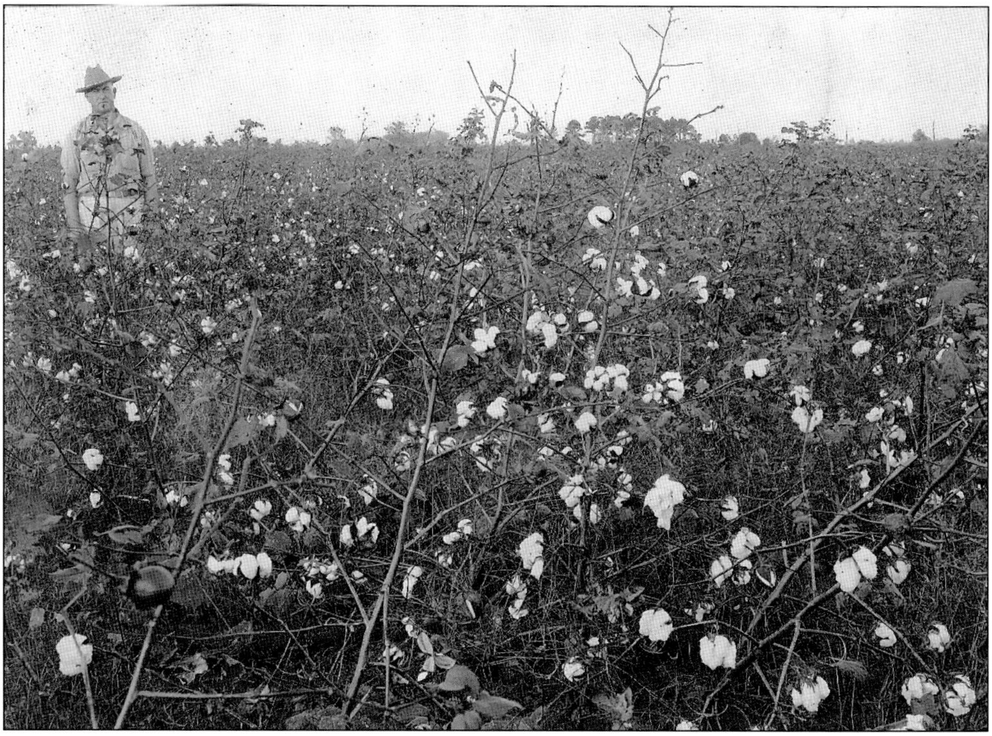

Cotton shaped the livelihoods of most families in the rural piedmont sections of South Carolina in the nineteenth century. In this image, Buck White stands amid a field of this valuable crop.

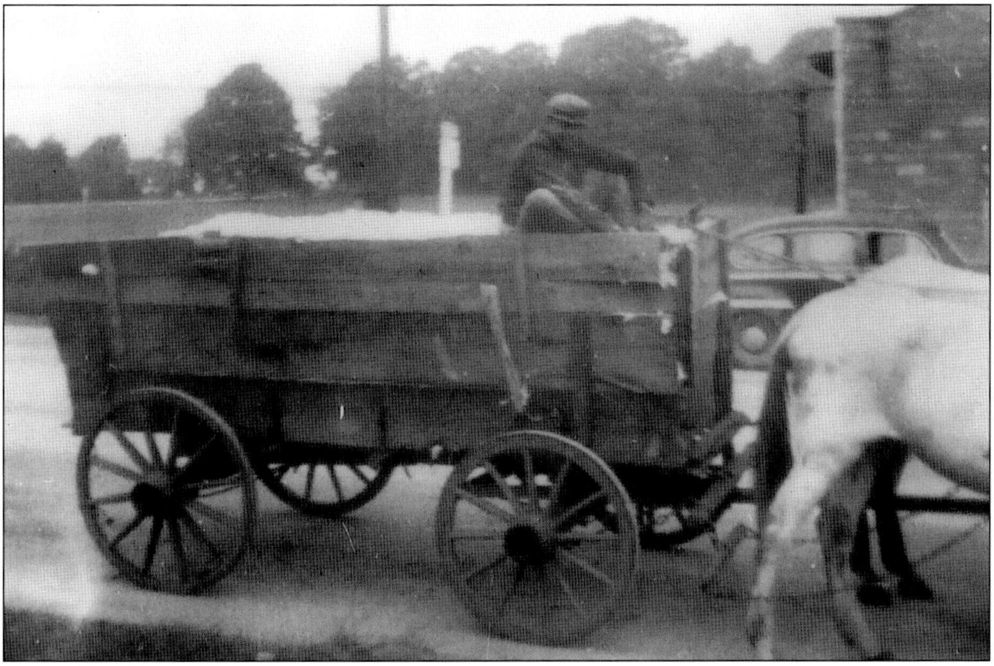

A wagon load of cotton is seen here headed for the Rainey Gin in Sharon, marking the transition in mule-drawn and motorized vehicles.

overwhelming majority of the white people of South Carolina—whether slave owner or not—supported secession. Yet, a study of the politics of the antebellum era reveals slavery was the ultimate consideration of every act of Southern legislators. It would appear that the Southern antebellum mind was preoccupied, or obsessed, with the institution and how to protect it from outside forces.

The crisis over secession continued through 1850. In 1851, the North was moving in a political direction that seemed to alienate the South. While the South was under much pressure from the abolitionists, a number of Northern states were making laws diametrically opposed to the equality they preached. For instance, Iowa and Indiana had passed legislation prohibiting the African American from migrating into their states, and Iowa was taking steps to forbid the sale of real estate to free blacks and even considering methods to remove the free black from it borders. Michigan, although granting citizenship to blacks, denied them voting rights. One man in South Carolina shook an accusing finger at Michigan saying, "they call a black man a citizen, but at the same time deny him the right of citizenship." That same year, Wisconsin joined her sister, Michigan, in abolishing capital punishment. These changes from traditional policies set the South against the North and fueled distrust.

In 1851, York County, as well as all of South Carolina, was divided into three distinct ideologies concerning the politics of secession—Secessionists, who wanted secession; Co-operationists, who refused to leave the Union without the other Southern states; and Submissionists, who took no side in the matter. Of the latter, it was said, "their soil was no higher than dollars and cents."

On July 14, 1851, a number of York County Co-operationists met at the courthouse to oppose secession, they were as follows:

J. Leander Adams
William R. Alexander
J.J. Allison
John Ash Jr.
D.K. Bales
Joel S. Barnett
Colonel J.H. Berry
Jefferson Black
Joseph Black
William C. Black
James Blair
Samuel Blair
Ross Bolin
Hugh Borders
Rufus Boyd
John S. Bratton
James Brian
John M. Brison
W.L. Brown
James Caldwell
Robert Caldwell
Captain Isaac Campbell
Jedediah Coulter
David Currence
John Davidson
Colonel H.H. Drennan
F.A. Erwin
Philip Etters
Dr. B.E. Feemster
Alexander Fewell
Theodore Fulton
William Glenn
D.F. Hall
John Hall
Michael Hambright
David Hamilton
William Hanna
Hugh Harris
Thomas C. Henry
Joshua Hudson
D. Franklin Jackson
Hugh M. Jackson
James Johnson
Dr. John Johnson
Dudley Jones
A.W. Kirkpatrick
John Latta
Edward Leech
Joseph Leech
W. Dixon Lesley
A.F. Love
Colonel J.B. Lowry
Dr. W.R. Lowry
Duncan McCallum
G.L. McCarter
John McClelland
Robert McClelland
Reuben McConnell
S.L. McConnell
James McElwee
J.N. McElwee Jr.
William McElwee Jr.
William McElwee Sr.
John McGill
William McGill Jr.
Dr. John McGowan
Alfred Moore
William Moore
William Nesbit
Joseph Poag
Richard Pressley
John Quinn
Joel Rawlinson
W.T. Roach
R.M. Roark
John Roddy
Dr. C.P. Sandifer
E.W. Smith
Miles Smith
Richard Smith
Samuel Smith
Jacob Starnes
Archibald Steele
John Steele
Samuel Steele
Reuben Swann
E.C. Thomasson
H.C. Thomasson
James Wallace
Dr. D.M. Watson
William Watson
William White
Thomas G. Wiley
Gassaway Wilson
Robert W. Wilson
Dr. John B. Withers
James Wood
J.L. Wright
Dr. Samuel Wright

Co-operationists generally held the following 25 reason for not seceding:

1. Session will not reverse the admission of California as a free state, nor fix the 36-30 as a Northern boundary.
2. Session will impose an intolerable burden of taxes.

3. Withdrawal will indirectly accuse other Southern states of a want of patriotism, intelligence and South Carolina would lose their sympathy.
4. The state would be placed in immediate collision with the federal authorities who would use force—"robbers are not governed by a code of morals."
5. Trade would be interrupted as the North would blockade the ports in an effort to regain their integrity.
6. The resulting blockade would be resisted and South Carolina would be transferred from peace to war.
7. South Carolina alone could not prevail against immense numerical force. The battle of the Revolution was not fought by the colonies alone—nearly the whole of Europe was at war with England at the same time.
8. Slavery has no friends beyond the South—it is impudent and unstatesman-like to desert our Southern allies.
9. The American Revolution admonishes us to seek for co-operation; our ancestors commenced a co-operation in 1764 that continued until 1776.
10. Secession will restrict slavery to the state—if the slave population doubles in 25 years, there will be 700,000 among us; a number too considerable to be employed or endured.
11. A new government would be dangerous to the public peace. Conflicting interests with neighboring states may result in civil war.
12. Fugitives now restored under the present laws would then only be surrendered at the point of a bayonet.
13. The state would not be able to dictate terms of a treaty without an immense army and navy. To raise up such a force would drain the state's resources.
14. Undisciplined men of neighboring states would be tempted to confiscate our property.
15. Deadly animosities would arise between citizens of adjoining states and result in constant warfare.
16. Unprotected seacoasts would allow abolitionists to carry off slaves by the shipload.
17. Security of a nation against aggression is found in the mouths of her cannons—without these, the flag will be insulted in every port—even her own.
18. Those who would protect us would only be borrowed strength and they would have the power to victimize us themselves.
19. Fear of general war will deter any foreign power from protecting commerce.
20. Secession would jeopardize the existence of a mighty republic.
21. We cannot involve other states in an issue they have expressly declined to raise.
22. Separate secession is unaccepted by every distinguished politician (with one exception) within the state and by all, (without exception) out of the state—including Calhoun.
23. Sister states have conceded all they will for the sake of the Union—they will concede no more—if we wait, we will be together.
24. South Carolina is bound by her honor, made at the Nashville Convention, to not desert her association with the other Southern states.
25. Submission is not the alternative of secession.

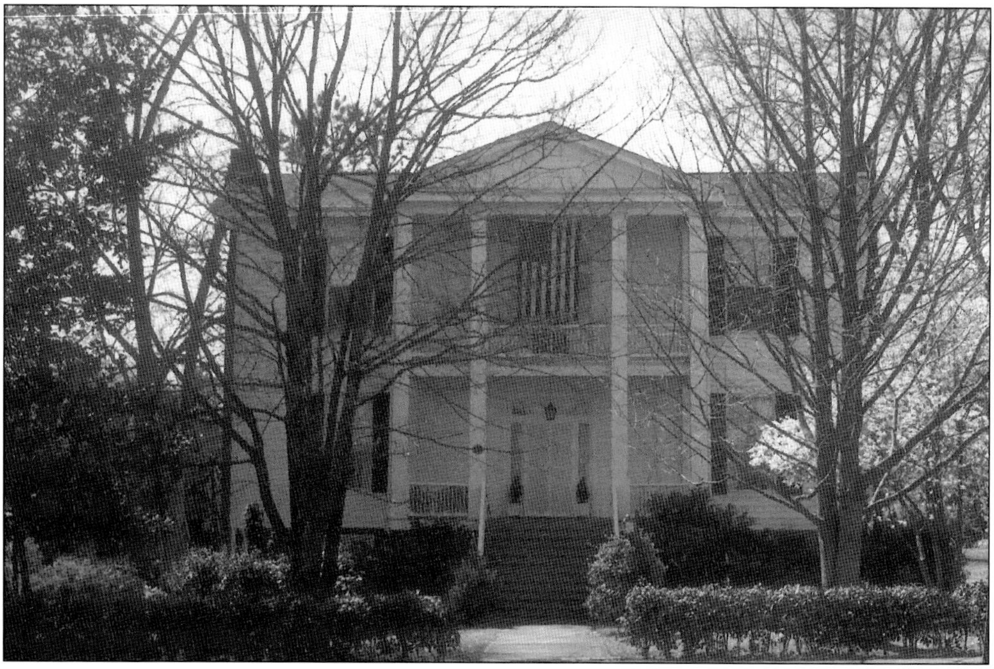

This Greek Revival–styled home, facing York's Liberty Street, was the home of newspaper publisher L.M. Grist. Several members of the Grist family were publishers of newspapers, one of which is the Yorkville Enquirer. *The* Yorkville Enquire *was started in 1855 and is still being published in York today.*

The issue continued to heat-up between the Co-operationists and the Secessionists as each side tried to draw out the position of the state's representatives. Senator I.D. Witherspoon of Yorkville was rebuked by one of the town's citizen who took exception to a statement he had made. Witherspoon had said he favored secession only if South Carolina had the cooperation of the other states. A short time later, he remarked that he thought secession was reasonable even if South Carolina had to stand alone. Mr. Witherspoon's constituency demanded to know how he could reconcile the two opposing remarks.

Even the local newspapers became embroiled in the debate. The *Yorkville Miscellany*, which was published by York's Lewis M. Grist, was anti-secessionist, while the *Remedy* was decidedly a secessionist paper. Each issued blistering editorials demanding proofs and apologies.

Seemingly, secession was settled at the ballot box the following October, but its adherents were not finished and they began working clandestinely. History reveals that most of these men who had opposed secession, if not all, changed their minds by 1860. According to historian Allen D. Charles of Union, South Carolina, one factor in the South's secession in 1860 was that a majority of native-born South Carolinians were living in other Southern states and voted to go out of the Union with their mother state.

The antebellum period was filled with problems that always seemed to hinge on slavery and drive South Carolina to the brink of secession. One of these dealt with labor and a budding industrial revolution in the South. When pro-slavery advocates were confronted with the possibilities of industries using free white labor, they argued that such a labor force would be detrimental to a slave labor republic.

In 1855, Benjamin F. Perry, under the belief that labor had fallen into disrespect because of its longtime identification with slavery, promoted the need for manufacturing businesses and a laboring class of whites. But Southern farmers and planters contended it would undermine the slavery system. James L. Orr was in agreement with Perry, saying the South was truly in dire need of developing factories and machine shops.

Being an agricultural society, most South Carolinians were dubious, to say the least. The *Yorkville Enquirer* expressed a fear of a white labor force, which might develop into "that most dangerous viper" and would bring death to slavery. The writer saw the possibility of an "organized, determined free-labor party, whose bond of union will be hatred of slavery competition" and would demand that slave competition be regulated or minimized and eventually lead to abolishment.

Visionaries such as Perry and Orr were often shouted down, if not silenced, by men like William K. Easley of Greenville District, who denounced their advice as an "insatiable thirst for advancement and amelioration" spawned by

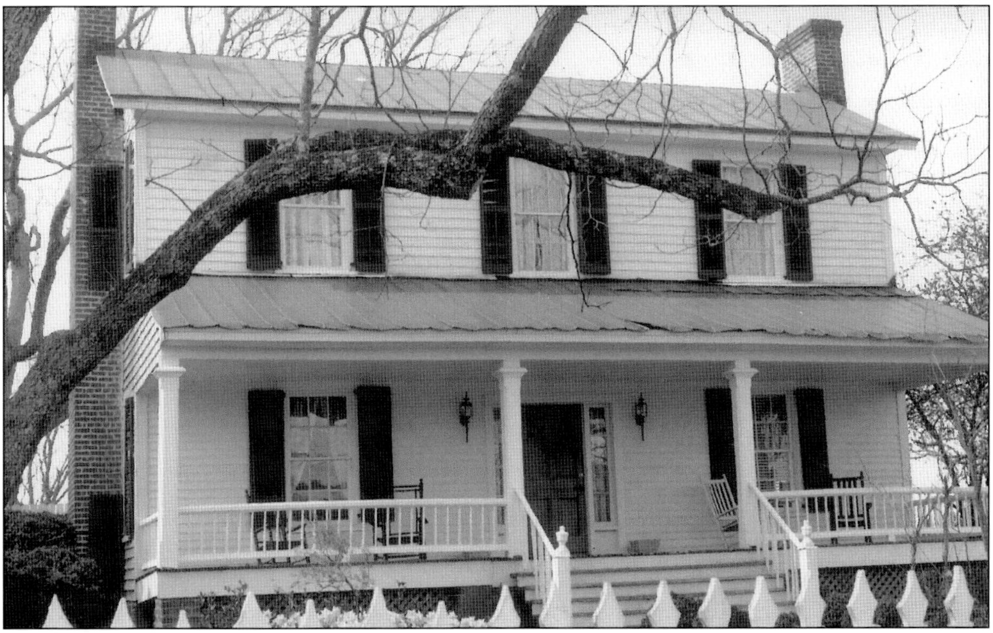

The Rainey Place, located 2 miles south of Sharon, was built c. 1835 by Charles Williams. The house boasts architecture identified as a typical example of an "I" house, sometimes referred to as a "Piedmont Farmhouse."

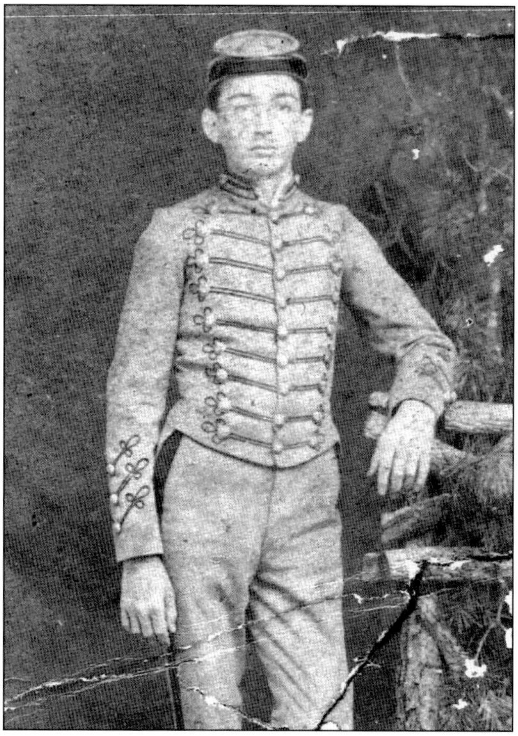

John L. Rainey (1844–1924) was a cadet at the Kings Mountain Military Academy in York during the period before and at the start of the Civil War.

Yankees. Easley put the matter at rest for the slaveholder saying, "For all intents and purposes, they [the North and the South] are two peoples, two separate and distinct national ties, differing in genius and spirit." If Easley's remarks are representative of the average antebellum Southerner, and there is no reason to think otherwise, it is easily seen that an eventual and terrible conflict between the two sections was inevitable.

While the country did not disintegrate in the 1850s, the destiny was all too apparent and the cool leaders were destined to be out-shouted. In Western York County and surrounding areas, there was a small but powerful planter class that exerted tremendous force in the political, economic, and social arenas. These planters, if one surveys the largest of them, felt themselves under attack by their Northern critics. And, in the Cotton Kingdom, it was these influential people who, in December 1860, would win the argument with the cautious Co-operationists. In the Upcountry of South Carolina, such as Western York County, these Secessionists propelled the country toward rupture.

In 1860, on the eve of the Civil War, the Carolina Upcountry was well populated and, unlike the Lowcountry, filled with small arms owned by yeoman farmers who, on the average, owned three to four slaves. It has been suggested that to qualify as a "planter" one must own at least 100 acres and 20 slaves. While the Upcountry was, by and large, occupied by yeoman farmers, there were a number of planters in York County. Dr. Lacy K. Ford of the University of South

Carolina states the distribution of farms by improved acres in York County in 1860 were as follows (by percentage):

0–50	51–100	101–500	Over 500
19.5	23.9	53.9	2.7

South Carolina, like most of the antebellum South, experienced alternating waves of economic booms and panics that pounded the state like so many breakers on the Carolina coast. Each wave sent both farmers and planters scurrying about making adjustments to their investments depending on the rising and falling tides of local and international markets. On the whole, throughout the period, South Carolina experienced some degree of increase in the standard of living as King Cotton mounted his golden throne. The regime of this hoary monarch was felt not only in the South, but in the North and much of Europe. Short staple cotton, a member of the royal family, flourished and ruled in the red hills of the upper piedmont, sharing the empire with the duke of grain—corn.

York County had few planters who could be classified as large slaveholders; that is, in comparison to the Lowcountry, where plantations may be the home of hundreds of slaves. While the Bratton family of York County had more than 100 slaves in the 1850s, Mrs. Bratton had sold or distributed a number of them among her children and the land had been subdivided so that no one family unit held the required number of 100 for this study. The same is true for the Davies of Chester County.

In York and the surrounding counties of Chester, Union, and Spartanburg, a number of landowners did meet the criteria of a planter. Robert Gadsden McCaw, a Presbyterian planter, was born 1821 in South Carolina and owned a non-resident plantation near Fishing Creek in York County. He married Belle Means Bratton and was educated at the University of Virginia, attaining the military rank of colonel. He served as a state representative, state senator, and lieutenant governor. He owned 135 slaves. Regarding the planter class in Spartanburg County, John Conrad Zimmerman was born in 1802 in South Carolina. He and his wife, Selina Pierce Wannamaker, owned "Rosemont" plantation on Fairforest Creek in Spartanburg County. Episcopalian by faith, he owned a cotton mill and served as a commissioner of public schools. He owned 107 slaves.

Chester County had numerous planters, as the following list of names shows. Thomas McCullough Boulware, born in 1829 in South Carolina, was a Presbyterian planter who lived in the Blackstock community of Chester County. He attended Davidson College and married Mary Jane Vinson. In 1860, he had a total of 157 slaves on this plantation. Born in 1785, William Cloud, M.D., married Margaret McCreary Homes and was a member of the Presbyterian Church. His plantation, "Beckhamville," was located in Chester District and was the home of 128 slaves. Tscharner Hobson deGraffenried owned "Oakland" Plantation on Sandy River in the Chester District. He was born in 1810 in South Carolina, was a graduate of the College of South Carolina, and married Mary

Eaton Johnston. They were members of the Baptist Church and owned 108 slaves. Richard Evans Kennedy was born 1811 in South Carolina and married Sarah deGraffenried. He was a member of the Baptist Church and a trustee of Chesterville Female Academy Society. His Chester County plantation contained 123 slaves. James Stringfellow McLure, born in 1834 in South Carolina, was the owner of the "RedCliffe" plantation in Chester County. After graduating from the College of South Carolina, he married Sallie E. Rice. He was Presbyterian and owned 120 slaves. John Joseph McLure, born in 1827 in New Jersey, was a graduate of Princeton College and admitted to the South Carolina Bar in 1851. A Presbyterian, he married Elizabeth Heathly McIntosh and owned a plantation in Chester County with 150 slaves. Henry Worthy, born in 1800 in South Carolina, married Nancy Elizabeth Hill. While probably not a member, he supported the Brushy Fork Baptist Church. His plantation, "Worthy's Bottoms," was located in Chester County where 107 slaves lived in 1860.

Like Chester County, Union County had a considerable number of affluent and influential planters. Nathaniel Gist, born in 1776 in South Carolina, and his wife, Elizabeth Lewis McDaniel, lived at the "Wyoming" plantation in Union County and owned 119 slaves. He served as a state representative and justice of the quorum and attained the rank of lieutenant colonel. Late in his life, he was associated with the Presbyterian Church. Mrs. Sarah Frances Gist was born in 1816 in South Carolina and was reared on her father's plantation, "Wyoming." She married John Gist, who graduated from the College of South Carolina and

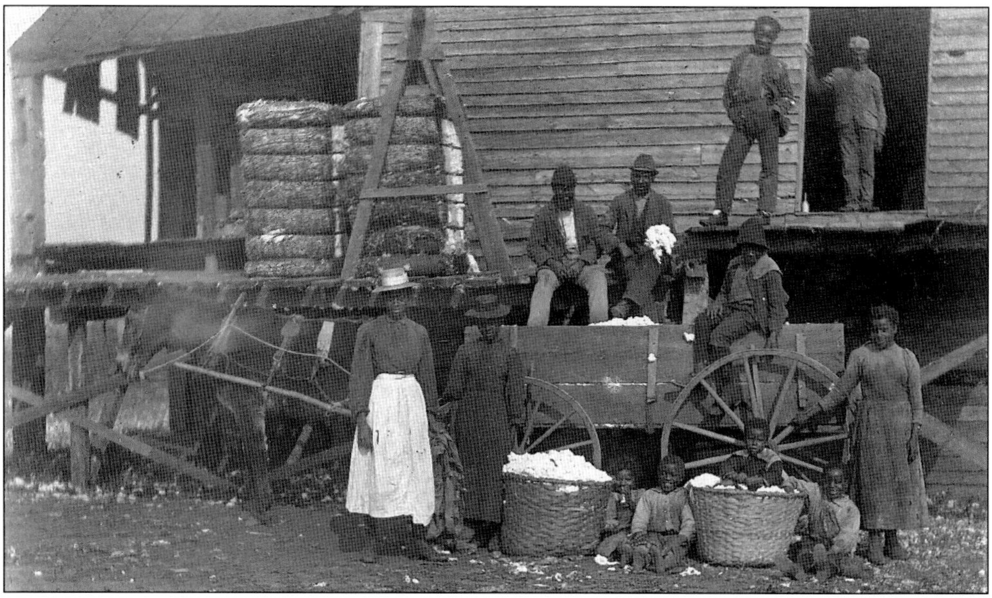

This scene at Strawberry Hill Plantation, near Rock Hill, captures a view of early African-American workers, of a variety of ages, bringing in a cotton crop. (Courtesy Winthrop University Archives.)

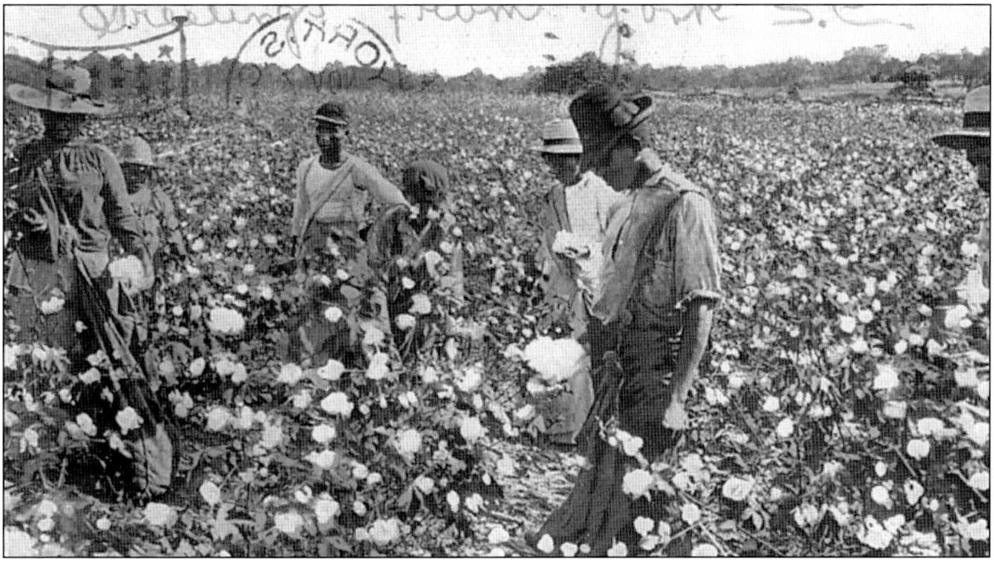

The plantation society across South Carolina's piedmont and the South depended on slave labor for their economic livelihoods. This postcard image from 1915 still indicates the importance of cotton in Western York County.

served as a state representative. A widow by 1860, Mrs. Gist, at her plantation near Pinckneyville, was the mistress of 145 slaves. William Henry Gist was the owner of "Rose Hill" plantation in Union County. Born 1807 in South Carolina, he graduated from the College of South Carolina and later married Louisa Bowen and Mary Elizabeth Rice. He served as a state representative, governor, and lieutenant governor of South Carolina, and a delegate to the Secession Convention of 1860 and was trustee of the South Carolina College and a noted author. They were members of the Methodist Church and owned 178 slaves. John Thompson Hill, born in 1816 in South Carolina, married Elizabeth Pickett Mobley and Anne E. Meng Wallace. His plantation, the home of 116 slaves, was near the Fish Dam section of Union County. Born in 1789, James Randolph Jeter was affiliated with the Baptist Church. He and his wife, Elizabeth Hobson, owned "Roanoke Spring" in Union County and 122 slaves. John P. Sarto was born in 1799 in South Carolina. He and his wife, Martha A.E. Sims, were Presbyterians and lived on their plantation near Fish Dam Ford in Union County with their 107 slaves. Born in 1789, Andrew Wallace Thomson, a Union County Methodist, was admitted to the South Carolina Bar in 1815, and married Nancy Henderson. He owned 186 slaves and served as justice of the peace and as a state representative.

Perceiving slavery to be under attack, South Carolina seceded from the Union on December 20, 1860. What followed was the nightmare of the Civil War, during which the planters witnessed their actions result in the destruction of the Cotton Kingdom. King Cotton was, in a sense, assassinated by the members of its royal court.

5. Yankees on the Broad River

The scars of the Civil War are fresh ones and they get opened on a regular basis because, in South Carolina, the conflict engulfed every family, black and white. Western York County is no exception. The area's white sons enlisted in the Lost Cause in 1861 while the white women cheered. Among African Americans of the South Carolina Upcountry, the dissolution of the Union probably meant very little—shackles and a hope for freedom continued without interval.

Wars, usually, are greeted with great enthusiasm—at least for a while, until the first count of bodies snaps the participants into reality. As historian Arthur Schlesinger Jr. has explained, "All wars are popular for thirty days." Then, the exhilaration gives way to casualty figures and homefront hardships endured by those left behind.

While no major battles occurred in Western York County, white males took part in most of the war's engagements. Many men from this area were members of the 5th, 6th, and 12th South Carolina Regiments. The first troops from Western York County marched with Edisto Island native General Micah Jenkins of the 5th Regiment, Company A and B. Other military units made up by Western York County volunteers were the Jasper Light Infantry, the Broad River Light Infantry (generally known as the Crosby Company), and the Turkey Creek Grays. In total, York County sent 16 companies of their finest examples of manhood to the bloody battlefields.

In the decades after Appomattox Courthouse, the war hovered above Western York County's people like a gray ghost. By 1888, veterans (and their widows) petitioned the state of South Carolina for financial assistance. The following is a list of Western York County men and women who made up the Confederate pension role for that year:

Catherine Bolin (Blacks[burg])
Margaret C. Bolin (Hickory Grove)
Mary Ann Bolin (Hickory Grove)
Leuticia Brown (Blacks[burg])
A.D. Burris (Blairsville)
Peter B. Byers Sr. (Blacks[burg])
Elizabeth L. Jackson (Clover)
John H. Jones (Hopewell)
Mary R. Lindsay (Clover)
Mrs. L.A. McCarter (Bethany)
Oran Newton McCarter (Bethany)
Carolina C. McKnight (Clark's Fork)

John L. Rainey, the father of the town of Sharon, served in the Confederate Army.

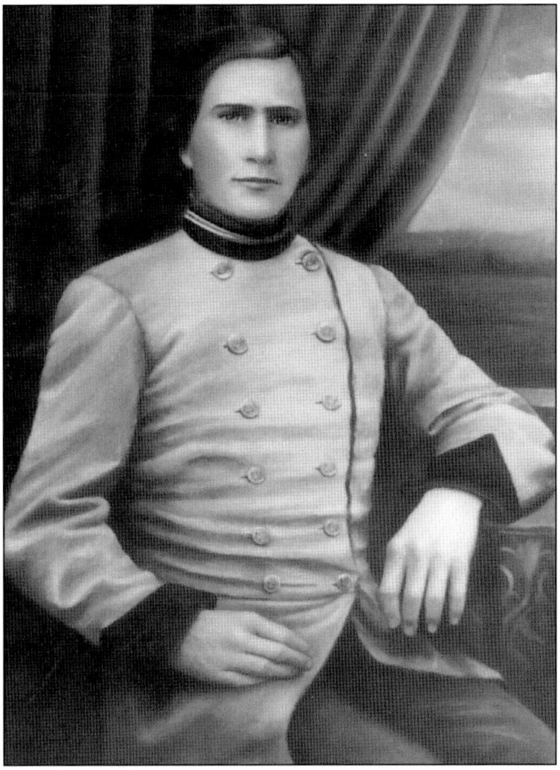

Sarah J. Camp (Bethany)
W.D. Camp (Blacks[burg])
Samuel L. Campbell (Clover)
Catherine Childers (Blacks[burg])
James Childers (Hoodtown)
Sarah D. Crawford (Bethany)
Michael Dover (Clark's Fork)
Elizabeth D. Garrison (Smith's)
Mary F. Gill (Zadoc)
Jane A. Hill (Blairsville)
Mrs. A.M. Howe (Bowling Green)
Margaret S. Miller (Zadoc)
Elizabeth Morris (Hickory Grove)
Jinsy Mullinax (Blacks[burg])
H.R. Neal (Hickory Grove)
Younger N. Neal (Hickory Grove)
Margaret Smith (Hickory Grove)
William Sprouce (Hickory Grove)
Nancy Turney (Zadoc)
Mary E. Whitner (Bethany)
M. Caroline Wilson (Blacks[burg])

The pension roll for Western York County had lengthened by 1896. Following are the names and communities of these veterans and widows of the Lost Cause:

Charles Allen (Hickory Grove)
John Barber (Zadoc)
A.D. Barnes (Lominack)
J.T. Bigham (Sharon)
J. A. Brandon (Hopewell)
W.H. McDaniel (Clark's Fork)
J.W. Martin (Smyrna)
J.L. Miller (Blairsville)
J.G. Minter (Blairsville)
Wylie A. Moss (Blacksburg)

H.B. Broom (Hickory Grove)
W.D. Brown (Hopewell)
John Cain (Sharon)
G.W. Campbell (Blacksburg)
James Childers (Blacksburg)
John Childers (Hickory Grove)
Sherod Childers (Hickory Grove)
J.A. Dowdle (Sharon)
John M. Gilfillan (Hickory Grove)
J.S. Gourley (Olive)
T.M. Grant (Hoodtown)
T.M Grant (Sharon)
George Harris (Valdora)
Thomas Harris (Hickory Grove)
H.J. Hullender (Kings Creek)
M. Hullender (Blacksburg)
F.J. Jenkins (Gould)
J.H. Jones (Hickory Grove)
B.W. Lindsay (Blacksburg)
R.F. Lindsay (McConnellsville)
J.A. Lockhart (Carp)
D.B. McCarter (Zadoc)
G.W. Mullinax (Blacksburg)
Jackson Palmer (Hickory Grove)
Ben Peterson (Blacksburg)
Robert Peterson (Blacksburg)
J.A. Pursley (Hickory Grove)
P.L. Pursley (Zadoc)
M.L. Randall (Blacksburg)
O.C. Robbins (Bullock's Creek)
R.K. Seaborn (Hickory Grove)
Cornelius Sexton (Blacksburg)
J.U. Shedd (Hickory Grove)
John D. Smarr (Cotton)
Thomas Spencer (Hickory Grove)
Alexander Wallace (Zadoc)
Daniel Wallace (Hickory Grove)
J.M. Whitesides (Smyrna)
R.G. Whitesides (Smyrna)
J.R. Williams (McConnellsville)
George Wilson (Carp)
R.M. Wilson (Clark's Fork)
D.D. Wright (Hickory Grove)

Widows

Adeline Bolin (Hickory Grove)
Catherine Bolin (Darwin's)
E.L. Bolin (Hero)
Martha Bolin (Hickory Grove)
Vicey Bolin (Clark's Fork)
M.M. Bowen (Blacksburg)
Loutitia Brown (Blacksburg)
Harriet F. Carter (Olive)
M.J. Caveny (Zadoc)
Catherine Childers (Hickory Grove)
Dulcenia Childers (Hickory Grove)
Jennie Childers (Clark's Fork)
Sally Crawford (Olive)
M.R. Dogett (Zadoc)
Elizabeth Dover (Smyrna)
N.J. Dover (Clark's Fork)
Winnie F. Feemster (Bullock's Creek)
Elivira J. Given (Zadoc)
M.E. Greer (Gould)
Jane A. Hill (Blairsville)
Catherine Latham (Hoodtown)
C.C. McKnight (Clark's Fork)
Mary Martin (Smyrna)
Sarah Martin (McConnellsville)
E.C. Patterson (Hickory Grove)
Nancy Quinn (Smyrna)
M.E. Robinson (Blairsville)
C.C. Shillinglaw (Zeno)
Dora P. Smith (Bullock's Creek)
Margaret Smith (Hickory Grove)
Nancy Turney (Zadoc)
Elizabeth H. White (Blacksburg)
Mary J. White (Blacksburg)
N.M. Whitesides (Clark's Fork)
M.C. Wilson (Blacksburg)
Sarah Wyatt (London)

Typical of the warriors of the Lost Cause was Captain William Beatty Smith, a veteran of the Jasper Light Infantry. He was born on his father's plantation on November 16, 1840. His father, Major Myles Smith, was a Western York County farmer who held a commission with the state militia. His paternal grandparents were James Smith, who was born 1741 and died in York County in 1821; and Mary Henry, who was born in 1749 in Augusta County, Virginia, and died 1821 in York County. James Smith was said to have given 6 acres to the Beersheba Presbyterian Church.

After receiving a formal education, William Beatty Smith worked with his father on the plantation, which was located about one-half mile west of the town of Clover. On April 13, 1861, he enlisted as a private in the Jasper Light Infantry. Two brothers, John I. Smith (who later became a merchant in Clover) and Robert B. Smith (who moved to Texas after the war), also served in the army of the Southern Confederacy. William B. Smith was transferred to Virginia and saw his first battle at First Manassas. He was promoted to second sergeant and later first lieutenant of Company G of the Palmetto Sharpshooters.

At the Battle of Seven Pines, 35 of the 65 men in his company were either killed or wounded. Smith was promoted to captain when the officer above his captain was badly wounded. At the Battle of Frazier's Farm, nearly two-thirds of his company were lost. He participated in the Chickahominy Campaign, the Battles of Boonesboro, Sharpsburg (Antietam), and Fredericksburg. In the fall of 1863,

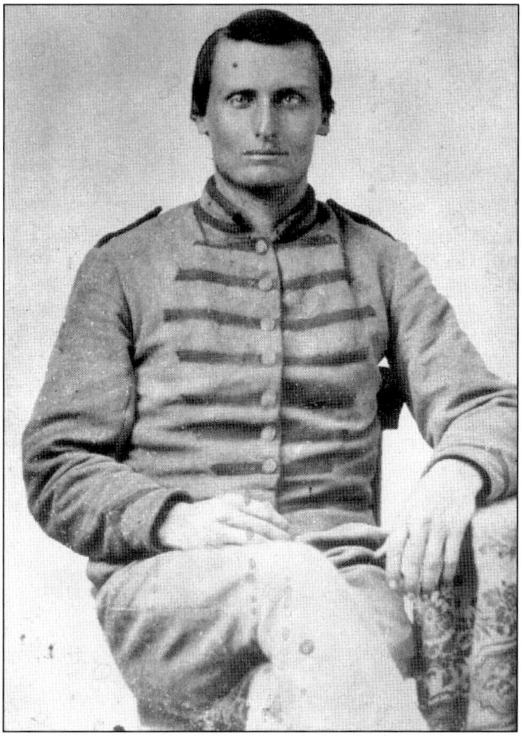

James L. Strain is pictured here in his Confederate uniform. Strain, like many men across the Upstate, volunteered for service with the Confederacy.

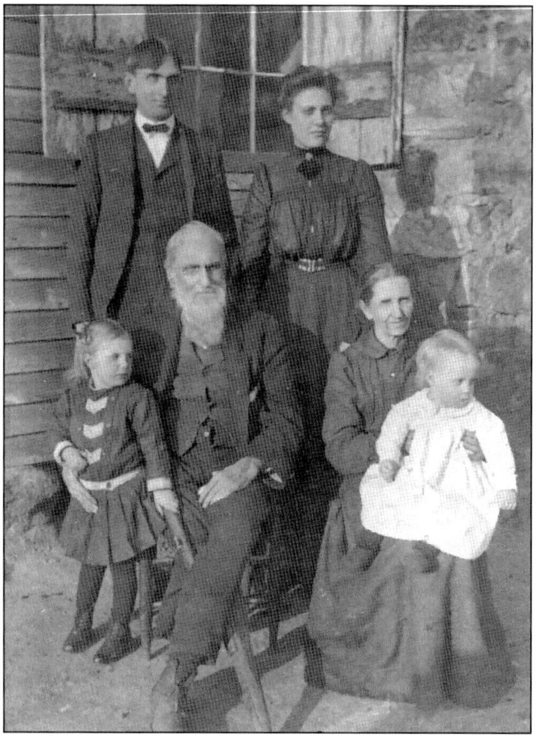

During the war, James L. Strain (seen on the previous page) served as a member of Union County's Holcomb's Legion and later had his leg amputated in a Richmond hospital. In this family portrait, Strain's granddaughter clutches his peg leg.

he went with Longstreet to Georgia and Tennessee and fought in the Knoxville Campaign. Returning to Virginia, he saw action at Wilderness, Spotsylvania Courthouse, and Cold Harbor. After Petersburg, he fought at Appomattox Courthouse, where the conflict ended.

After the truce, he returned to his home in York County and followed in his father's footsteps as a successful planter. In 1867, he married Frances Biggers, daughter of Alexander Barnett Biggers, a Confederate calvaryman. Captain Smith continued to farm until 1876, when he opened a mercantile business near his home and the new Chester and Lenoir Railroad. Tradition says that this was the founding of the town of Clover, making him the father of the town. He continued his business for 15 years, when, in 1889, he, among others, organized the Clover Cotton Manufacturing Company. For the rest of his days, he was president and principal stockholder until he was succeeded by his son, Myles L. Smith.

Both Captain Smith and his brother, John T. Smith, vowed they would not cut their beards until the South was victorious over Northern aggression. Captain Smith sported "the best beard in York County." His wife plated his beard every Monday, and during the week, he tucked it inside his shirt. On the Sabbath, she combed it out to for worship services.

Following the fall of Richmond, the capital of the Confederacy, in 1865, President Jefferson Davis, with his cabinet, escorted by 2,000 cavalrymen, fled southward. After holding their final cabinet meeting at the home of William E.

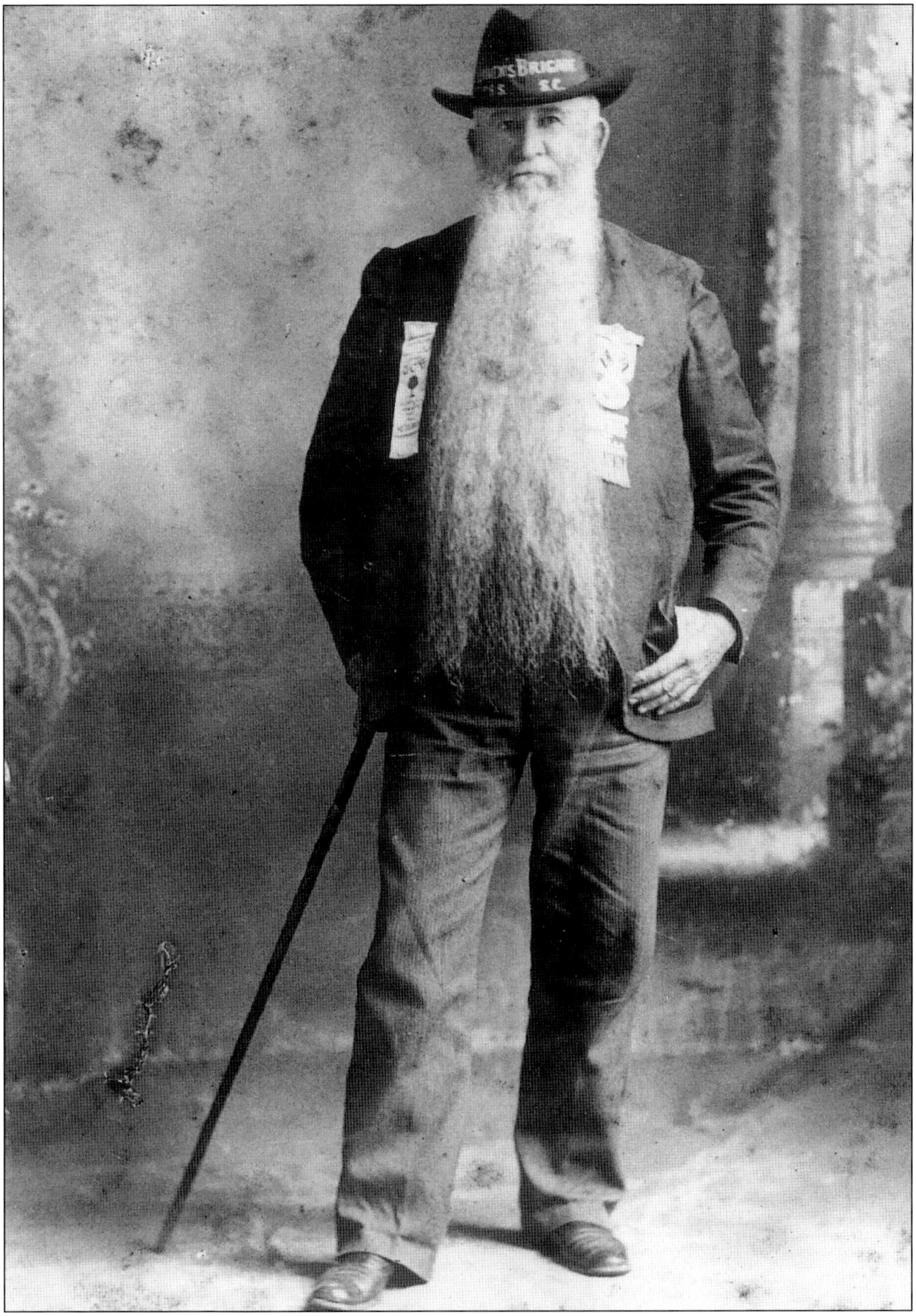

Confederate veteran William Beatty Smith, of Clover, is seen here in his later years. According to local legend, Smith wore his beard in a braid during the week, and his wife would comb it out for church attendance on Sunday.

White in Fort Mill, the entourage came to Yorkville, where Davis stayed at the home of Dr. Rufus Bratton on South Congress Street. He was accompanied by Secretary of War John C. Breckenridge and Secretary of State Judah P. Benjamin. A reception held in the evening of Davis's visit gave many Yorkville citizens an opportunity to meet the president. The townspeople gathered around Bratton's home to express their respect and sympathy to their president. They were addressed by Breckenridge, who spoke from the second-floor balcony of the Rose Hotel, next door to the Bratton home, urging the people to keep the faith. But the curtain was coming down on the Lost Cause and faith had died on faraway battlefields.

On April 27, 1865, a chain of events commenced that brought the War for Southern Independence to Western York County. On that day, United States Secretary of War Edwin M. Stanton telegraphed General George H. Thomas, commander of the Army of the Cumberland, headquartered in Nashville, Tennessee. Stanton informed Thomas that President Davis had left Goldsboro, North Carolina, with 6 to 13 million dollars in gold and silver, heading to Charlotte. Stanton ordered the commander to stop Davis and seize the Confederate treasury at all costs.

In turn, General Thomas telegraphed the following to General George Stoneman: "If you can possibly get three brigades of cavalry together, send them over the mountains into South Carolina to the westward of Charlotte and toward

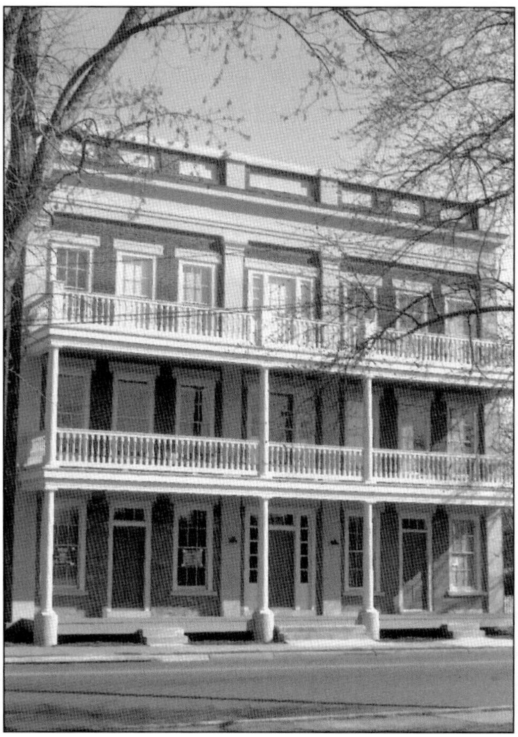

York's Rose Hotel was built in 1852 by Doctors Rufus Bratton and E.A. Crenshaw and soon purchased and opened by Edward Rose. This public house was reported to be one of the most modern hotels in the Upcountry. It was here, in April 1865, that the Confederate Cabinet spent the night while on their flight southward.

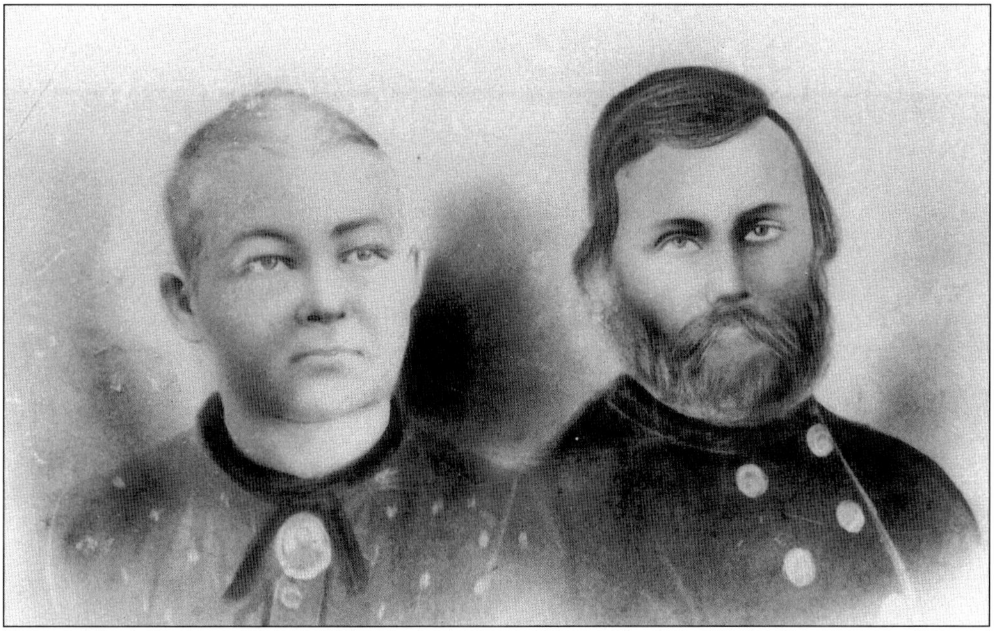

A prominent figure in Hickory Grove, John Whitley Mitchell is seen here in an artistic portrait with his wife, Jemina Plexico Mitchell, during the Civil War.

Anderson. They may possibly catch Jeff. Davis, or some of his treasure . . . Give orders to your troops to take no orders except those from you, or me, and from General Grant." Unknown to Stoneman, a group of raiders under General William J. Palmer, was within 60 miles of the Davis entourage. Leaving Rutherfordton, North Carolina, the troops headed southward. Palmer was near the old Cowpens Battleground on April 29, when he received Stoneman's message to capture Davis and the treasure. By that time, Davis and his three brigades had passed through Yorkville and were headed down the Pinckney Road, which would lead to Blairsville, Bullock's Creek, and the Pinckneyville Ferry on the Broad River.

Traveling with Davis was his personal staff and several cabinet members: Secretary of State Judah Benjamin, Navy Secretary Stephen R. Mallory, War Secretary General John Breckenridge, and Adjutant General Samuel Cooper. Other staff members in the entourage were John H. Reagan, John Jules St. Martin, and Burton N. Harrison, the president's personal secretary. Because of rough roads, the portly Judah Benjamin forsook his horse for one of the ambulances. As Davis traveled through Western York County, which had been spared by Sherman's torch, the president became more relaxed and his mood brightened. Historian Shelby Foote wrote, "He spoke of Scott and Byron, of hunting dogs and horses in a manner his fellow travelers found 'singularly equable and cheerful.' " On that particular Saturday morning, the sky was bright and clear. Sometime before noon, the entourage reached the intersection of Quinn's Road near the home of Reverend Robert Y. Russell. The major portion of the cavalry was ordered to proceed along that road which would take them to present-day Hickory Grove and then advance to Smith's Ford, where they could cross into Union County in the shallows. The president, his staff, cabinet members, and personal guard continued on the Pinckneyville Road. Around noon, they entered the Bullock's Creek area and found the road lined with well-wishers. Davis and the entourage stopped at a tavern just before crossing the Broad into Union County, and spent some time speaking to the local people.

Six miles to the north, General Palmer and his Union troops arrived at Smith's Ford just as the last Confederates were preparing to cross the river. Approximately ten were captured by Palmer and questioned. These prisoners supposedly told the general that the Confederate treasury consisted of 100 boxes of gold and 60 kegs of silver Paso's—about 10 million dollars. Lying about the size of the Confederate force, the rebels told Palmer that Davis and the treasure were guarded by 3,000 to 4,000 troops. Hearing this, Palmer decided not to attack such a large force.

On May 3, 1865, York County's only newspaper, the *Yorkville Enquirer*, reported the presence of the Yankee cavalry on the Broad River, although its size was overestimated:

> A force of the enemy's cavalry, estimated at from three to four thousand, crossed Broad River at Smith's Ford on Sunday Evening and came within eleven miles of this place [Yorkville]. They subsequently recrossed and are reported to have moved in the direction of Limestone Springs. A flag of truce bearing the recent order of Sherman was dispatched after them but failed to reach them at last account.

Several area families have oral traditions of seeing these Yankee troops along the York County side of Broad River and that a subsequent skirmish had taken place as well. Their presence was reported at Thomson's Quarters, the Hamilton plantation, and the Osborne plantation, which was south of the Pinckneyville Ferry, where Davis crossed into Union County, and some 7 miles south of Smith's Ford. Without any written accounts to prove the oral traditions of the Yankee foray into the area, it was first assumed that these may have been some stragglers, or "bummers," from Sherman's column some 40 miles to the east. None of the York County historians had ever heard mention of Yankees on the Broad. It was not until 1993, when the above newspaper account of Stoneman's troops was rediscovered, that the oral traditions were given solid credibility.

York County, safe from the ravages of war, must have seemed like easy pickings to the Yankees, as they began to loot and pillage the area of all livestock, foodstuffs, and valuable household items. When Dr. W.P. Thomson received word that Union soldiers were looting just north of his plantation, he sent his personal servant out to bury the family's silver items. Upon returning, both Thomson and the servant attempted to hide under the house. Dr. Thomson, being a small man, was able to squeeze under the lowest part, while the servant, who was much larger, could not crawl under but a short distance. When the troops arrived, they discovered the quaking servant and forced him to go with them. Family traditions tell that many years later, he was seen in Winston-Salem, North Carolina, where he had been abandoned by his captors. The family's silver was never recovered.

Jack Hill, a small, cone-shaped prominence located just north of the Thomson plantation and on the Hamilton plantation near the old Pinckney Road, was said to have been the site of a skirmish between the Union troops and local farmers. Occurring on Sunday, April 30, this would have been one of the few incidents which happened after the truce was signed at Appomattox, ending the four-year war. It was here in the spring of 1865, on the banks of the Broad River, that the Civil War came to Western York County—but it was a war that had already ended. Peace would not cover the area for another 11 years because now the people faced the degrading ordeal of Reconstruction.

Many years later, in April 1939, Hugh H. Sherer of the Blairsville community was interviewed by news reporter Ernest Jackson. At the time, Sherer was celebrating his 93rd birthday and was one of the two Confederate veterans still living in York County—the other was Ernest Lowry of York. In response to the reporter's question as to which were better times, the old or the new, Sherer quickly replied, "The old times were the best; people lived more sensibly then. There is a lot of foolishness now."

Sherer had joined the Confederate army early in 1864, and served in the 17th South Carolina Regiment, commanded by Colonel McMaster. The regiment

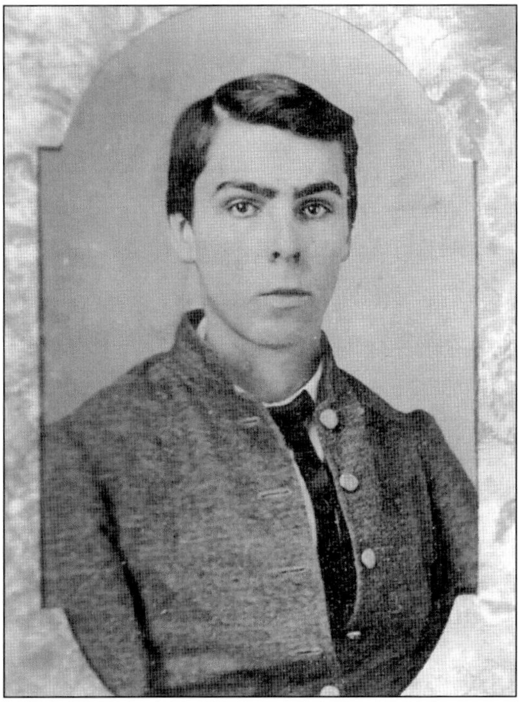

John T. Scoggins, of Hickory Grove, serves as an example of the area's patriotism toward the Southern cause. In 1864, at the young age of 15, Scoggins enlisted into the Confederate Army and was sent to the Cold Harbor battlefield. Upon discovery of his age, he was sent home, but within a few months, he became 16 and immediately re-enlisted.

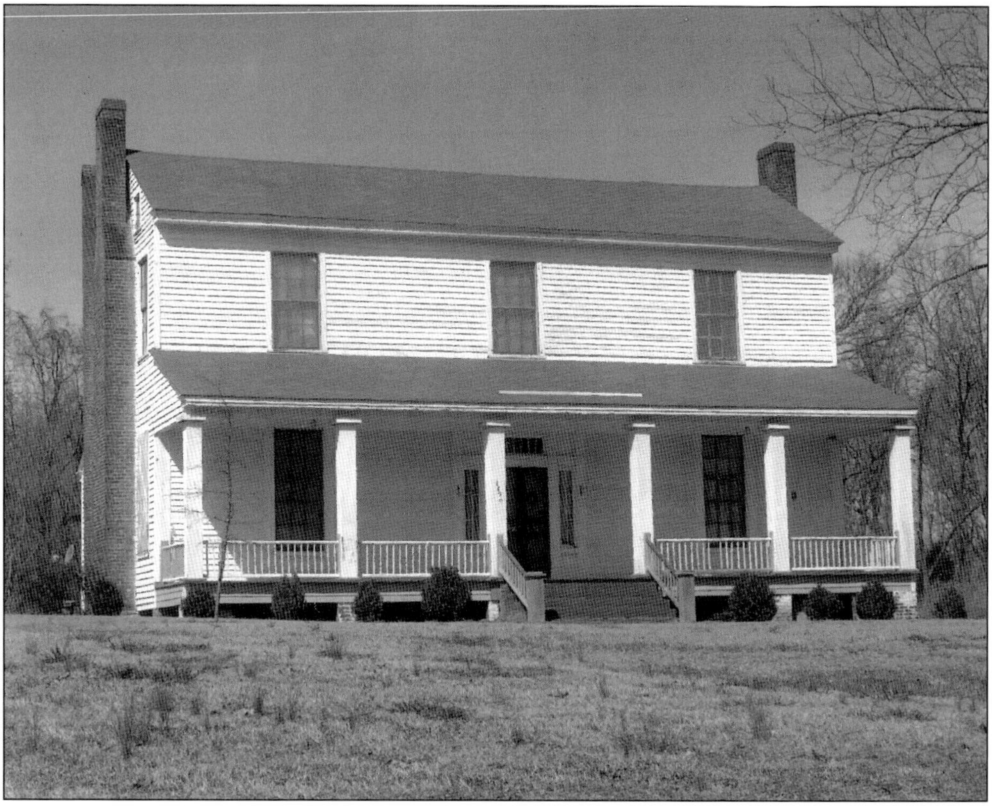

The antebellum home of Alexander S. "Buttermilk" Wallace is situated on the old Pinckney Road. During Reconstruction, this Republican legislator supposedly signed warrants in this house for the arrest of men accused of "Ku-Kluxing." He also raised the ire of neighbors and local community members by hosting integrated parties and dances.

was sent to the Virginia battlefields and suffered increasing hardships as the war ground to its terrible end. He recalled, "I slept in the rain, snow, and sleet; but this life didn't hurt me. What did I eat? Just anything I could get and sometimes not much of that. You can't pick where you sleep or eat in a war—you just have to take what comes your way." Ironically, he went through the war unscathed by enemy fire, but was wounded in the arm when his own rifle discharged while he was trying to keep it dry in a heavy rain.

During the tumultuous times of Reconstruction, he and his three brothers, James, William, and S.H. Sherer, were tried and convicted of "Ku-Kluxing." Like dozens of other York County men, all four were sentenced to serve 18 months in a federal prison in Albany, New York. At the end of 17 months, they were released, having been given time off for good behavior. "After they let us out of prison, they drove us to the railway station in a sleigh drawn by four horses. They gave us ten dollars to come home on. It was a long trip and a tedious one, but we managed to get home at last," Sherer observed.

"How was prison life? Well, it was pretty tough. For one thing the fare was very poor—sour Irish potatoes for dinner and mush and molasses for supper. But we managed to live—and that is about all you can expect to do in prison. While there, we worked, most of us at shoe making. Each man learned a special part of the job. My work was to cut heels."

Even in his 93rd year, Hugh Sherer was in good health. He rose early and ate heartily. He took pride in reading without the aid of glasses and enjoyed reading the local newspaper to keep abreast of current events. After awakening, he stayed up all day and walked freely about the house and spent many peaceful hours sitting on his front piazza. His mind remained clear and he tried to participate in life as usual. Just prior to his birthday, he had wanted to go to Sharon, some 3 miles away, to vote in a school election. Only after much pleading from his family did he submit to staying home.

When questioned about his longevity, he said he did not know how to account for it except that he had always been temperate in his habits and that longevity was not rare in his family. His father lived to the age of 92 and a brother died at 83. While he enjoyed chewing tobacco, he did not consider himself a "heavy user of the weed." His daughter-in-law, Zettie Robbins Sherer, believed his long life might have been connected with his vegetarian diet; he ate meat very sparingly, she said.

A few months before his death in 1924, Sharon's John L. Rainey, another Confederate veteran, commented on his diet. "I do not eat any hog meat any

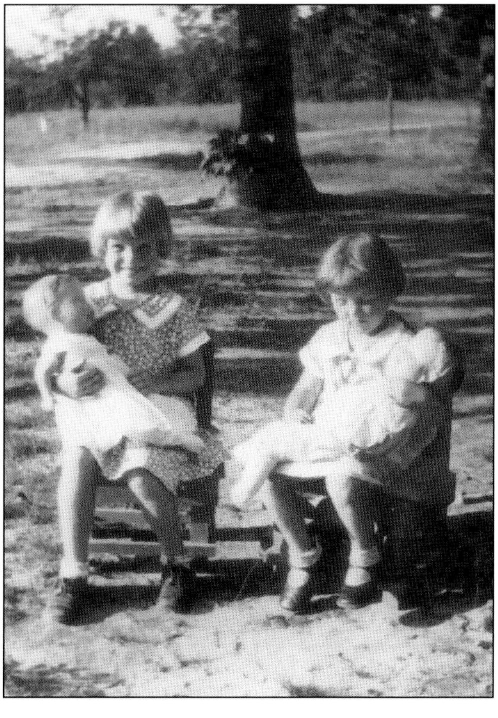

Sisters Barbara and Carolyn Sherer play with their dolls at their home in 1933. They are the daughters of farmer, furniture maker, and controversial Western York County citizen Hugh Sherer and his wife, Sarah Russell Sherer.

more—that is no fresh pork," said Rainey. "I can eat beef or chicken and it does not seem to hurt me—partridge too, I can eat partridge all right." When it was suggested that mutton was healthy and had no side effects, Rainey responded as follows:

> No mutton for me, I have not eaten a piece of mutton in sixty years, and I'll tell you what fixed me. It was during the Civil War. We had had nothing to eat for several days, because we had been fighting all the while. We came upon a pasture in which there were a number of sheep and the men shot some of them down for food. I got hold of the leg of a sucking ewe, roasted it and ate it without any bread or even salt. That fixed me. It made me sick. One man died from eating those sheep. I have never tasted mutton since. . . . We were under fire at the time we ran upon that sheep pasture, but we did not mind that so much as we did the terrible hunger from which we were suffering. I suppose I would have tried to eat a buzzard about that time if it had been all that I could have got hold of.

Reporter Jackson closed his article on veteran Sherer musing, ". . . when his memory tracks back across the years he sees again, in mental vision, the familiar

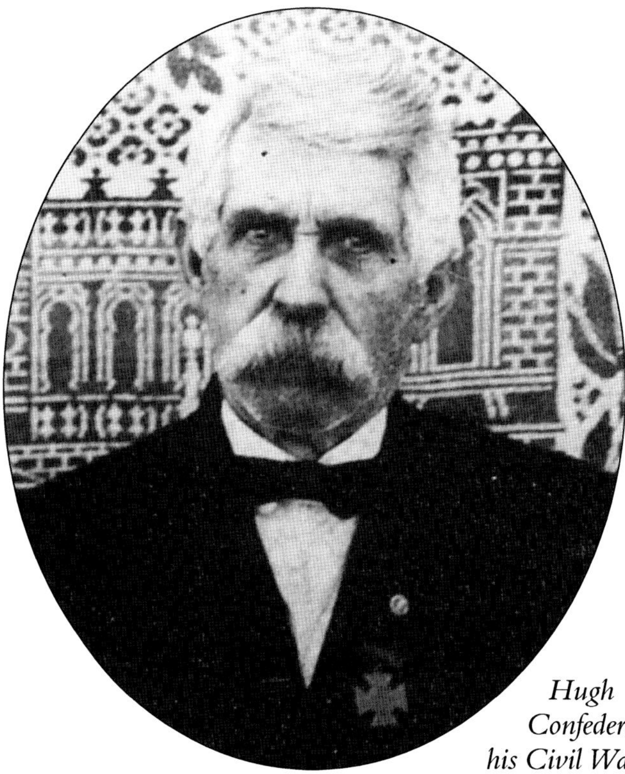

Hugh Sherer, like many of his Confederate compatriots, proudly displayed his Civil War medallion of service.

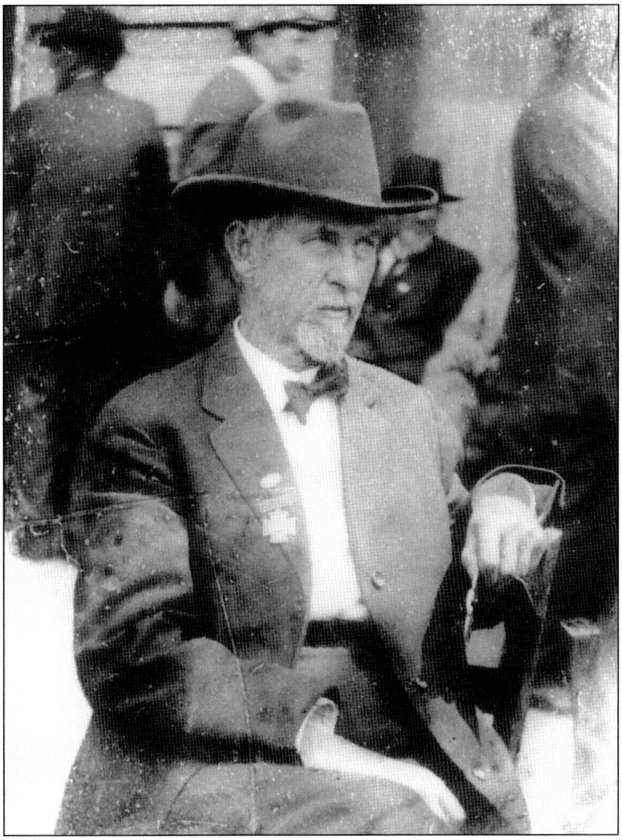

At the outbreak of the Civil War, William S. Wilkerson, son of Thomas Jefferson and Lucinda Howell Wilkerson, enlisted under the command of Captain W.B. Smith of Clover. At the time of Wilkerson's death in 1925, only two members of his company remained alive. Note the Civil War pin on his lapel.

scenes of Virginia in war time—the long columns of marching infantry, the artillery toiling forward, the cavalry hurrying into action. There falls on his ear, too, the thunder of cannon and the rattle of musketry as the ragged but dauntless Army of Northern Virginia come to grips with the foe. And directing all, he sees a gray bearded, slouch-hatted man astride a white horse—the grandest soldier that every drew sword, still swear his handful of living followers—'Marse Robert' himself." Hugh H. Sherer died the following year.

While the major battles of the Civil War were fought on fields far from Western York County, the repercussions were no less felt in the hearts and homes of the people. The deafening thunder and bloody scenes of places like Manassas, Cold Harbor, and Petersburg permeated the heart and fiber of every individual living in the South—including residents of Western York County. Defeat, extirpation (the pulling up by the roots), the scorched-earth policy of the federal government, and the tragedy of America's most deadly war traumatized and molded the people of the old Confederacy. "Yankees on the Broad!" is a symbolic shout of terror, charged by the emotions of a "lost cause" defended by men in gray who witnessed their world turned upside down. The survivors, all casualties, never forgot the images and sounds.

6. Along the Old Line of the Charleston, Cincinnati & Chicago

A casual walk up the drive of the Bullock's Creek Presbyterian Cemetery is bound to give the observer a sense of patriotism found in the people of York County. Shortly after the Broad River Basin Historical Society erected a memorial marker to the more than 20 Revolutionary soldiers buried there, the Cemetery Committee decided to commemorate all veterans buried within the confines of that historic cemetery. Scheduled to be completed by 2010, seven more monuments will join those of the Revolutionary War, the War of 1812, and the War with Mexico, with the Civil War marker scheduled for the spring of 2002.

While Bullock's Creek Cemetery may be unique in its decision to honor the war dead in such an uncommon fashion, it is not unique in its contents of patriots who loved this nation. All across Western York County, the bodies of those who served in the multiple wars of the United States lie in peaceful slumber. When this nation needed its men and women to defend and protect its interests, the people of York County rallied at every alarm.

From the great American Revolution to Desert Storm, not only the men, but the women of Western York County have put their shoulders to task and gave it all they had. While men and resources were sent to the battlefields, the women bravely deprived themselves of their loved ones and daily necessities.

The most devastating war this nation has known was the Civil War, sometimes known to Southerners as the Southern War for Independence. Devastation was not limited to its many battlefields, but a major portion of the nation's wealth and welfare were lost and never to be regained. And as destructive as it was, out of it was developed an undying romanticism so needed in the lives of humans as well as symbols that exemplify the need for bravery to fight for principles found in lost causes.

Sometimes, patriotic Southerners are accused of making too much of that war and are questioned, "Why can't you people just leave the Civil War alone?" The answer is simple—it was the most devastatingly destructive and deadly event in American history. The war and the aftermath of Reconstruction forever shaped the minds of Southerners, and those descendants living in Western York County are no exception.

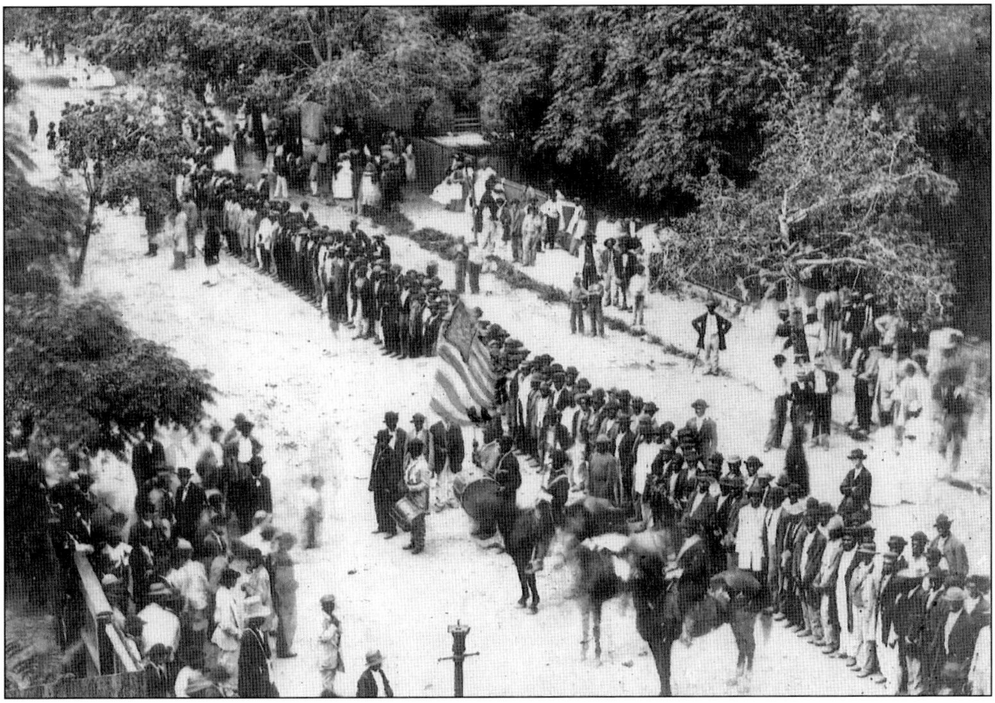

During Reconstruction, Union Leagues were established throughout the county to educate freedmen on their rights. This large assembly in Yorkville of the Union Leagues may have taken place during a day of political campaigns.

To suggest that third- and fourth-generation descendants should "forget about it" must be seen as arrogant and insensitive. The families of those Confederate veterans might reply, "Did the Federal government ever suggest a 'forgive and forget policy?' " Should veterans of World War II, or Vietnam, or Holocaust victims and their descendants be reminded they should forget about it?

As the Civil War came to a close, most York Countians found themselves struggling under the reality of broken homes and families, dire financial straits, and adjusting to a new world created through war. M.S. Carroll, in 1924, reflected as follows on the situation the people of York County found themselves:

> From the close of the Civil War in April 1865 until 1976 was a period never to be forgotten by those who lived through it. A horde of Carpet Baggers from the North descended upon us, and they, in conjunction with the meanest, most detestable creatures that ever wore the skin of a white man (I mean the Scalawag); Scamps, who turned traitor to their own people in order to rob them. The Negroes, having been freed and given the right of suffrage, were easily the dupes of these scoundrels and were told that they were entitled to forty acres and a mule and if they could not get it any other way, to burn out the whites and take it

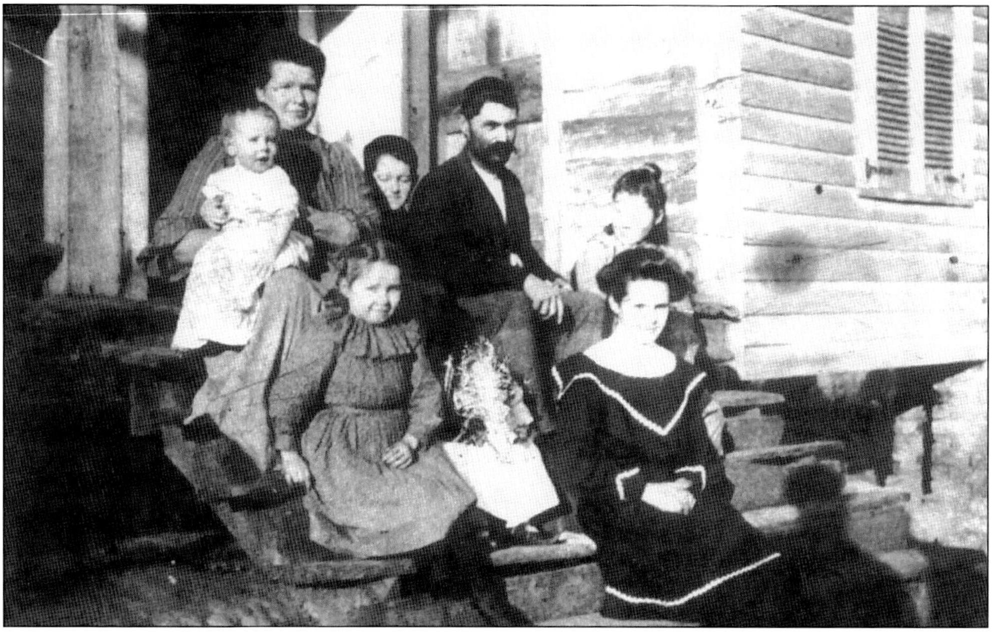

The William Preston Whisonant family, dressed in their "Sunday Best," gathered on the sunny steps of their Hickory Grove home after the Civil War, a time of great difficulty for many families across Western York County.

> by force, even to the killing of the whites from the cradle to the grave. While I don't recall any murder committed, they did proceed to burn hundred of dwellings, gin houses, and barns. Until about 1869 and 1870, there was scarcely a night passed without a fire in some direction.

Radical Republicans had a death hold on South Carolina, and they were determined to punish the state for its sins against the Union. Using freedmen as their instruments of power, they filled nearly every local and state political office and ignored the real needs of the people. In the spring of 1868, the Ku Klux Klan, made up of white Democrats, appeared on the scene in hopes of breaking the Republican hold. Intimidation and violence sprang up across the county like weeds in a cotton field after a spring rain—mostly in Western York County. Every fire set was retaliated with beating, intimidation, and sometimes murder. Against the warning of a civil war by more moderate whites, "carpetbagger" Governor Robert K. Scott, in February 1871, placed three companies of all-black militia units in the county to implement disarmament of whites. Violence and destruction of property escalated.

Fearing an outbreak of war, President Grant placed several companies of the Seventh Cavalry in Yorkville along with Colonel Lewis Merrill to investigate, arrest, and prosecute anyone involved in the activities of the Ku Klux Klan. By the end of 1871, fear of incrimination spread across Western York County and in the wake of arrests, men began to flee across state lines from their once safe homes. The Yorkville jail was cramped with men arrested on suspicion; some were later released, most were held for trial by authorities based in the Rose Hotel.

By November 1872, 25 indictments were handed down for the lynching of militia Captain James Williams, which took place near Brattonsville. Every indictment was for men from Western York County. Eighteen more were indicted for riot and assault on William J. Wilson, and another 18 for riot and tumult on John R. Faris, a white man.

Washington and the people of the North grew weary of Reconstruction and began seeking for reasons to abandon the Southern project and spend their time with more successful endeavors. Although many Klansmen were imprisoned in Albany, New York, they had been successful in that it wore out the Federal government and brought Reconstruction to an end. While many may argue that the Klan was destroyed by Federal intervention, it cannot be denied that they did not cease their activities until they accomplished their task of breaking political powers and disrupting Reconstruction.

When the engineers of the Union and Pacific Railroad began demanding protection from Indian attacks, the government saw a perfect opportunity to distance itself from the South by moving the Seventh Cavalry out of York County.

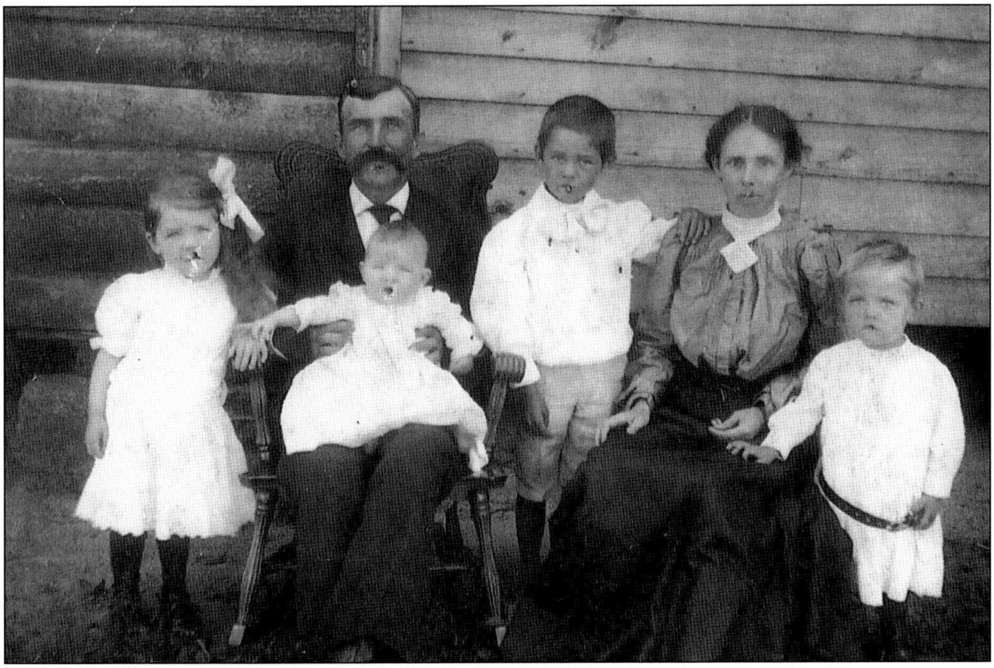

James Newell Russell (1865–1948), of Blairsville, grew up in the Reconstruction South and was shaped by its hardships. In this 1905 family portrait, he is seen with his family; they are, from left to right, as follows: Sarah, James Russell (holding baby Lewis), unidentified, Barbara Chambers Russell, and Robert Young "R.Y."

Many of the "blue coats" who had been part of the peace-keeping force in this county would later be found dead and mutilated on the hills of Wounded Knee.

As the Ku Klux Klan began to fade into history, another paramilitary wing of the Democratic Party began to form. In preparation for the state and national election of 1876, the Red Shirts of South Carolina began devising plans on how to "redeem" the state from Radical rule and ultimately dismantle the government created by carpetbagger Republicans. Led by the Democratic candidate for governor, Wade Hampton, his Red Shirts began their work in the Carolina piedmont where they had the most support.

What was termed as the "Last Grand Stand of the Republicans in York County" took place on September 25, 1876, at Wilson's Chapel, a black church located in the Blairsville community. Republican Party leaders had planned the political rally when a large delegation of Democrats arrived and suggested a joint program. The chairman of both parties met in a 30-minute, private session and outlined the program with ground rules. They agreed that all banners had to be furled and put out of sight, except for the United States flag and that the utmost courtesy must be shown to all candidates. Each party was allowed three speakers with a 30-minute time limit, with closing remarks to be made by United States Senator A.S. Wallace (R).

Satisfied with the program, Isaac D. Witherspoon spoke to the assembly of about 400, which was equally divided racially. Flattering the black Republicans, he assured them they had nothing to fear from the Democratic Party, that it was an "utter impossibility" to deny the black man his rights, and that the Democrats

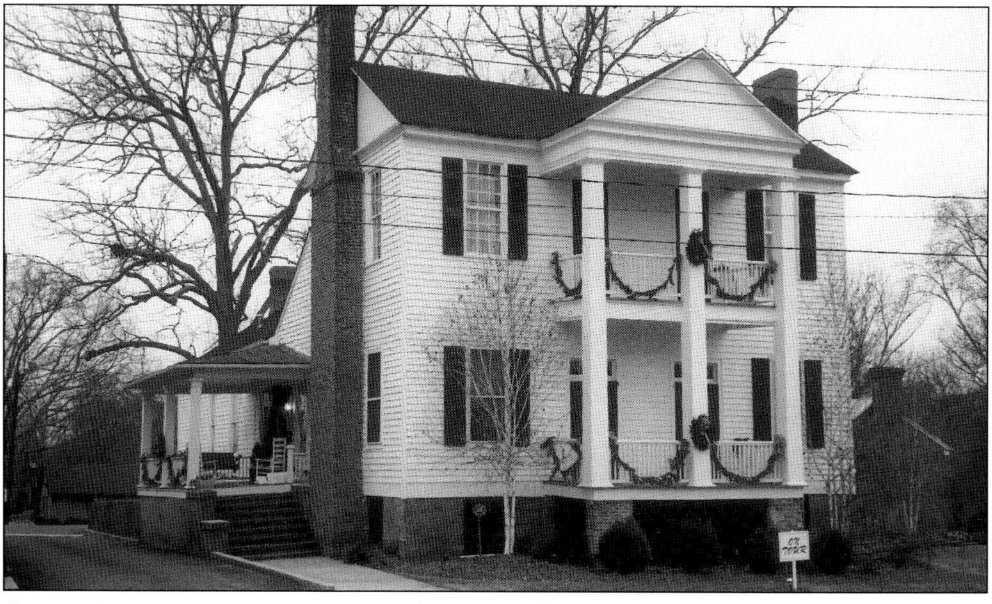

During Reconstruction, Isaac D. Witherspoon, the owner of this York home, became an important Democratic Party leader.

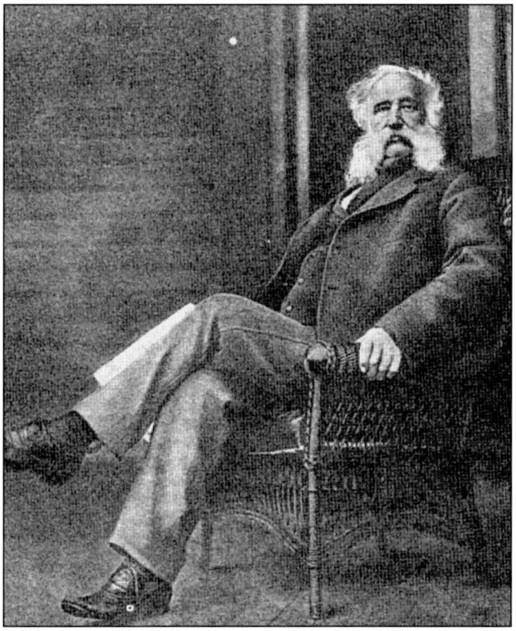

Wade Hampton, former Confederate general, rallied supporters in his campaign for South Carolina governor to put an end to Reconstruction.

were committed to the state constitution that protected these rights. He addressed the corruption of the Republican Party and of the South Carolina government headed by that party.

John Hannibal White, a black state senator, was the next speaker. White warned the members of his race against believing that the Democrats would protect their rights—that they had not really changed. He declared that should the Democrats gain control of both houses, they would pronounce the amendments and Reconstruction null and void and a bloody war would ensue.

Major James F. Hart, chairman of the York County Democratic Party, followed Witherspoon's lead saying the party had changed and that is was and always had been the true friend of the black man. Pointing out that it was white men who had approved the Fourteenth Amendment, he did not bother to say that Congress had withheld statehood until it had been ratified by South Carolina.

As hypocritical and patronizing as these speeches may seem, they were effective, as the election would prove. As civil and courteous as the meeting at Wilson's Chapel was, Democrats had not totally forsaken their old ways. They still believed that the threat of violence was a good reminder and intimidation a handy tool. Shortly after this meeting, the Democrats agreed to hold a military-style parade of a regiment of Red Shirts in York on Election Day.

Just one month before the November election, Hampton's campaign trail led him to York, where a huge parade of Red Shirts greeted him. More than 600 men, all dressed in red shirts, representing the Democratic Clubs of Bullock's Creek, Kings Mountain, McConnellsville, Clay Hill, Rock Hill, Bethel, Hickory Grove, Cherokee, Ebenezer, and York paraded behind their "Redeemer."

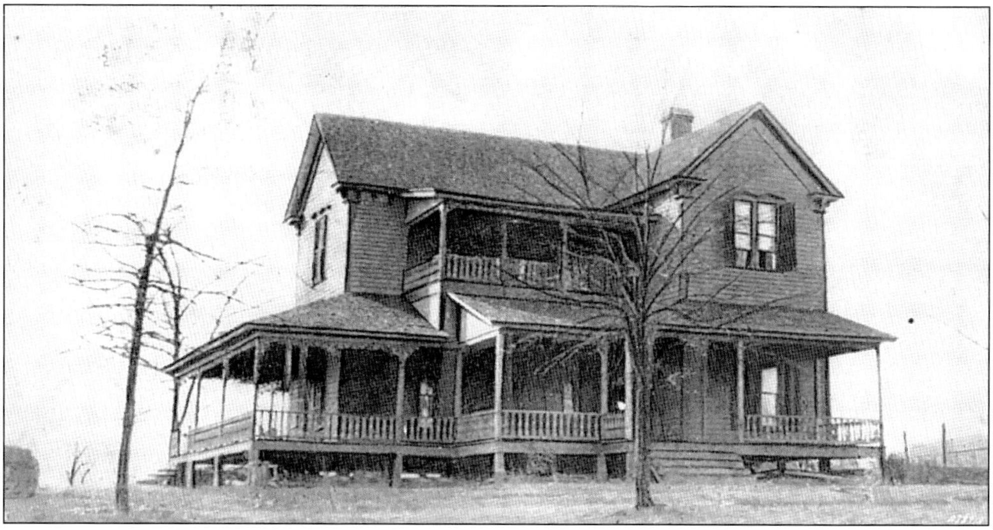

Standing solitary and bleak, Leech's Hotel, one of Hickory Grove's early businesses, was frequented by salesmen and drummers who came to peddle their wares to the merchants of the small town.

In January, after a prolonged counting process, Hampton was declared the governor of South Carolina. Eventually, the Federal troops were withdrawn from the capital, and the Democrats were free to attempt to rebuild the old aristocracy.

Within the townships of Bullock's Creek and Broad River lie the three main communities of Western York County—Hickory Grove, Smyrna, and Sharon. Spawned by the 1888 and 1889 advent of the Charleston, Cincinnati & Chicago Railroad, these havens, at times, have been referred to as the "Tri-Cities." Of these three small towns, Hickory Grove has the longest history in association with the postal service.

Hickory Grove's post office, located in the store of James McKinney, was established in 1831. Hickory Grove, however, was not the first in Western York County to have an established post office; in fact, several offices were established some years before Hickory Grove. Some 20 years earlier, in 1808, a post office was established at Thomson's Tan yard several miles east of Hickory Grove. Others predating the one at Hickory Grove were Blairsville in 1815, Henderson's in 1816, Hopewell in 1817, Harmony in 1819, and Smith's Ford in 1826.

But it was the establishment of a crossroads store by James McKinney at the intersection of Quinn's Road and Smith's Ford Road that was the genesis of the town. Apparently, James McKinney came up with the name "Hickory Grove" when he applied for the position of postmaster. In 1846, McKinney sold his holdings to Thomas G. Wylie, and by the following year he was the new postmaster. At that time, the name changed simply to "Wylie's" and remained so for a number of years. In 1868, the voting precinct for the crossroads community was designated "Wylie's."

Early in the twentieth century, a journalist filed this profile of Hickory Grove in 1904: "Hickory Grove is a lovely place and healthy. Its main street, with a handsome block of brick and frame shops, is short, as it becomes a lovely avenue with big armed leafy trees and green wards and be-gardened houses, over which four churches and a two story school are guards and sentinel."

In this "lovely place" at the turn of the twentieth century dwelt a number of people and families who played an important role in the town of Hickory Grove. One of them was Professor W.T. Slaughter. He was born in Georgia, three days after South Carolina seceded from the Union, and by his father's friends was dubbed "Little Secession" and afterward, "Sech." Coming to Hickory Grove, he purchased the home of J.H. Martin, an elegant house with a broad verandah on three sides, and fronted by a beautiful lawn on which stood stalwart oaks. Slaughter made additions and opened it as the Slaughter Hotel. Many of the older residents recalled the parties and dances at the hotel, as well as fights, stabbings, and shootings. Before become a hotel owner, he ran a business in town dealing with stationary, novelties, and "talking machines."

J.N. McDill, well known throughout the county, had been a merchant in Hickory Grove since just after the Civil War. After some years, John R. Allison,

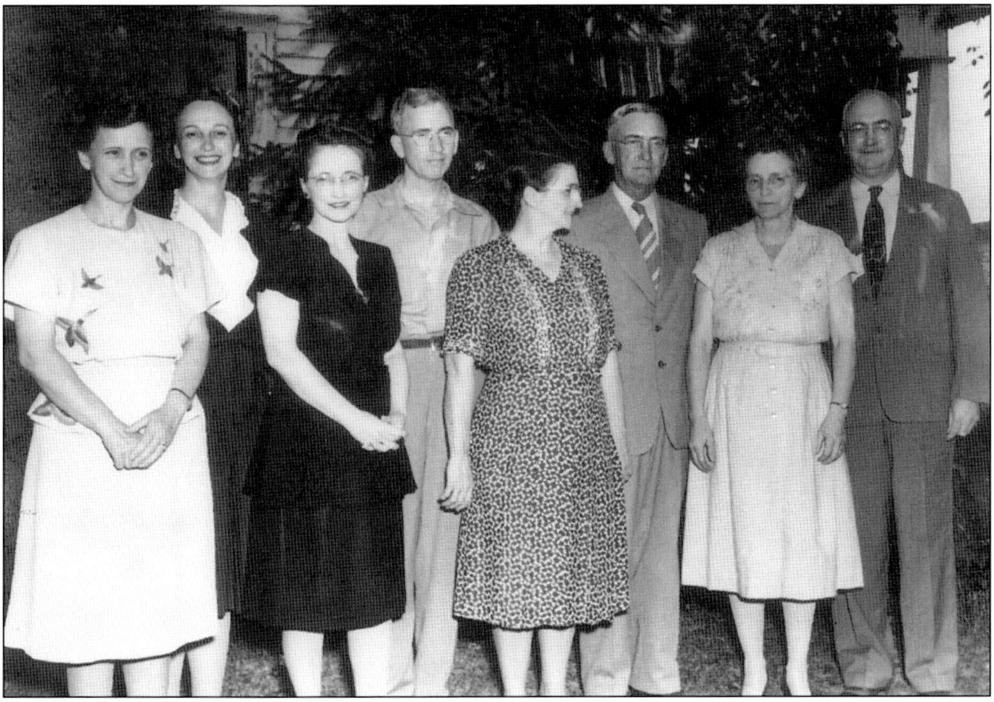

"Family" has always had a special meaning to the people of Western York County, where traditions are closely guarded. Families continue to gather at their home places on Sunday afternoons. These children of John Calvin and Anna Trout Wylie, of Hickory Grove, have assembled at a family reunion in July 1948.

a planter in his own right, was hired by McDill and soon became his righthand man in management. McDill owned a steady undertaking business, and after some years he sold his mercantile store to give his full attention to the dead. The town's post office was conducted within McDill's store, and about 1896, Allison was appointed postmaster. In 1904, the town received four mail delivers by rail and had two rural routes. John W. Leech delivered the mail on Route 1 and John H. Wylie traveled Route 2. Allison's assistant was Nixon M. McDill, a graduate of Erskine College, and he handled the four mail delivers.

Doctor T.S.R. Ward came to Hickory Grove before the town was incorporated and established a wide practice in the area. Like most physicians of the time, he also had other profitable business concerns. He owned a well-stocked pharmacy, farm, and bought and sold real estate. Dr. Benjamin N. Miller, a graduate of Johns Hopkins University, soon joined Doctor Ward and continued to practice in the area for approximately 50 years.

The Whitesides family earned their prominence in Western York County through successful farming and later in business and local politics. This family was well represented in mercantile business in each of the towns of Hickory Grove, Sharon, and Smyrna. In the early 1900s, the Whitesides Brothers Mercantile Company in Hickory Grove was thriving under the leadership of I.J. Whitesides as the general manager of the business as well as the ginning and milling interests.

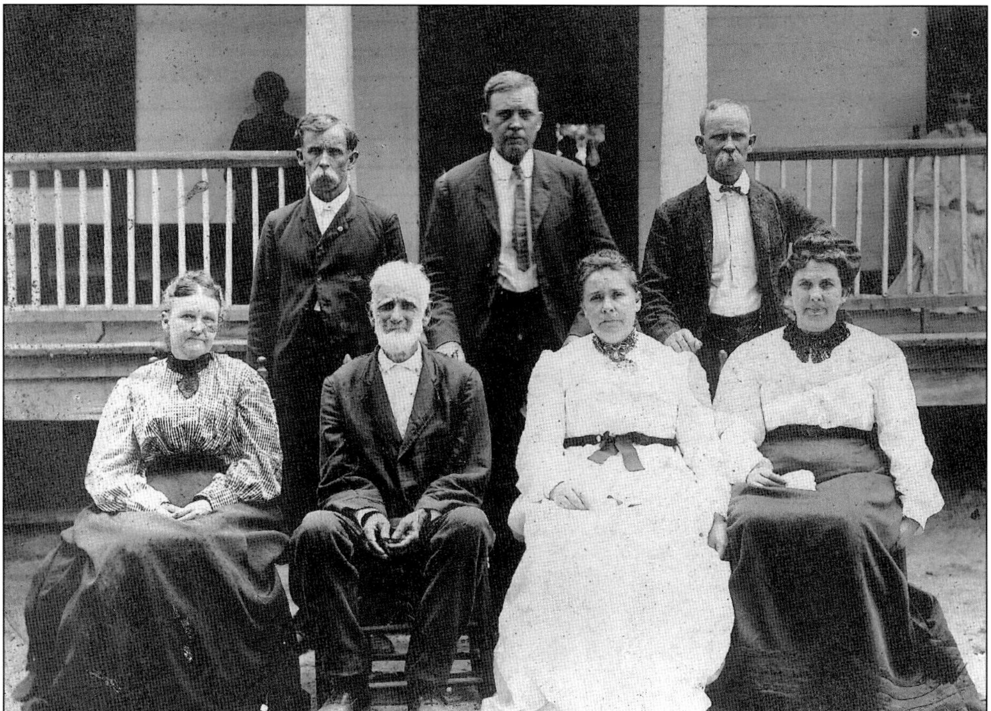

The McGill-Whitesides family appears here in a c. *1900 portrait.*

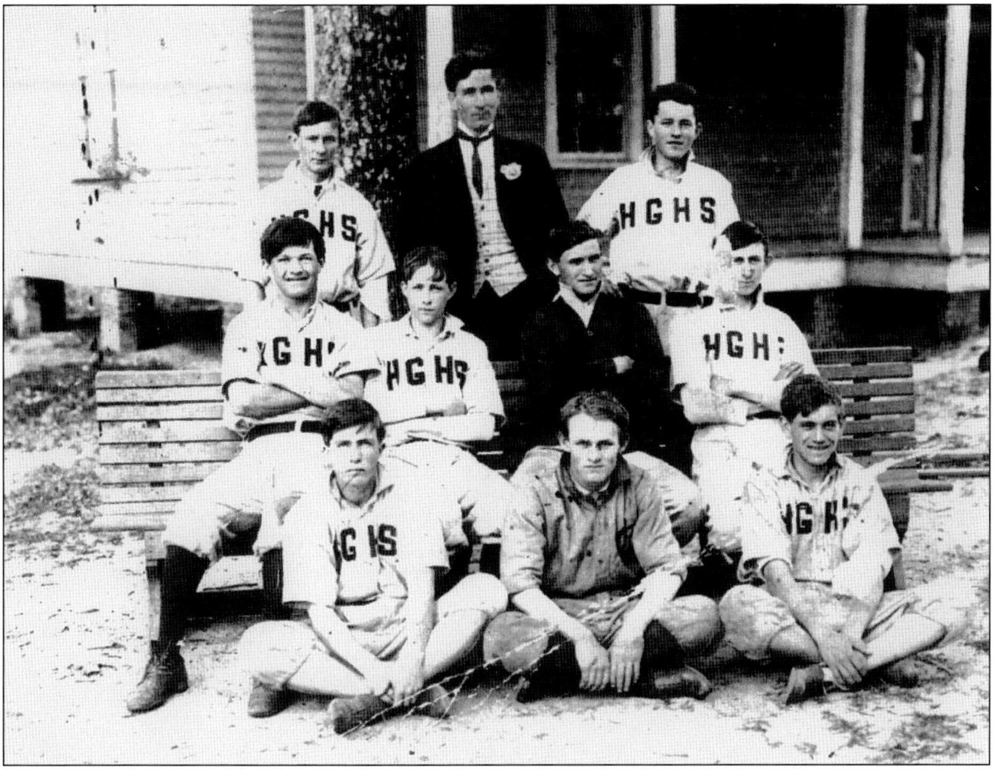

Hickory Grove High School's 1912 baseball team consisted of several young men from the town's more prominent families; they are, from left to right, as follows: (front row) Barron Whisonant, Clarence Castles, and Grover Slaughter; (middle row) Stark Slaughter, Joe Leech, W.T. Slaughter, and Ralph Castles; (back row) Harry Allison, Professor Holiday, and Daniel F. Whisonant.

At the same time, he was running both his mother's farm and leasing properties, which required his talents in supervising 25 plows.

Another of Hickory Grove's prominent mercantile-planter families were the McGills. I.N. McGill began operating a livestock company before the turn of the twentieth century, chiefly buying and selling mules. Soon after the Civil War, he began keeping bees, becoming "a champion apiarist of the region," and in 1905, he was caring for 60 patent gums. That same year, his son, T.M. McGill, was managing the family's mercantile business in one of the town's new brick buildings.

Soon after the town of Hickory Grove was chartered by the state, Walter J. Moorehead moved into town from Mount Tabor in Union County. Moorehead began his training in merchandising under his uncle, W.A. Moorehead, at Wilkinsville, across the Broad River from Hickory Grove and later at Mount Tabor. By the turn of the century, Walter Moorehead had built a brick store building with about $6,000 in stock with a branch in the nearby Hopewell

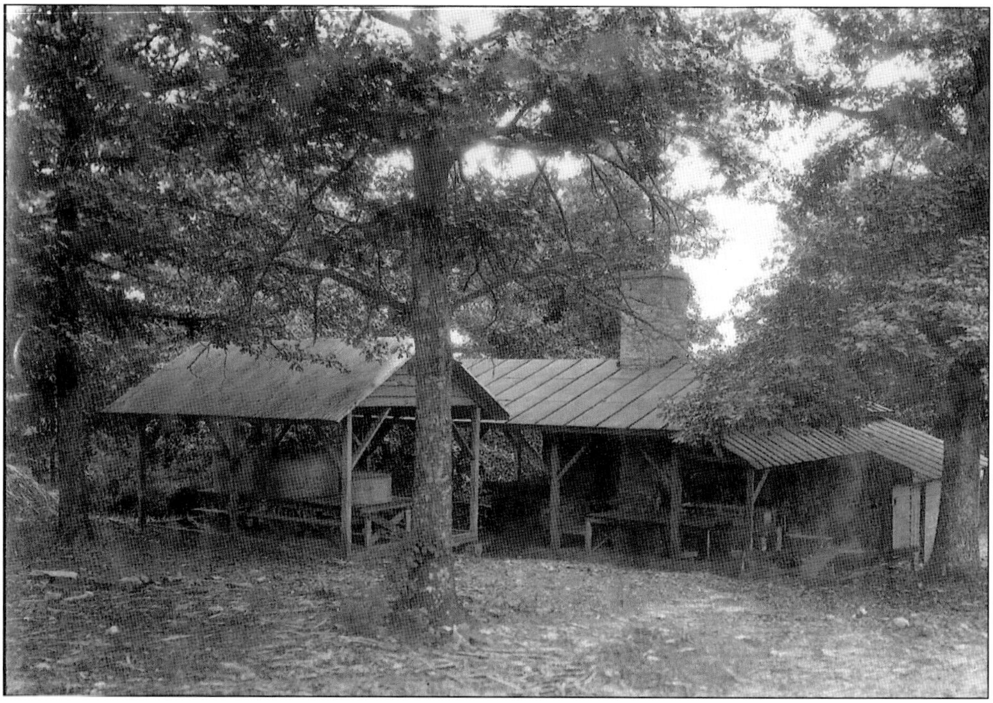

By the first decade of the twentieth century, William Smith Wilkerson of Hickory Grove was known as the "Sorghum King." At this mill, he invented a faster way to process sugar cane and increase production.

community. He was also a cotton buyer and had developed another business in which he was handling about 15,000 dozen eggs a year.

W.S. Wilkerson was Hickory Grove's star entrepreneur, though not always successful in his many financial ventures. In the summer of 1895, he and Samuel Hunt, S.B. Lumpkins, A. Tripp, and J.B. Martin applied to the secretary of state to incorporate the Hickory Grove & Lockhart Shoals Transportation Company. The object of the company was to charter steamboats on the Broad and Pacolet Rivers and to run a line of hacks for river travel. The Lockhart Cotton Mill was under construction at the time and the engineers believed it would be economical to off-load building supplies and equipment in Hickory Grove, deliver it to Howell's Ferry, and then ferry it down the river to the mill site. It appears Wilkerson's river company never got in the water since the mill engineers found another route to the mill at Lockhart Shoals.

Inventor of a new processor for sorghum milling, W.S. Wilkerson became known as the "Sorghum King of Western York County." From his farm just south of Hickory Grove, he operated various agricultural concerns; he was not only a planter of some success, but operated a cotton gin, sawmill, thresher, and haybailer. Wilkerson served as county commissioner many years and president of the Farmer's Mutual Life Insurance Company. Also in 1905, his son, John S.

Wilkerson, began stepping into his father's entrepreneurial shoes when he opened a mercantile business in Hickory Grove with a stock of $5,000.

Reflecting on his long life, Hickory Grove's W.S. Wilkerson delivered a speech in 1921 about the changes he had seen in that community over the years. He pointed out that during his boyhood, there were "three distinct classes of whites": first was the wealthy—slave holders—ladies and gentlemen of leisure; second, the middle class of whites, too industrious to associate with the lowest class, but ignored and scorned by the wealthy class; third was the very poor whites, scorned and despised by both the other classes. "Castes and classes prevailed and there was no mingling of people as there is today," he said.

Continuing with his reminisces, he said, "Much of the land was taken up from the government at 10 cents an acres"—his grandfather's farm of 58 acres, then owned by a Mr. Lattimore, was purchased for $25. Wilkerson related that the people in the country in those days were selfish and that each class was for itself. He believed that had the country continued under those conditions it would never have reached the condition of today. He recalled that money was very scarce in those days, that his first job paid him 35¢ a day for work that lasted from sunrise to sunset, and that he had to walk 4 miles before beginning to work.

Postage, he told his audience, was paid by the receiver. The Yorkville to Atlanta stage and mail coach passed through Hickory Grove once a week, making the

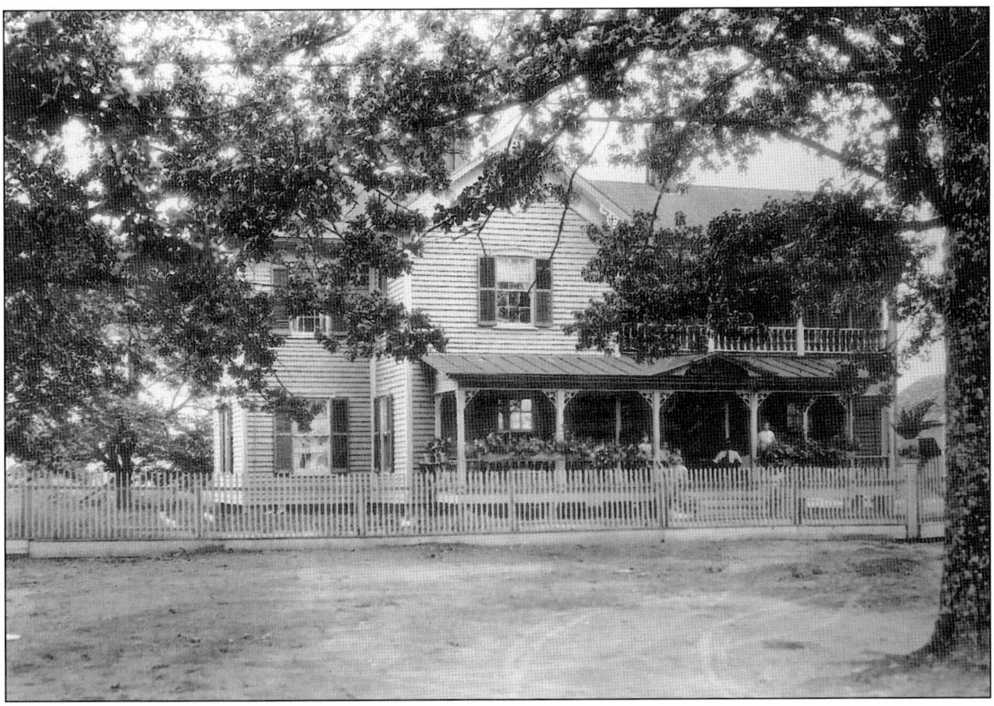

The stately home of William Smith Wilkerson was located south of Hickory Grove. This residence later was destroyed by a fire in the 1950s.

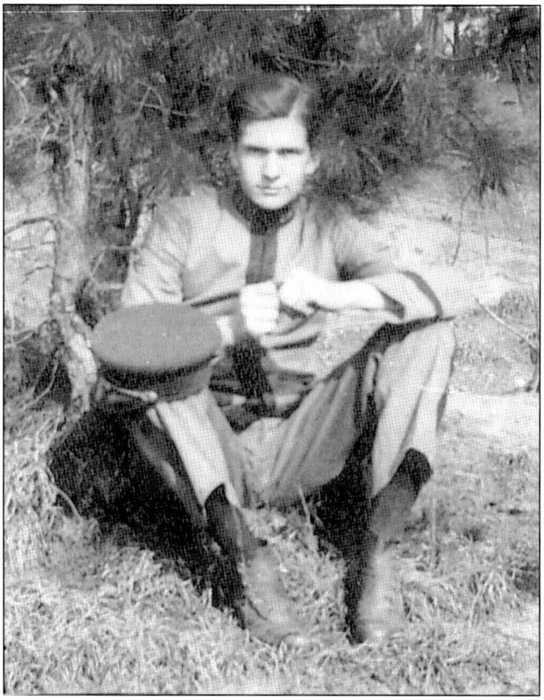

William B. Wilkerson Sr., seen here, was the son of W.S. Wilkerson of Hickory Grove and sorghum industry fame. William B. is pictured in his Clemson Cadet uniform in 1914.

trip in one week—if the weather was good. The driver had a long bugle, 5 or 6 feet long, made of 10 pieces of wood, which he would sound as he neared the town, ensuring that the mail and fresh horses would be ready. Clothes, according to Wilkerson, were mostly of the homespun variety. Few of the people rode horseback and few still were in carriages—most traveled on foot. There was only one carriage maker in Yorkville and he produced no more than five or six vehicles a month.

Like most towns in Western York County, Smyrna began with the establishment of a church and sometime later, a store at a nearby junction of roads. In 1842, the Smyrna Associate Reformed Presbyterian Church was organized and would, some 50 years later, give its name to the small town spawned by the Charleston, Cincinnati & Chicago Railroad.

While it seems likely that a crossroads store would have existed on the site, the first mercantile business on record was that of F.D. Horn, which was built soon after the arrival of the railroad and the establishment of a depot in 1888. At that time, Junius L. Duncan was appointed the first railroad and telegraph agent for the Smyrna Depot. A year or so after Horn established his business, Dr. J.W. Allison opened a grocery store and drugstore near the depot and telegraph office. Also in January 1891, Milton Wylie established a dry goods business. The town was not chartered by South Carolina until January 5, 1895, and shortly after that, the town held its first election, at which time Uranus Meek Pursley was elected mayor and Julius A. "Tony" Hope was appointed the first postmaster.

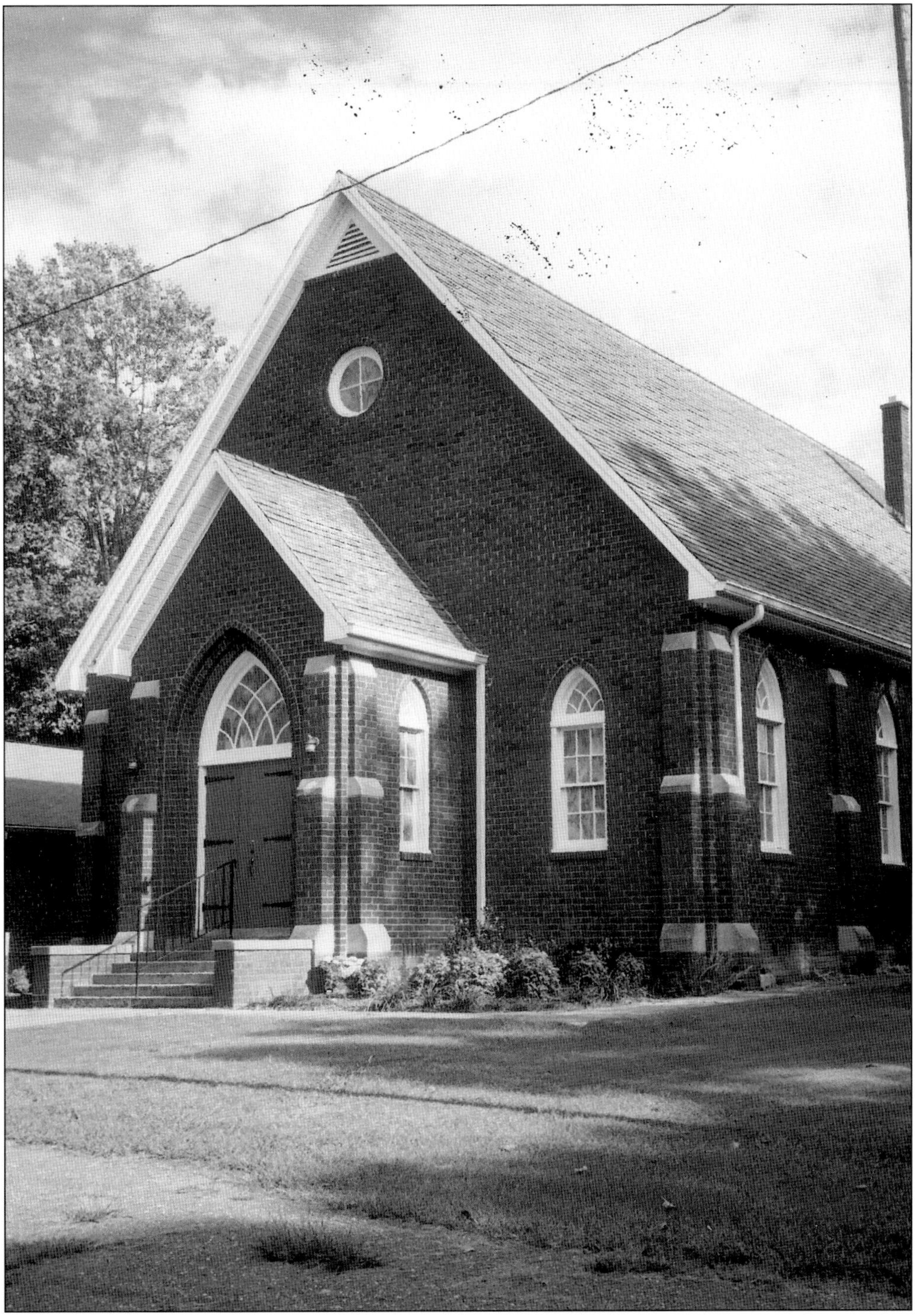

This photograph shows the Smyrna Associate Reformed Presbyterian Church, a long-standing congregation in the community.

In 1924, the "West Road" was completed from Smyrna to York, through Hickory Grove and Sharon, providing a safer and faster route across the county. A road that leads in, also leads out, and within five years of its completion, Smyrna began to decline. About the same time, school consolidation was in progress and the high school was closed and its students bussed to Hickory Grove. Due to a decline in business, Southern Railway could no long justify keeping the Smyrna Depot open. The town father's made an appeal to the South Carolina Railroad Commission, but to no avail. In 1929, on the eve of the Great Depression, the depot and telegraph office was closed—by the end of the year, only three stores were still open for business. One of Smyrna's residents remarked, "Smyrna's all right as long as we have a post office." And maybe that is so—Smyrna still has a post office and it carries proudly the distinction of being one of the smallest incorporated towns in South Carolina.

Just beyond the town of Smyrna lies a land of mystery—"The Nation." No one seems to know how this indefinable area got its name, although there are numerous theories. In April 1926, Samuel Lawrence of Clover, while reminiscing about fishing trips to the Ninety-Nine Island area on Broad River, referred to the Nation as follows:

> The country around Ninety-Nine Islands was always and is today extremely backward—it is poor farming country. The people are ignorant, and have few schools and churches. This section was formerly

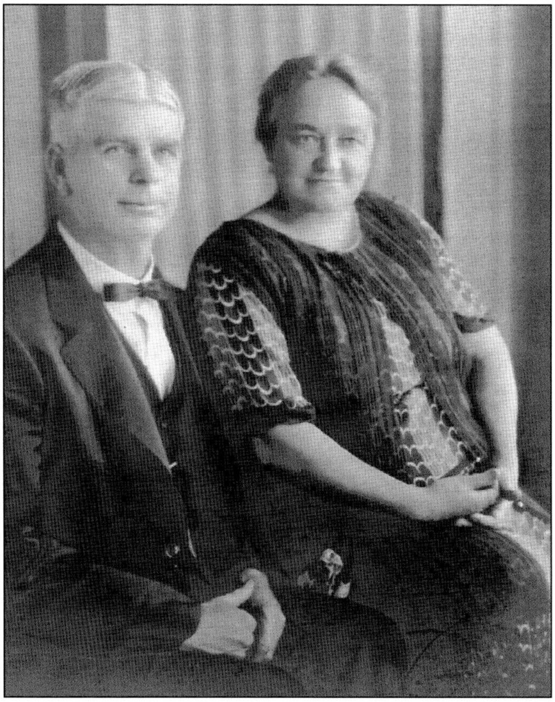

Uranus Meek Pursley was elected the first mayor of Smyrna, the smallest incorporated town in Western York County and the entire state of South Carolina. Mayor Pursley poses here with his wife, Alice Hope Pursley.

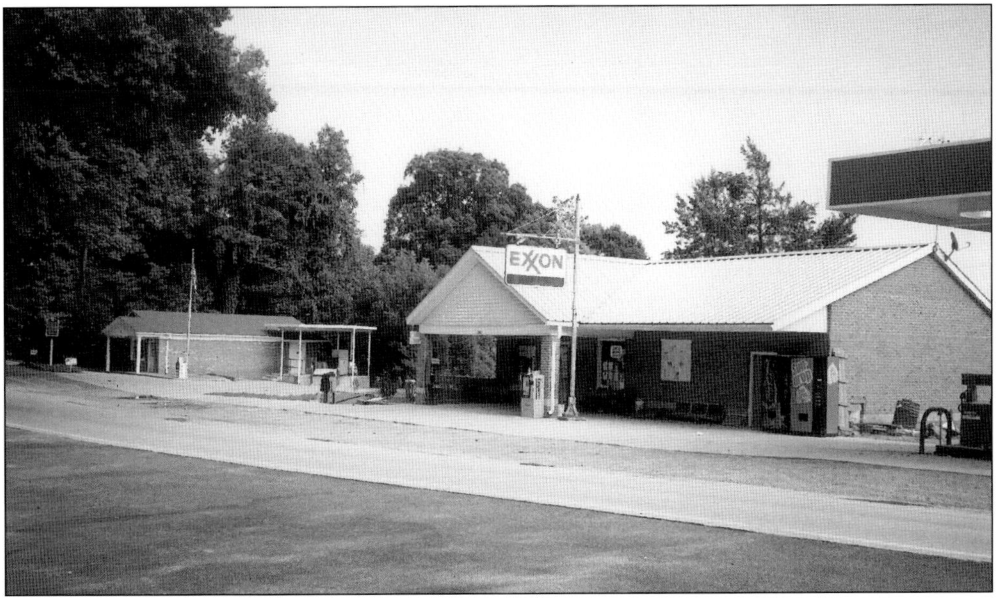

Although quite small, Smyrna is still represented today by a post office, seen here to the left of the Whitesides & Company store.

> called "The Nation" whether it was [because it had been] occupied by the Cherokee Nation of Indians or because the people lived as a nation unto themselves, cut off from all intercourse with the rest of the country. To illustrate the condition of affairs—reports came to the Governor of South Carolina that men and women were living in open adultery in the Nation. He sent officers to investigate and it was found men and women living together and raising large families without having been married. They had no ministers or civil officers to perform wedding ceremonies and they just mated anyway. There was no intentional wrong doing. The governor then sent officers to perform wedding ceremonies and countless fathers and mothers stood in the midst of their children and was married . . . Schools and churches have been built and "The Nation" is now only a memory to the oldest inhabitants.

Lawrence seems to have some understanding of several facts, albeit they are confused with various suppositions. He is probably right in his ideas about a people living "as a nation unto themselves" since German Lutherans would have had little to do with Presbyterian Scots-Irish—either socially or religiously. The term "the nation" may have been a derogatory title given by the Presbyterians to distinguish themselves from these early settlers, and may have carried a note of disdain for those who intermarried with Indians living in that area. All along the frontier, from Virginia to Georgia, there were pockets containing people who had intermarried with local Indians. These pockets usually had distinguishing names

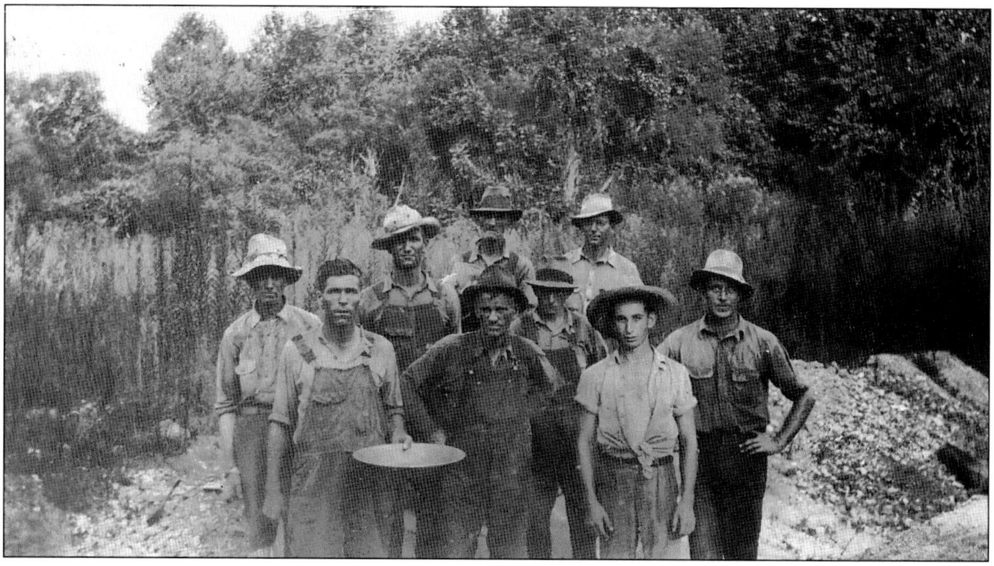

Among the 51 active gold mines listed, most were situated in Western York County, and 35 were located within a 6-mile radius of Smyrna. The first bullion from the area was sent to a mint in 1829.

given by the more ethnically pure settlers. Lawrence, however, made a common mistake in believing the Indians in that area were Cherokee. In most probability, they were of the Catawba tribes. The Cherokee nation was farther west in the mountains of North Carolina. Lawrence mentions the lack of ministers in the area. There were, however, Presbyterian ministers and congregations within their reach had they taken advantage of their proximity.

In the spring of 1855 a destructive fire swept across the most western regions of the county that many said symbolized the Day of Judgment in the minds of those who observed the chaos. Not only in Western York County, but all across the state, fires whipped by high winds were raging out of control. Mary Elizabeth Boyce of Fonti Flora plantation in Fairfield County wrote as follows:

> We have all been in great uneasiness nearly all day in consequence of fire breaking out near here—all hands turned out to try and put it out but the wind blowing so terrible it was impossible. It burned over about a hundred acres in a short time and consumed a great deal . . . They succeeded in arresting its progress and I hope no more harm will be done. We heard that fire was out in different parts of the neighborhood doing great damage . . .

Western York County, however, was not as fortunate as those around Fonti Flora. It was reported that the wind blew like a tornado all day from nine in the morning to sundown. Houses were unroofed and shaken to the very foundations.

Fire from Union County leaped across the Broad River on to the Manning plantation, just above Kings Creek. To compound the situation, houses destroyed by the wind had the contents of their fireplaces hurled ahead of the wind, igniting fires everywhere. Mothers grasped their babies in their arms and ran for open fields out of the reach of fire and falling timbers. Some, with the few things they could save, huddled in open places as they watched the flames consume their homes, barns, fencing, and other property. By three in the afternoon, the sun was scarcely visible from the smoke and raging fire.

In the coaling ground above Kings Creek, thousands of acres of timber land was so burned over that scarcely a house or a cord of timber was left. Hardly a plantation in Western York County did not have to contend with fire that day. Hopewell Independent Presbyterian Church, 3 miles from Blacksburg, was only one of the many buildings destroyed. Men rode for miles to protect the property and lives of their neighbors. The shouts of men and the frenzied screams of women and children were muffled by roaring winds and surging flames.

The winter of 1855–56 offered its own hardships. James L. Strain, who lived near Salem Presbyterian Church, recalled that winter saying that snow had started to fall on Saturday, December 21, and did so for five consecutive Saturdays. For 2 months and 21 days, to March 10, 1856, lingering mounds of snow remained on Bullock's Creek.

Christmas in 1889 was especially festive that year in the budding town of Sharon. On December 24, the South Carolina Legislature granted a charter that brought the town into legal existence. Although the people of the area were jubilant then, only a few months before, there was widespread fear that the

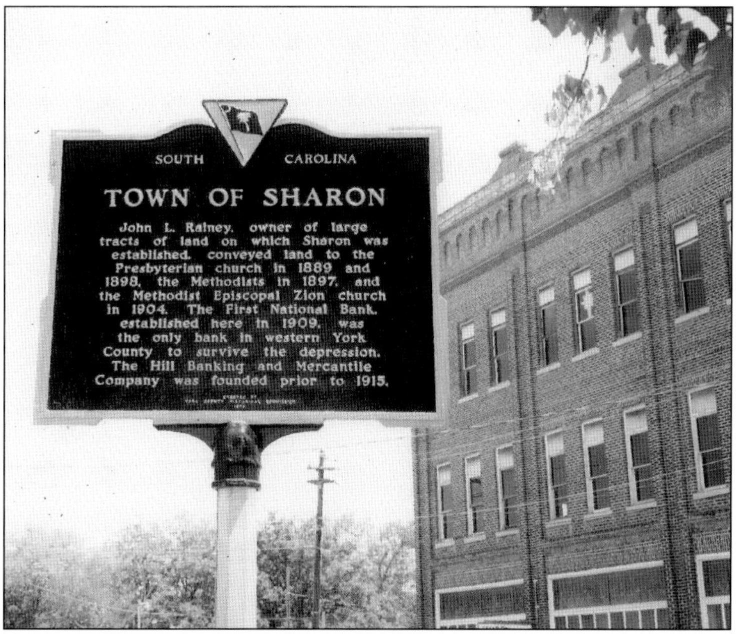

The Sharon town marker stands on the east side of town and welcomes those traveling from York and beyond. In the background is the Hill Building, Sharon's most outstanding landmark. The historic structure was built by W.L. Hill in 1913 to house the Hill & Company Mercantile and Planters Bank.

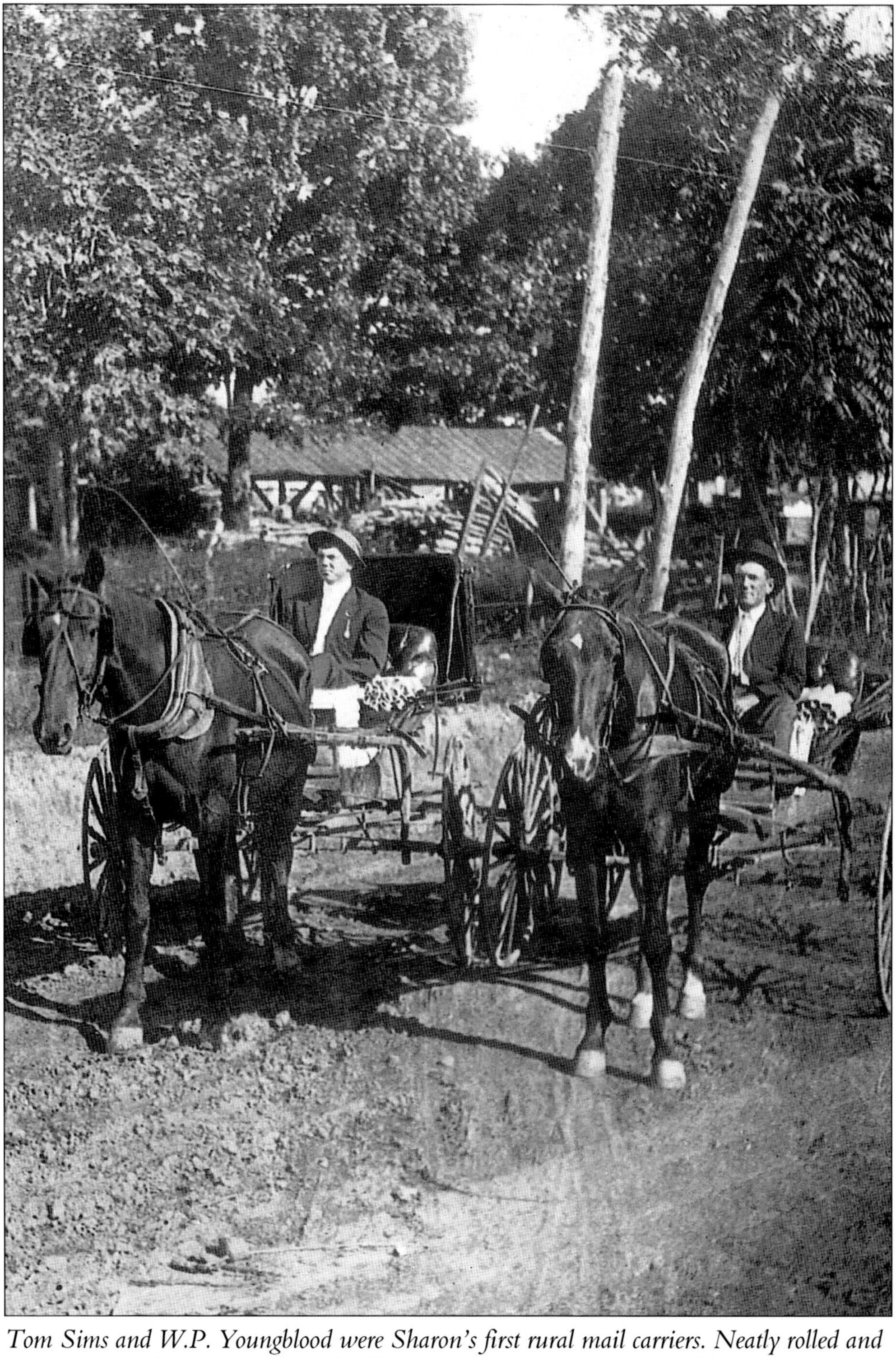

Tom Sims and W.P. Youngblood were Sharon's first rural mail carriers. Neatly rolled and resting next to the carriers, the Yorkville Enquirer *newspapers await delivery.*

promised boom was about to go bust. The town fathers and the railroad officials has previously reached an agreement that a depot with full facilities for passengers, freight, and telegraph would be established at the junction of the railroad and the Shelby and Chesterville Road. No permanent depot had been constructed, but John L. Rainey had given 6 or 7 acres of land for the site and a temporary depot had been placed there for immediate use.

Suddenly and without warning, the officials of the Charleston, Cincinnati & Chicago dismantled the temporary depot and told the community leaders it had no plans, now or ever, to build a depot in Sharon. The town's jubilant spirit was crushed! Disappointment turned to anger when a rumor began to circulate that the merchants of York had offered the railroad officials $10,000 to scrap their plans for a depot in Sharon.

Whether the rumor was true or not, it had a suspicious ring of truth and greed. The merchants in York could already see that Hickory Grove was in a tremendous boom because a full-service depot had been positioned in that town. Three new stores had opened by the previous September and two more were soon to be in business. W.S. Wilkerson was completing his store, a 25-by-70 foot frame structure. T.M. Whisonant was building a large home there and soon Jason Caulter would build himself a new home. Over 700 bails of cotton had been purchased and shipped out of Hickory Grove, and it was drawing business from the eastern portion of Union County, up and down the Broad River, as well as the far reaches of Western York County.

Sharon would be no exception. Sitting on the edge of an economic boom, Sharon was becoming a magnet for the farming communities of Blairsville, Hoodtown, Bullock's Creek, as well as much of the northwest region of Chester County. It was reasoned that the merchants of York feared that a depot in Sharon could shift the center of economy farther west than they desired.

Three miles away, in the farming community of Blairsville, the folks had shared Sharon's excitement over the prospects of growth and prosperity. The Blairsville correspondent for the *Yorkville Enquirer* was indignant toward the businessmen of York concerning the possibility of their involvement against Sharon. With fiery courage, he lambasted them for their interference in Sharon's progress and for their greed and lack of prudence. But the correspondent in Hoodtown considered the businessmen of York to be too kind to be involved in such shenanigans. The editor of the York-based paper expressed his appreciation for his Hoodtown agent.

Blairsville remained allied with its neighbor to the north, and when a celebration was had in the town in the spring of 1889, the Blairsville Cornet Band was there to supply music for the festivities. They were especially proud that spring; in the preceding June, they had purchased a new set of Parson's instruments and were ready with a full repertoire of music. No mention was made if the Hoodtown Brass Band was present.

The town fathers had made an appeal to the South Carolina Railroad Commission and had been promised it would be thoroughly investigated. The summer of 1889 seemed to drag long and tedious as the little town waited for the final decision, which could make it boom or bust. Since the temporary depot had been dismantled, anyone wishing to catch the train had to go out of Sharon to the waterstop to board.

On August 19, the commission arrived in Sharon to begin its investigation "of the sudden and previously unannounced withdrawal of railroad and telegraph facilities from Sharon." Court was assembled in the new, but unfinished, store of S.S. Plexico. The citizens of Sharon were represented by W.B. Wilson Jr. of Rock Hill and D.E. Finley of Yorkville.

John Rainey testified that on July 24, 1888, Dr. John G. Black of the Charleston, Cincinnati & Chicago requested the people of the area to select a suitable and convenient location for a depot. He said they met the next day and selected a spot which was to be known as "Sharon." He further testified that on the September 25, Major John F. Jones called on him at his home and secured a deed for 6 acres of land at the selected site. Major Jones told Rainey that he approved of the location that had been selected above "those d—d swamps and hills!" But Jones argued that he had obtained the land from Rainey only as a starting point for locating a depot and that it was their normal way of doing business, for often the company did not use the titles they procured.

Testimony proved that the Charleston, Cincinnati & Chicago Railroad had

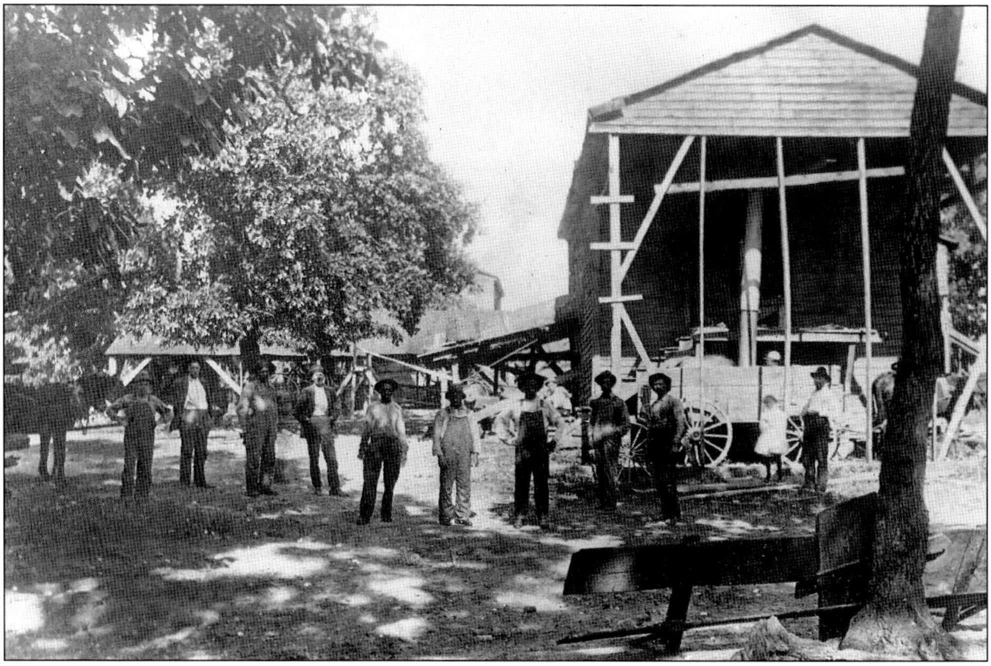

At one time, John L. Rainey owned and operated two gins: one in Sharon and an older one near his home in Raineytown. At the Raineytown gin, workers assemble for this photograph, while in the background, a wagon is being emptied of its load by a vacuum pipe.

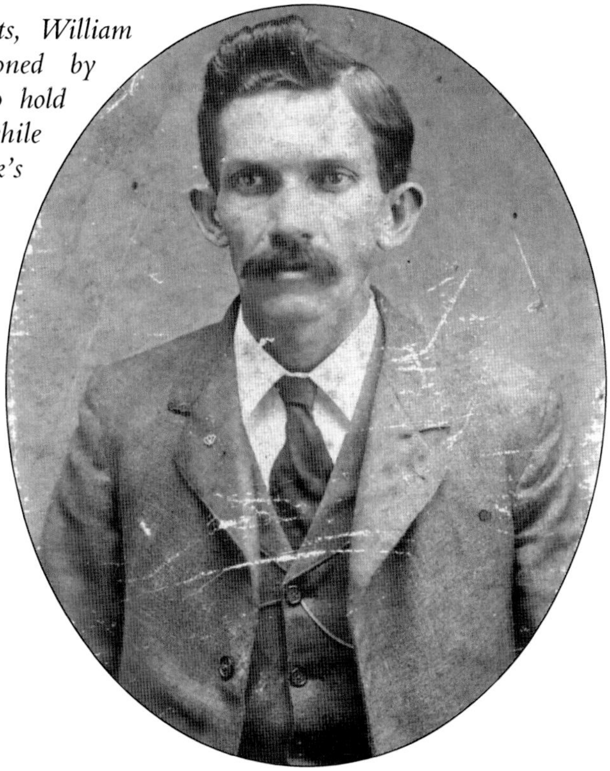

One of Sharon's first merchants, William Smarr Plexico was commissioned by the South Carolina Assembly to hold the town's first election while serving as magistrate of Bullock's Creek Township.

done all to give the town officials every impression that a depot would be placed there and that numerous people had located their homes and businesses there because of that impression. Dr. John May Jr. testified that he would not have opened an office in Sharon if he had not been assured of a depot by Major James F. Hart, attorney. J.A. Thomas came forward with further proof that the railroad did have prior plans to build a depot on Rainey's site. He told the commission that timber for the Sharon depot had already been delivered by a Mr. Arrowood, a contractor who had built the depot at Hickory Grove, as well as several others along the line.

It was further shown that when the railroad company placed a temporary depot on the site, this proved they had plans for a more permanent one. It was proved, however, that the depot was not there just for the convenience of the railroad construction. It was pointed out that W.I. Moore, an agent for the railroad, had placed the car at the site and had functioned as agent and telegraph operator, selling tickets, receiving and loading freight, and giving shelter to passengers the whole time.

As further proof that the area people believed the the railroad would make Sharon a stop on the line, Colonel R.A. Johnson, general manager of the Massachusetts & Southern Construction Company, placed a letter before the commission. The letter stated that the people of Bullock's Creek Township had

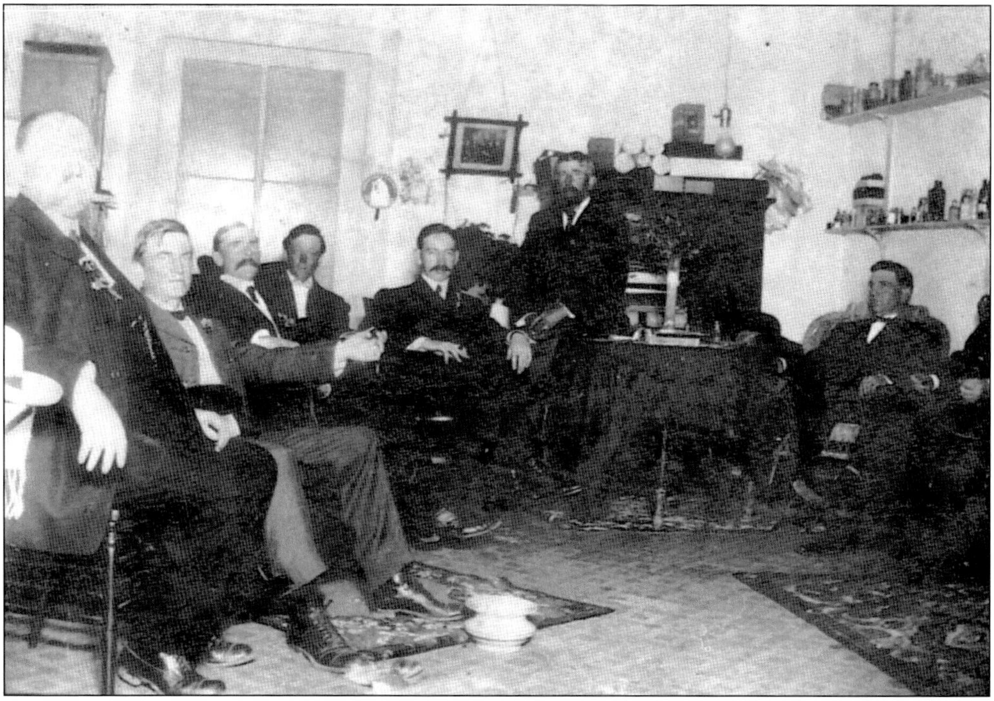

This may be a c. 1910 meeting of county physicians or other officials. Dr. Joseph H. Saye, of Sharon, sits atop the desk.

agreed to raise $15,000 for the construction of a depot. As a point of technicality, J.A. Hope testified that he had assisted in surveying the lines and that Sharon did not fall into the Bullock's Creek Township, but in the Broad River Township.

Dr. J.H. Saye supported Rainey's testimony that the site was a good location for both the area people and the railroad, as it would be a center of trade for 15 square miles. It was estimated that about 5,000 bales of cotton would be shipped by rail in a season if the depot was located in Sharon. James Ross came forward saying that shipments to and from Sharon had already amounted to $10,000.

The commission came to a quick and swift decision. They were confident that the officials of the railroad had promised the town fathers a depot on the line and that they were in breech of promise by withdrawing those plans. The town of Sharon received a letter dated August 31 from M.L. Bonham, chairman of the Railroad Commission. The letter stated if the Charleston, Cincinnati & Chicago Railroad did not comply with their resolution to re-establish the depot in Sharon within 60 days, the matter would be placed in the hands of the attorney-general.

In compliance to the resolution, a conference between the town committee and railroad representatives was held on September 17, 1889. At this meeting, the representatives agreed to make Sharon a stop on the line and that a depot would be built by the town. With this news, the little village returned to a jubilant mood. Soon W.A. Robinson and Robert R. Plexico announced they would locate a furniture store in Sharon and in October, William Lawrence Hill purchased a lot to relocate his mercantile business from Sandersville (near Blairsville) to Sharon. Sharon was underway.

While a heterogeneous and mobile population usually peopled railroad-spawned towns of America, it was not so with Sharon, Hickory Grove, and Smyrna. The people that made up these towns were mostly old, well-established families. There were a few Germans that had migrated into the area, but these had no effect on the development and were soon integrated into society. Living in Western York County around the turn of the twentieth century, one might grow up knowing nothing of other cultures and never meeting anyone but those like themselves. The people of Sharon and the surrounding area were either kin or shared kin, a people who for 150 years had quietly thinned the soil and thickened the blood. When they came together as a community, whether on sale day, revivals, picnics, or ball games, it was a family affair. Some Western York County people, after the 1930s, may have had some limited contact with the few Roman Catholics or a Jewish merchant in Rock Hill. Yet, there would have been little opportunity to have a long-term relationship. Western York County, until the establishment in the 1930s of York's Divine Savior Catholic Hospital, was overwhelmingly Protestant.

Building a new town is not only an opportunity to make money, but a new way to define oneself and attempt to rise to the top of a social class. The merchant class

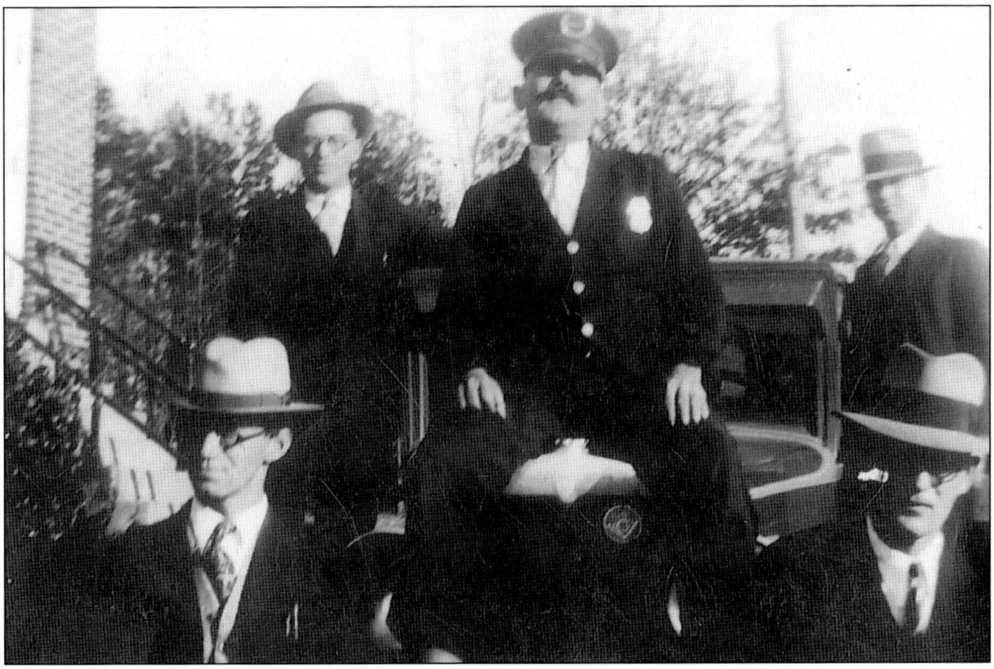

Sharon's 1928 local government consisted of the following officials: (bottom) W.S. Gibson, mayor, and Bratton Plexico, councilman; (center) Bob Broom, policeman; (top) Odes Spurlin, town clerk, and Dr. Floyd.

of all three towns was the first to define themselves as the elite or upper crust of local society. Among those who attempted merchandising businesses, some soon distinguished themselves as astute businessmen, gained respect of their peers, and gradually acquired a highly respected place in society. However, some in this struggle had the misfortune of floundering and falling, and subsequently lost any hope of a rise to the top of the social strata.

The ways to climb the social ladder are as varied as the people themselves. Some ignored their past and hoped others would do the same while they reinvented themselves. Others did it by community service, and some by marriage. There were several cases throughout the area where men of lesser business success or social standing were fortunate enough to marry a woman with some degree of gentility, charm, social grace, and charity. Through these marriages, the husband was automatically elevated—provided he maintained an acceptable degree of respectability.

For the first 30 or 40 years of the small towns on the line of the Charleston, Cincinnati & Chicago Railroad, women were not defined as their own person, but by their husband, or if unmarried, their father. For example, the wife of Dr. Saye would not be referred to simply as Ella Saye, but rather "Mrs. Joseph Saye, "Dr. Saye's wife," or sometimes, "Mrs. Dr. Saye." Before the 1890s and on into the twentieth century, women were instruments of defining a man's success and his place in society—her own self-pride was found in how well she kept house, the children, and her husband. As always, the proper marriage into the right family

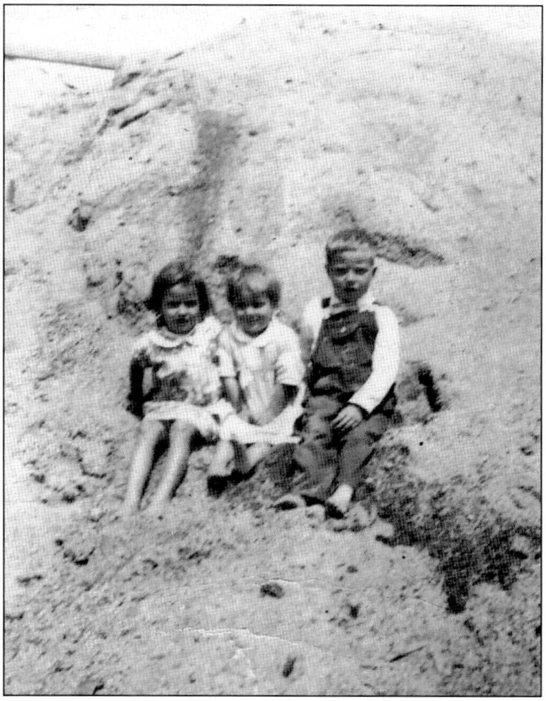

Pausing from a moment of play, these children from Sharon are, from left to right, as follows: Doris, Lyconia, and Horace Moss.

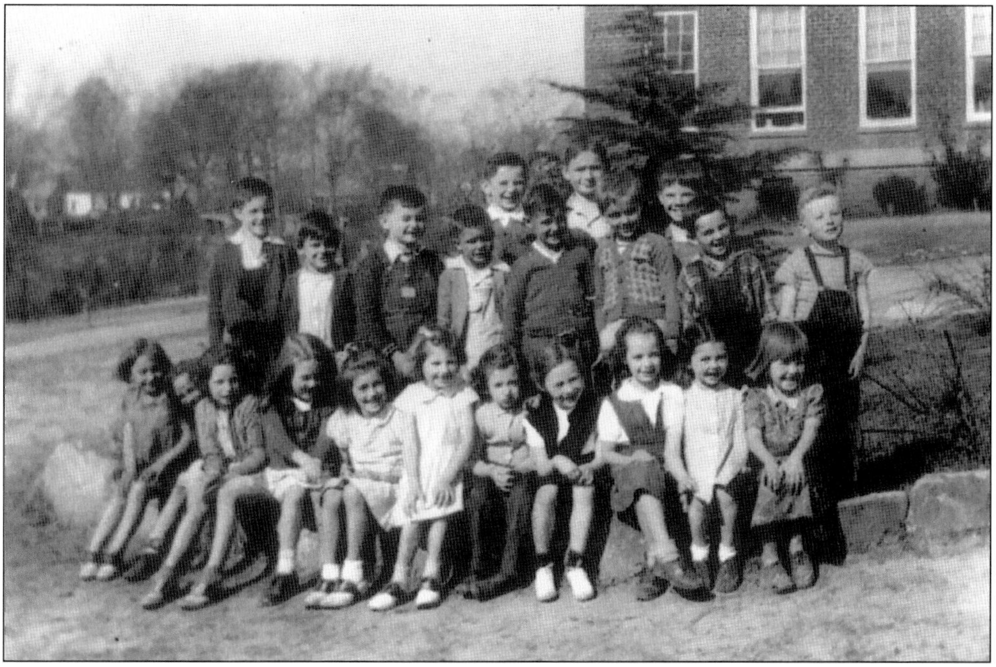

This 1946 first grade class from Sharon Elementary School was taught by Adeline Rainey. When schools in York School District 1 were consolidated nine years later, many of these youngsters were separated from their classmates, and two years later, they graduated from Hickory Grove and York High Schools.

might secure a young man or the newly rich a more suitable place in society. Although one man may be quite familiar with another, and on first-name basis, a certain reserve was maintained regarding the wives using terms such as Mrs. so-and-so or if the first name was used, prefixed with "Miss."

As time went on, women were beginning to find new ways of defining themselves. As women obtained higher education and became certified teachers, their worth in defining themselves, as well as a husband, greatly increased. The profession of the wife, like the profession of the husband in earlier years, reflected on the spouse. Fortunate was the farmer or blue-collar worker who married a schoolteacher—not only was the family income increased, but so was his social status and prestige as well.

Of course, the amount of money and the things it can buy is always a tremendous consideration in social acceptability. Things, all too often, are a way to define one's self- importance. In cases where the man prospered enough to purchase a new appliance or the latest technology for his wife, it opened a door of admiration from her peers. Even shopping at a particular store would lend the air of money and importance to the easily impressed. Well into the 1950s, a shopping bag from Ivey's Department Store in Charlotte had the ability to raise an eyebrow or two. These shopping bags were a prized trophy to cleverly exhibit

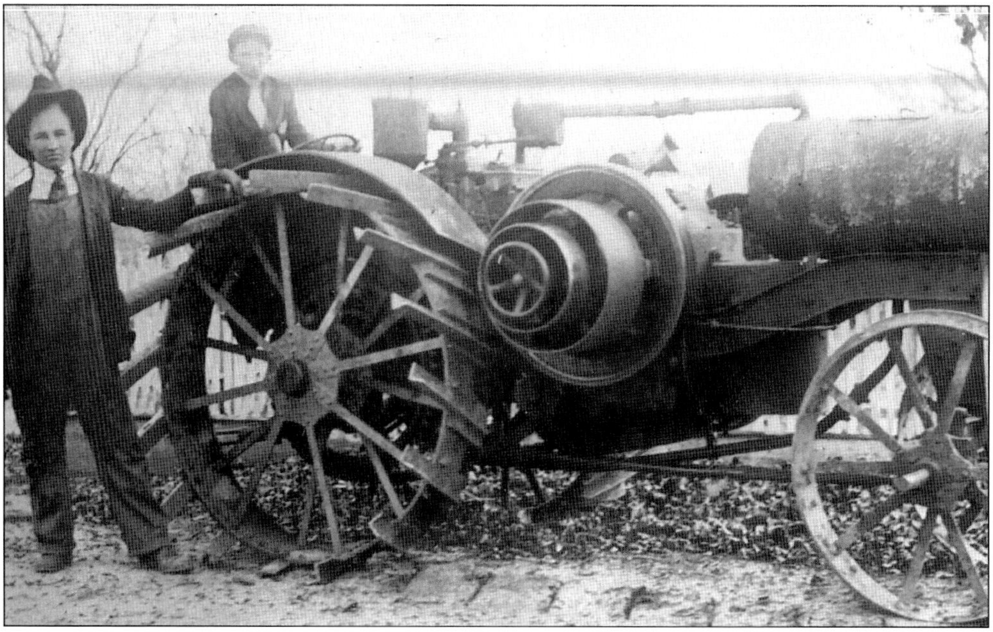

In 1919, this odd-looking piece of farm equipment was the height of modern technology in Western York County and a thing of great pride to its owner, Oscar Burgess, who operated a farm between Hickory Grove and Sharon.

before other women. The most usual way to let her neighbor know she had been to Ivey's was to send a few tomatoes or squash from the garden to the one chosen to be impressed. It is suspected these bags circulated among the womenfolk until they were in tatters, none being sure from whom it originated.

At the incorporation of the "Tri-Cities," distrust between the farmer and merchant was already developing. Before the coming of the railroad and the establishment of Sharon, Hickory Grove, and Smyrna, distrust of Western York County farmers most likely focused on the well-established merchants of Yorkville. But when the new towns began to grow and planters rose to the merchant class, the focus and resentment was then on their own people, men of whom were their kin.

Securely embedded in the psyche are two diametrically opposing symbols of the South: palatial homes and the poverty-stricken tenant farmer. While the former symbol is certainly unreal and rare, the latter unarguably has more validity. In 1890, farm tenancy in South Carolina was 61.1% percent of its population, second only to Mississippi's 62.4%. Sharecropping and tenancy was the post–Civil War answer to labor problems brought about by emancipation. Former slaves and unlanded whites needed access to employment, but landowners had little capital to compensate labor. As a solution to both, farmers allowed these laborers to work 20 to 40 acres on a crop-sharing basis. To support these workers during the growing season, the landowners extended credit for food and necessities, secured by a lien on future crops. These liens were most often worked out with a local merchant who was a general supplier of feed, seeds, fertilizer, farm implements, and household items. Many farmers in Western York County had their own pantry or commissary from which they supplied their tenants and sharecroppers with food or small necessities. Like the merchant, the landowner kept accounts that were settled at harvest time.

The farmers' contribution, the need for credit, and how closely the farmer supervised the laborers defined the two levels of tenancy—tenants and sharecroppers. Tenant farmers often own mules, a few pieces of equipment, household furnishings, and were able to supply some seed and fertilizer. Their portion of the crops would run from two-thirds to three-fourths, less advances and interest. Sharecroppers usually owned no tools or implements, and contributed only labor. Totally dependent on lien credit for all their necessities and working under full supervision, their portion was no more than half the crop, minus advances and interest.

Crop-lien tenancy was developed as a viable substitute for slavery. Like slavery, it was paternalistic and easily exploited. The planter was an intricate part of the power structure and was in position to exploit the tenant by charging exorbitant interest on advances or confiscating the entire crop. A landlord suffering under a burden of mortgages, rising prices, and taxes could easily cut into the tenant's or cropper's share with little challenge from the poor who were wholly dependent on the landowner.

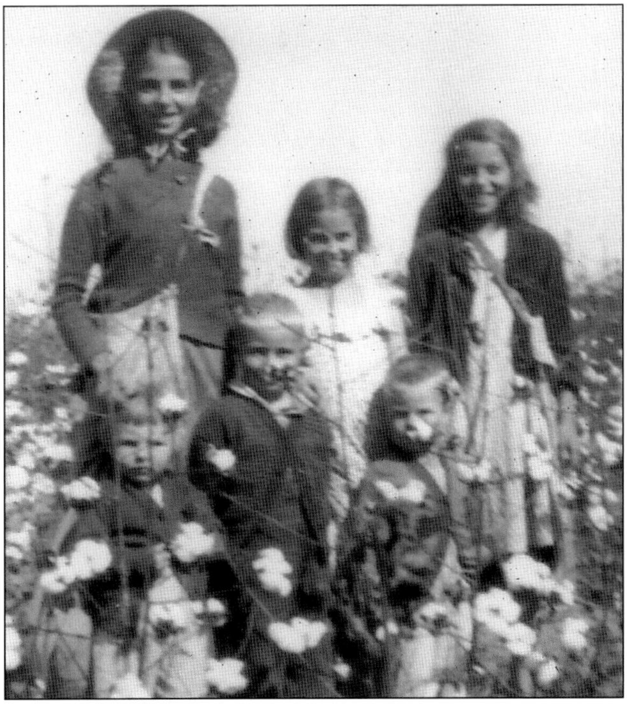

Sharecropping and tenant farming in the 1940s often required the entire family to spend the major part of their day in the fields. The older children worked or tended to the younger children, who played along the edge of the field. With a sack slung over one shoulder, Doris Moss (in the hat) is prepared for a day of cotton picking in this photograph. Next to her are her sisters, Lorene and Lyconia; standing in front are Ann Traylor, Ronald Moss, and Jimmy Moss.

From the outset, the sharecropper system developed an unsettling attitude between the landowner and the cropper. In many instances, one did not trust the other. The landowner often felt he did not get enough labor for his pay, and the laborer was suspicious of the honesty of his employer. These feelings of distrust caused many families—both black and white—to move from one farm to another during the lull of the agricultural years in December and January. As early as 1870, this was noticed first among the freedmen, as the following shows:

> . . . the teams [of horses and mules] have begun to do their share of the work of the season, which is chiefly the transportation of household plunder . . . the present generation of Africans are decidedly migratory in their habits. They resemble a pack of cards, which must be shuffled and dealt out fresh at the close of each game, and it is seldom that any farmer will hold the same hand two years in succession.

The tenant had no security and little opportunity to learn a skill that would free him from this slave-like life. They worked under year-to-year verbal agreements that offered no security beyond the growing season. With so much unskilled, landless labor available, it was a landowner's market. The owner could easily

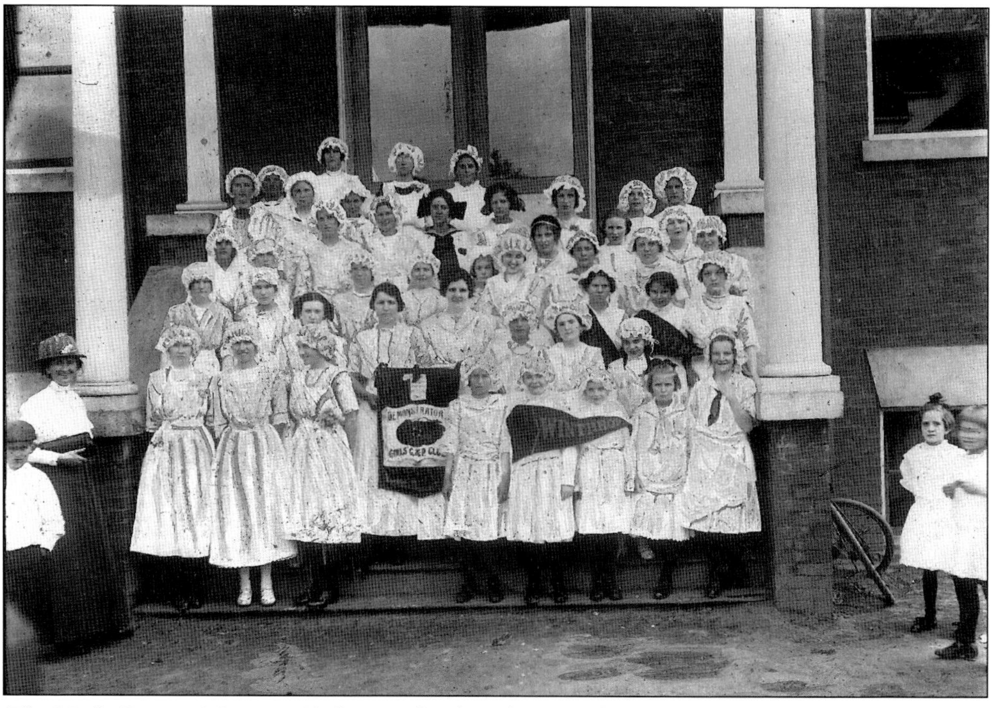

The York County Tomato Club poses for this photograph during a rally at Winthrop College in 1914. Groups like these stressed the importance of agriculture on the overall welfare and commerce of York County.

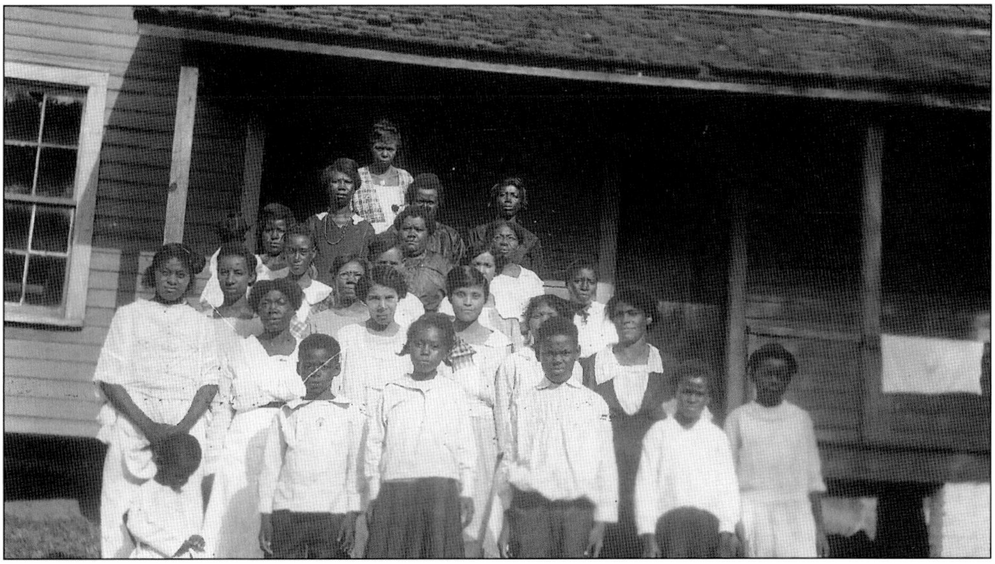

Pictured here in 1921 is an African-American agricultural club in York County, which instructed children on the process of gardening, farming, and canning. (Courtesy Winthrop University Archives.)

dispense with his tenants at settling time and had no incentive to retain dissatisfied or unwanted laborers. The tenant system was not only destructive to the land as it gave little incentive to maintain farm property, but also to the tenant, who was deprived of a role in the community, and his children, who did not receive an education, which insured the continuance of the poverty cycle.

A strange mental attitude was sometimes developed in sharecroppers, particularly so with those who lived in extreme Western York County. Due to their geographical and social isolation, they became extremely sensitive to landowners. They would often take a peculiar spin on a situation, imagining some injury or insult and "fly off mad." This little quirk increased their isolation as no real relationship could be developed.

There was a funny thing about poverty. From the nineteenth century and well on into the twentieth century, the lower-class farmer and tenants—both black and white—offered comic relief to the middle and upper classes. A perusal through any local newspaper during that time will reveal a steady flow of jokes, humorous stories, and tales that make the illiterate, poor farmer the laughing stock. Making the poor the butt of jokes was a pastime wherever two or three gathered, laughing at him broke tension, and balanced the psyche.

Although much of the area's population was made up of African Americans, burdensome laws of segregation virtually made them nonexistent in York County society. As a suppressed element of society, and whites being nearly identical in ethics and religion, racial prejudices were openly and unashamedly exhibited. The term "nigger" was in common use and jokes about blacks were relished. Even newspaper reports were obviously slanted with prejudice. One such article about "an old darkey" began, "Here is a little story that is somewhat refreshing, even if the subject of it is a colored man . . ."

As dreadful as the life of the white sharecropper was, the black sharecropper's existence was worse. This fourth class was defined wholly on race. The policy of "separate but equal" had quickly degenerated into "separate and unequal" and denied equal access to education, banking, credit, and insurance, as well as political and legal rights.

One incident regarding Planters Bank of Sharon obtaining insurance for a black sharecropper reveals the unwillingness to insure an African American and how far landowners were willing to insure their crops. On March 30, 1922, Cashier James D. Hambright of the Planters Bank wrote R.W. Buice and G.W. Wilkerson concerning their laborer, "Today the insurance company has called on the policy of Craig Gaston on account of him being a Negro. We thought it best to call your attention so that you can take whatever steps you think best." Wilkerson replied four months later, ". . . if you can get a crop mortgage from Craig Gaston we will carry the note until fall, otherwise we could not carry more than $300.00 for him."

Remaining as a vestige of slavery, social contact between the races was frowned upon and nearly nonexistent. While it was acceptable to meet and speak in a public place such as the street or in a store; it was strictly avoided in a social setting. While

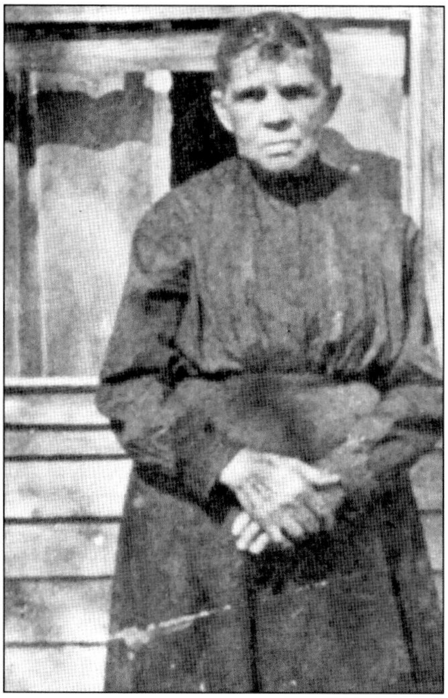

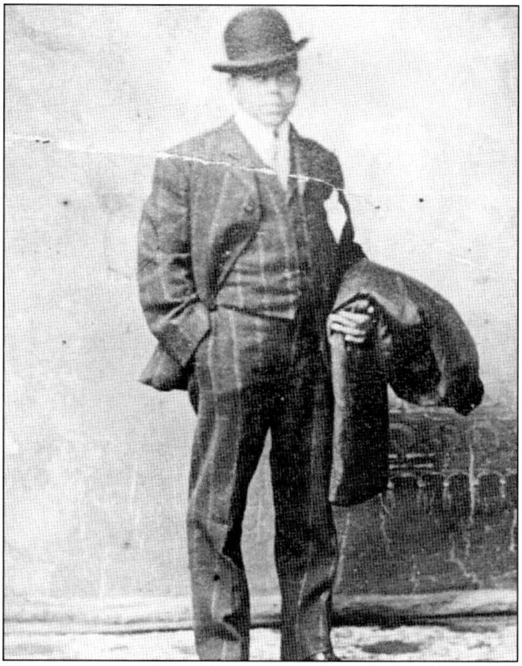

Both born as slaves, Louisa Sandifer (left) and Exodus Sandifer (right) worked at York's Rose Hotel.

Even well into the twentieth century, Western York County farmers continued using the agricultural methods of the antebellum era.

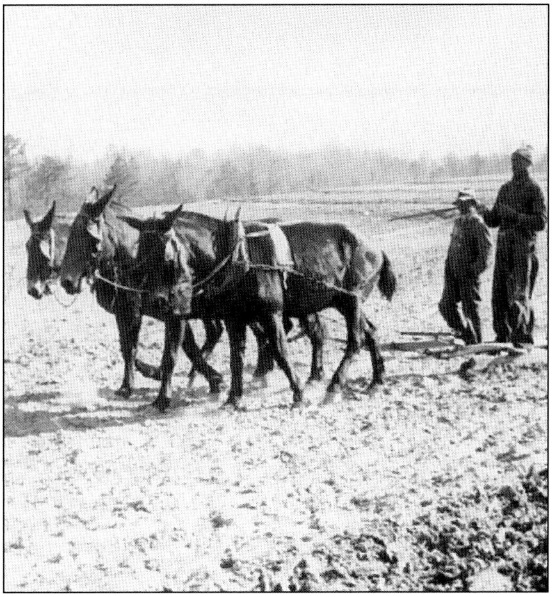

both races may work together all day in a field as equals, a public work place was not acceptable. Blacks, banned from public employment, were confined to farms or part of the support system to the white village: washing, cleaning, yard work, etc. Two white men of York summed up the general feelings toward blacks, "I have nothing against them. They are human beings, like we are. But I don't want to have to eat with them or associate with them socially." The second confided, "They might as well realize right now that we will *never* permit them to mix socially with us . . . we are just not going to accept them as social equals."

As part of the one-fourth of black farmers that obtained land in the South, several African-American farmers near Sharon owned their farms. By being landowners and escaping the depleting cycle of sharecropping, these black families participated in the community to some extent and educated their children. Whites often publicly praised these families as good and unusual examples of their race.

While "separate but equal" was the unfurled standard of race relations between blacks and whites, many facets were neither separate nor equal. Superficially, any sexual contact between the races was particularly frowned upon by the white society, yet several examples of on-going affairs between white men and black women were well known in the community—and probably a number not known. More than one of these affairs produced children that became the town's "pet" enigmas. In such cases that the fathers were prominent in the community, the male offspring was more visible and sometimes was given special duties about town or simply hung-around as the father's pet. In every case where a white man had fathered a child with a black woman, he still voiced his prejudices and in whatever degree of his power or influence would attempt to keep the black race "in its place."

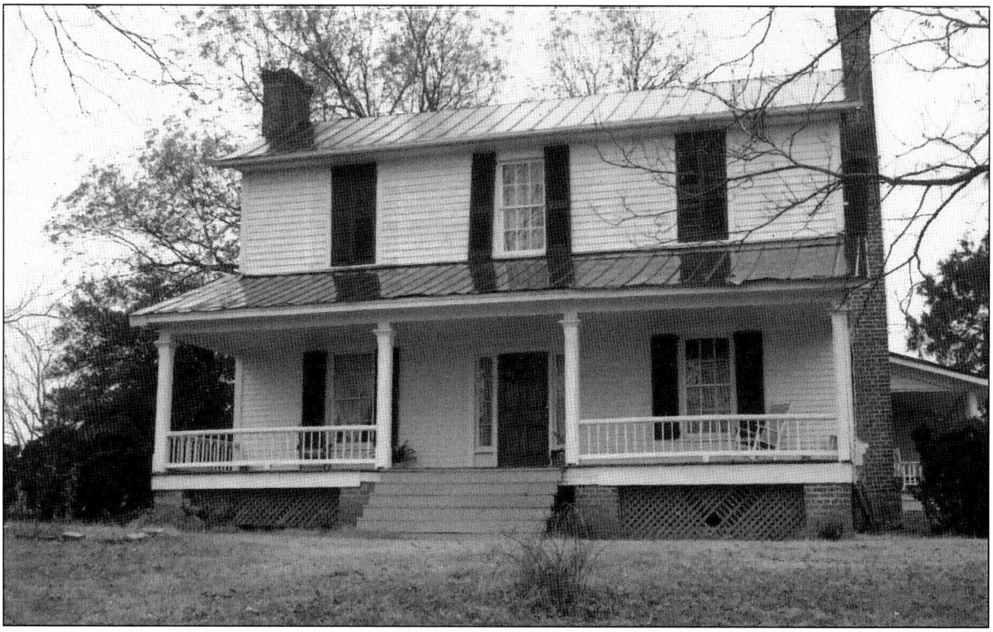

Upcountry homes, such as this one between Sharon and Hickory Grove, are monuments to the hard work of this Southern Eden's families.

Architecture, or the style of homes built by people, is a perfect indicator of their place in society or class distinction. Most of the houses built in Sharon just after the turn of the twentieth century have modified pyramidal roofs. The pyramidal roof was developed from the Georgian style of homes built along the Georgia and Carolina coast. Originally, the new style was constructed with a square floor plan that supported a pointed or pyramid roof with two chimneys. By the early twentieth century, the pyramidal roof was being built in upper South Carolina.

Cost and availability made these houses popular among the middle-class Southerner and are best described as representing economic security and the working, independent class. By the second decade of the twentieth century, this style of architecture became more complex with addition of gables and extended gable roofs. Often the roofs on Sharon homes did not complete a peak, falling short by 3 or 4 feet.

More than 20 of these homes built in Sharon during the second decade are still standing and testify that much of the town was made up of a middle, working, and independent class of people. The architecture of Sharon stands in sharp contrast to the style of choice exhibited in Hickory Grove. Few examples of the pyramid roof are seen in that town, rather larger and more ornate homes spot the countryside.

Around 1906, John S. Rainey, began constructing a home in Sharon which would typify "old money." His stately, columned home easily depicted an image (real or imagined) of "aristocratic" rule—precisely the message the third-generation

Rainey wanted to communicate. Overlooking his immediate business area and nearly the entire little village, the house site not only gave him an advantageous view, but he was in full view of anyone doing business in the town.

The house necessarily had to remind his peers that his roots ran deep and long through the red soil of York County. The symmetry of the house relays balance and dependability; the four Tuscan columns standing forward and boldly exhibiting themselves said something of its owner. The double-front porches and the obvious features of the Neoclassical Georgian style reflected the family's position and the widening gulf between him and his neighbors. Rainey's choice of architecture also seemed to reduce the importance of most of Sharon's public buildings. It was as much a symbol of stability and authority as any seat of religion or government.

Across town, on the road to York, a contrasting symbol of "new money" was completed by December 1925. The Colonial Revival dwelling with its light yellow-brick and red-tile roof, now deemed as the "Hill Mansion," was built by W.H. Peeps of Charlotte, North Carolina, for William Lawrence Hill. Hill, having operated a small mercantile business at Sandersville near the York–Chester County line that had been inherited from his grandfather, William Minter, came to Sharon in 1889 with everything he owned in a farm wagon. In partnership with

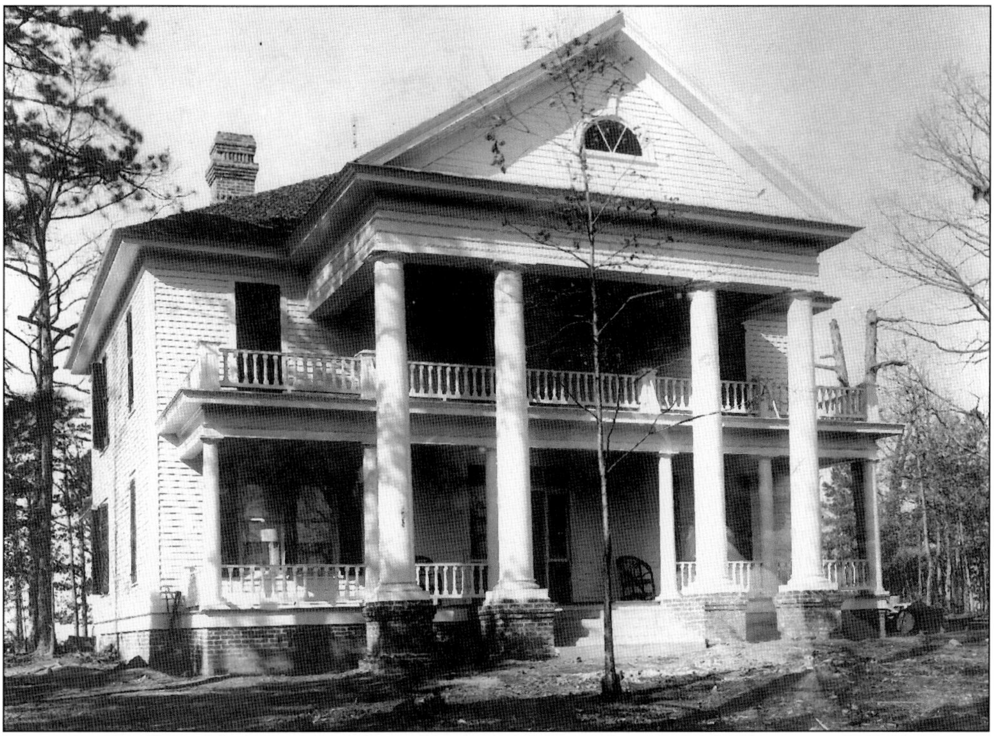

Sharon's Grove Hill, built by John S. Rainey, represents the magnificence and opulence of some of the grand homes that dotted Western York County's countrysides.

brothers Christopher L. and Porter B. Kennedy, he opened a mercantile business in a long clapboard building. This partnership dissolved about 1908. At that time, he began to make plans to expand his business and become the largest dealer of merchandise in the area. Without a doubt, Hill was the arch rival of Rainey. Here, in this tiny town "new money" and "old money" faced off for a battle that lasted for decades.

By the time Sharon and Hickory Grove had received their charters from the South Carolina General Assembly, the Farmer's Alliance had swept across the Cotton Belt and made its controversial move to political involvement. Although some had questioned that the move might undermine the Democratic Party, they soon realized, however, this was an opportunity to fight the process that afflicted the nation's farmers. In 1889, the Farmer's Alliance claimed 662,000 Southerners—4 out of 10 South Carolina farmers were members.

The Alliance promised relief for hard-pressed farmers through economic programs and political advocacy, pressing for reform of the banking and currency system, and creation of a federal sub-treasury system. In some counties the Alliance provided for the establishment of commodity storage facilities in rural areas, and farmers could receive cash using stored crops as collateral. This helped to break the cycle of indebtedness to the merchant who furnished his necessities

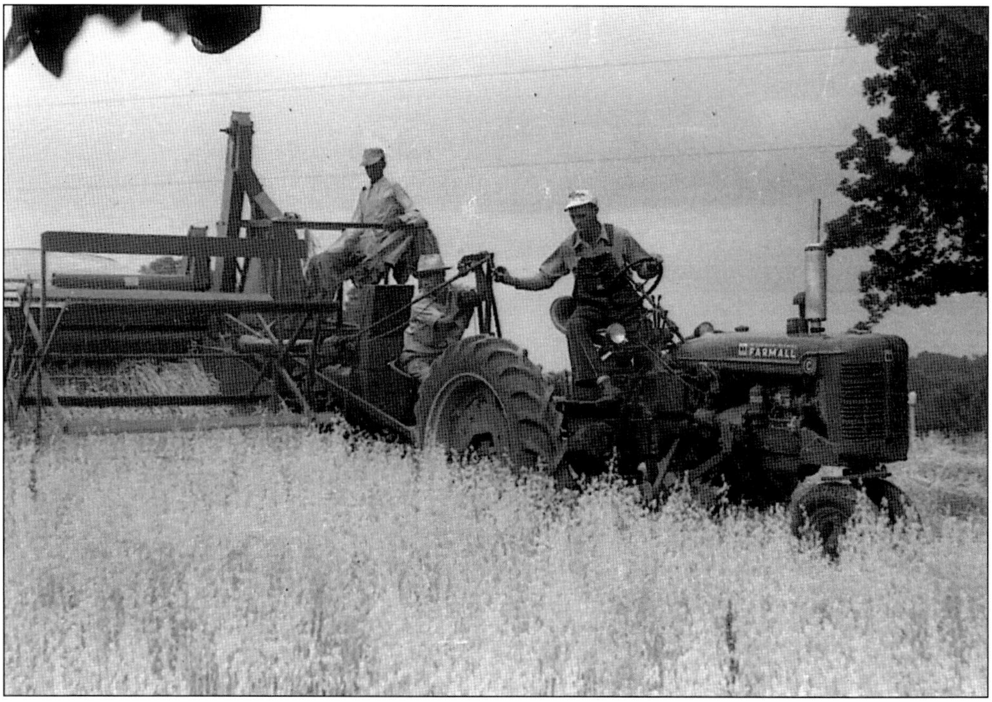

The operation of harvesting oats like this scene near Hickory Grove has all but disappeared in Western York County; however, agriculture shaped the lives of most of the county's residents in both the nineteenth and twentieth centuries.

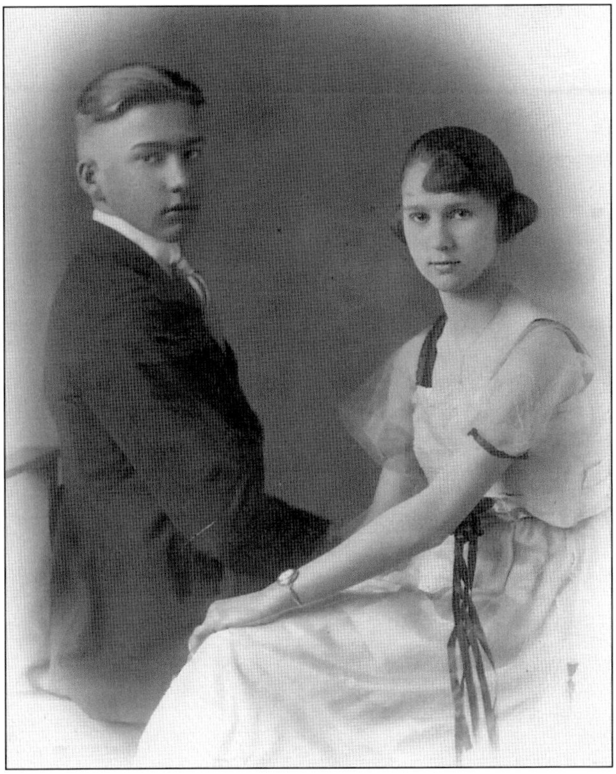

Hoodtown's James Flay Plexico poses with his sister, Sarah Lucille Plexico, for this 1920 portrait. James Flay Plexico was known locally as the "Sheik of Sharon" because of his deep set eyes, reminiscent of Hollywood's Rudolph Valentino.

on credit. By 1891, however, the Alliance membership was declining because they could not resolve the credit and marketing problems facing the farmer. When the Alliance was absorbed into the Populist movement, many dyed-in-the-wool Democrats dropped out.

Just a little over ten years after Sharon's incorporation, a local chapter of the Daughters of the American Revolution (D.A.R.) was organized in Yorkville in March 1898. This event was in keeping with the class revolution that was taking place all over the nation. Of the 105 patriotic orders founded between 1783 and 1900, 34 were formed before 1870 and 71 between 1870 and 1900. The rapid growth of these organizations may well be contributed to psychological fears of the old families who were losing status in the class revolution.

The D.A.R. specifically limits membership on the criteria of descent, length of residence, and participation in the American Revolution. The fears of loss of position were bandaged by recounting family glories of the past. The charter member of Yorkville's Kings Mountain Chapter included many old family names such as Bratton, Gist, Moore, Neal, White, and Witherspoon. Since Sharon women were not involved in its charter, it may be because they did not feel threatened—or simply because they did not have the time or access. When several Sharon women were inducted at a later time, it simply may have been a way of bolstering their new status as wives of leading men.

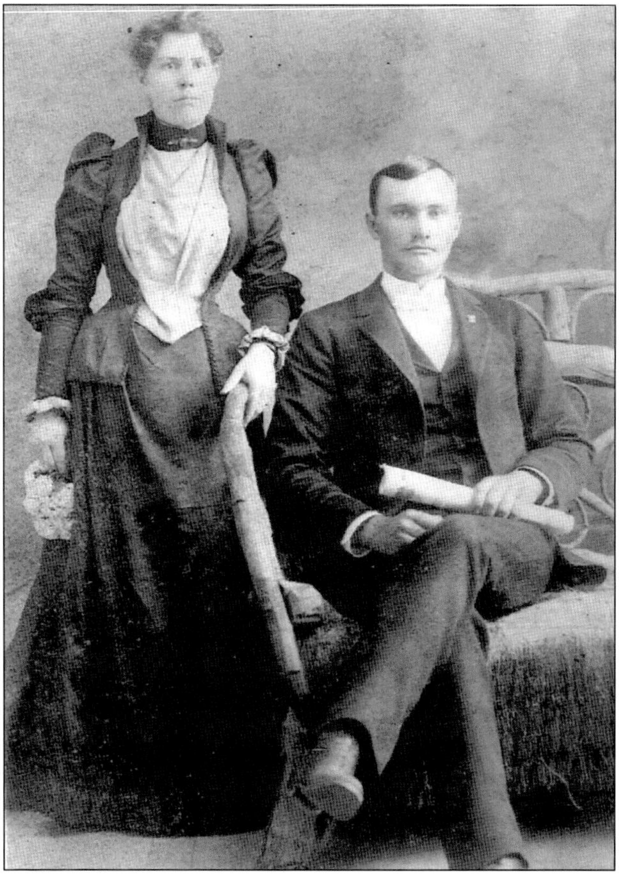

John Craig Kirkpatrick Sr. was the second Grand Master of Western York County's Palmetto Lodge. He and his wife, the former Aggie Hafner, are seen here in an early photograph.

The Palmetto Lodge No. 289 of the Masonic Order was chartered on December 3, 1911. In the beginning, the lodge met about 4 miles out of Sharon at the Hoodtown School on present-day Highway 97. Membership incorporated men from the "Tri-Cities" as well as all the small agricultural communities of Western York County. In 1926, the membership requested permission from the Grand Master of the Rock Hill lodge to relocate to Sharon due to poor roads. The letter cited the fact that the road used by the Hickory Grove members was in disuse and they had to travel to Sharon and then to Hoodtown a distance of 12 miles. Those who lived farther west had to travel about 20 miles. The Masons may have set up shop in the grammar school building upon moving into town since in the fall of 1935 they had to vacate the building because the school needed the space. At that time they rented the second floor of the Shannon Building.

Since the Masonic Order had been an important part of social life of Southern communities, it is a wonder why a lodge was not formed until 1911. The formation of a local lodge may have coincided with the time Sharon women were finding their place in the D.A.R.; if so, perhaps men were also reacting to the class revolution with feelings of insecurity. The Order, with its secret and elaborate ceremonies, rituals, and mysterious titles, has always helped members escape the humdrum of life while catering to elitism.

Sometime during December 1921, J. Clyde Plexico began studying the possibility of organizing a post of the American Legion in Sharon. Several servicemen resided in Sharon and were members of the post in Yorkville, but due to distance, they seldom had the opportunity to attend the meetings or enjoy the clubrooms. On February 24, the Hope Byers Post No. 99 of the American Legion was organized of ex-servicemen of Sharon and vicinity. Elected officers were J. Clyde Plexico, post commander; H.L. Mickle, vice commander; Joe W. Sims, adjutant; Ralph H. Cain, finance officer; Brown Baird, service officer; J. Palmer Hope, sergeant at arms; Sidney W. Sherer, Carl Jones, A. Bratton Plexico, C.H. Jenkins, and Glenn Blair, executive committeemen.

Following the organizational meeting, a banquet for the 32 assembled soldiers was served by the ladies of the Sharon Sewing Club, which was chaired by Mrs. O.M. Spurlin. After Reverend Carl McCully asked the blessing the men enjoyed their "chow." After a meal in the second-story hall of the Shannon Building, the dinner resounded with a number of short talks. James D. Grist of Yorkville outlined the aims of the American Legion. "What the Legion Means to Me" was the subject chosen by Ralph Cain, and J. Clyde Plexico told "Why I Want that Bonus." Baird spoke on "Some of My Experiences as a Military M.P."

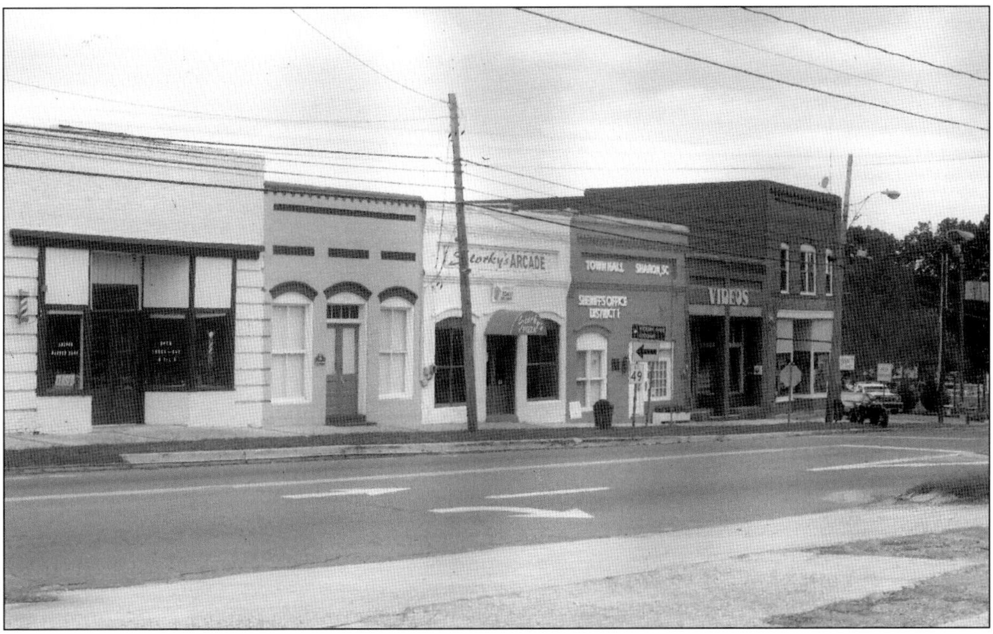

These buildings, which comprise Sharon's oldest business district, have been nominated for the Historic Register, and they will create the main Historic District of the town. The upstairs of the Shannon Building (far right) once served as a meeting hall and movie theater.

The principal speaker was Reverend McCully, who said although he was never a "jiner," he was of the opinion that the American Legion was a worthwhile organization in that it represented the best and highest ideals of more than 4 million men who served overseas during the war. He thought the aims of the Legion were to protect the interests of the country and its servicemen. In closing, he charged the ex-soldiers to remain soldiers—soldiers of the cross—and to serve under the greatest commander—Jesus Christ.

By April, the Sharon Post was reported as "just dragging along" with about 11 members. It appeared the servicemen of the area were like Reverend McCully and not much of "jiners." Regardless of their small membership, the post commander was hoping to be able to put together a ball team in the summer, and other officers were planning several activities. Soon the Post became defunct. During the 1930s, there was some talk about organizing another post, but lack of interest failed to make it a reality.

The longest existing and most prominent social organization formed in Sharon was the Woman's Club, which was organized in the fall of 1911 under the name "Literary Links." Two unmarried women, Julia Titman and Margaret Byers, were the primary organizers. It is said Miss Byers went about in a horse and buggy soliciting membership from certain farm women. The club, though small in number and influence, was Sharon's first attempt at "high culture." The charter members were as follows:

Miss Sallie Allison	Mrs. Lee Good	Mrs. J.H. Saye
Mrs. W.B. Arrowood	Mrs. Lester Good	Mrs. Ed R. Shannon
Miss Libby Byers	Mrs. W.L. Hill	Mrs. H.W. Shannon
Miss Maggie Byers	Mrs. E.B. Hunter	Mrs. J.A. Shannon
Mrs. W.Y. Boyd	Mrs. C.L. Kennedy	Miss Julia Titman
Miss Winnie Crawford	Mrs. J.S. Rainey	Mrs. D.A. Whisonant
Mrs. A.M. Erwin	Mrs. Claude Robinson	

The Ladies' Book Club, or more simply, "the Book club," aimed to help members "keep abreast with current literature and provide social contact." Lives of "homebodies" were improved through reading, the sharing of ideas, and demonstration of learned social manners. Annually, each member selected a book from an approved list, which was in turn passed through the membership for reading and discussion. But these homebodies were not content to be readers and discussers of books.

The club became associated with the South Carolina Federation of Woman's Clubs on October 27, 1921, and from that point, it became known as "the Woman's Club." In 1935, the Woman's Club was united with the General Federation of Woman's Clubs. Just prior to their joining the South Carolina Federation, the ladies beautified the depot area with several beds of canna lilies assisted by a Mr. Street, the section master. Their labor transformed "a rather dismal and dreary looking railway station into a place of some attraction." Another

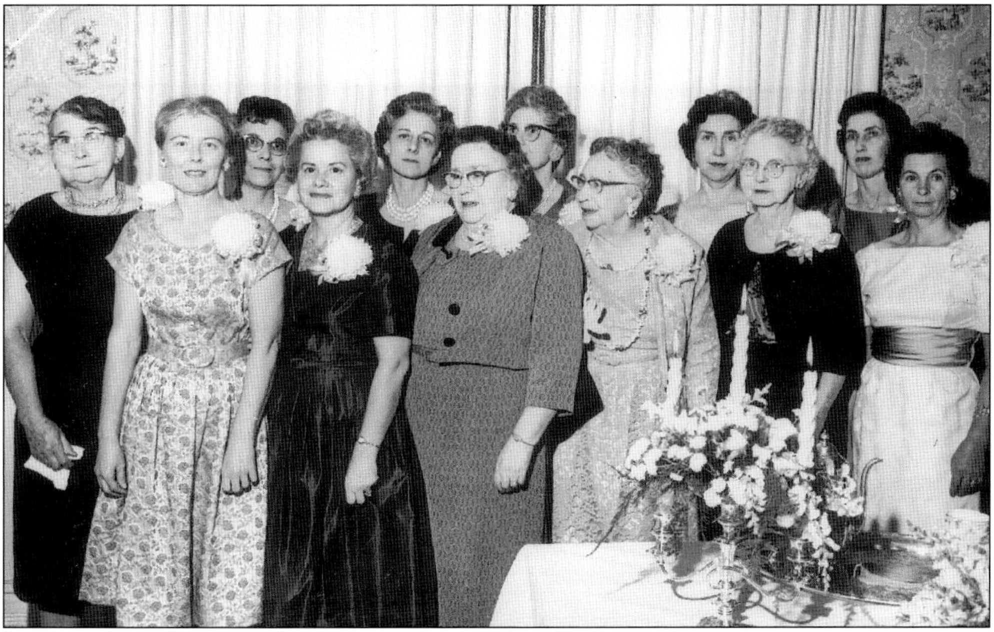

This view shows the full membership of the Sharon Woman's Club in 1961.

project sponsored by the Woman's Club in 1935 was a "beauty show," which was held at the high school. The winner was crowned "Miss Sharon," but because the *Yorkville Enquirer* is missing a number of the September issues, today's generations will never know who won the crown.

The Woman's Club also dealt with weightier matters than planting lilies and sponsoring beauty contests. In March 1935, a letter from the club was read in the House of Representatives stating they were in favor of "strict prohibitive liquor legislation." Mrs. Fred H. Youngblood, secretary, signed the letter. When an industrial survey was done in the 1930s, members of the Woman's Club were described as being ". . . talented musicians, poets, teachers both in public education and church, Red Cross workers, business women, . . . handwork artisans, artists who won many honors in club work and most important—good mothers, wives and homemakers whose influence would be felt for years to come."

If one can believe this synopsis, and there is no reason to doubt it, the majority of the members were educated, talented, and willing to serve the community around them. In their beginning they were striving to be well read. This within itself is admirable when one realizes that most of those living in the area cared little for reading. It may be for this reason, i.e. their love of literacy, and others having little appreciation for books and being unable to relate to the social facets of life, that this club was seen as "snooty" by some.

In the 1930s, under a Clemson University plan, Home Demonstration Clubs came about throughout the state. The Sharon Home Demonstration Club

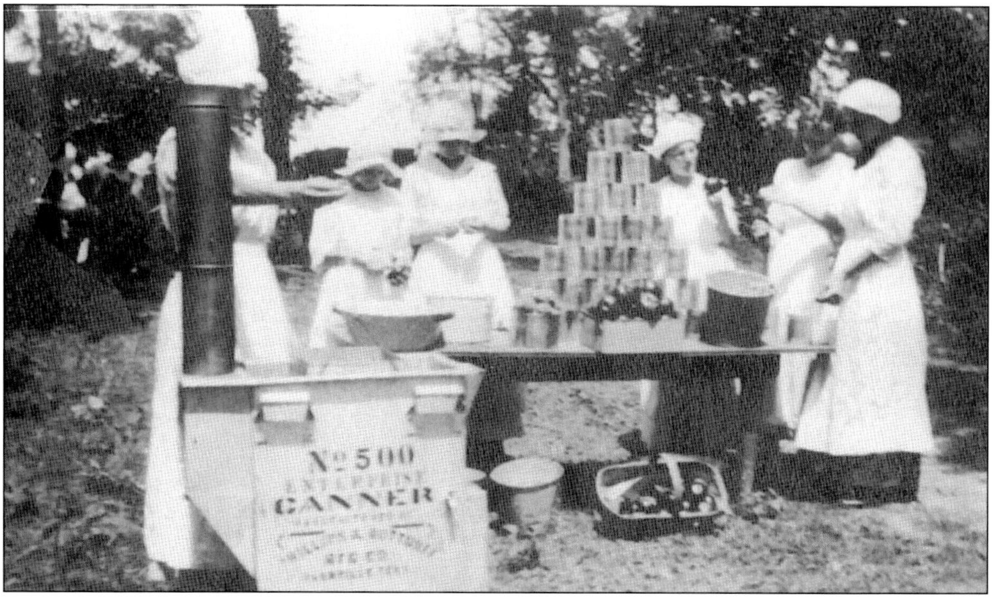

Local women were taught the economics and healthiness of home canning among the many programs of the Home Demonstration Clubs.

became active with a number of the town's women, and continued well past the half-century mark of the town. In 1934, Mrs. W.L. Hill was president and some of the members were as follows: (Mmes.) J.M. Maloney, K.L. Bankhead, W.A. Faris, Luther Hartness, S.A. Gilfillan, Darwin Howell, P.B. Kennedy, John Latham, W. Lon Plexico, E.M. Ricker, Horace Whitesides, L.B. Sherer, Will Shedd, B.C. Erwood, Ernest Dowdle, and C.L. Kennedy; and (Misses) Fewell, Edith White, and Eudora Maloney. That year, Mrs. Hill formed a committee to help serve hot lunches at the Sharon schools. Later in the year, the club was entertained in July by Mrs. K.L. Bankhead "in her beautiful outdoor living room," which consisted of black-and-white furniture. Later in the year, in October, Mrs. Kell stressed the importance of selecting becoming hats, how to wear them becomingly, and how to help them keep their shape by placing them on a hat stand made of an oatmeal box.

Several of the women of the Sharon Home Demonstration Club had their favorite recipes featured in the *Yorkville Enquirer* in February 1935. Mrs. S.A Gilfillan offered her congealed chicken salad, Mrs. Joe Maloney shared her butterscotch pie, and Mrs. L.B. Sherer presented a recipe for french toast. Mrs. W.A Faris gave her recipe for oatmeal drop cookies; Mrs. F.M. Martin, a recipe for Canadian war cake; and Edith White offered one for chocolate fudge.

In the first decades of the twentieth century, the tracks of the old Charleston, Cincinnati & Chicago served as economic and social portals—taking cotton to the cities of the North and bringing relatives for visits from neighboring counties such as Cherokee, Chester, Union, Mecklenburg, and Gaston. Travelers could board trains at hamlets like McConnells, Bullock's Creek, and Smyrna, settle into comfortable quarters, eat fine meals served on tablecloths, disembark in states like Ohio and Illinois, shop in Charlotte, or cheer Hickory Grove native son Bob Bolin as he pitched for the San Francisco Giants.

Still, Western York County held fast to its cotton kingdom heritage even as a new mobile generation, born in a new century, were able to sample life far away from the rivers that had always defined the region. In effect, the railway system, even after its tracks rusted in the latter half of the twentieth century, propped open a cultural alleyway, through which citizens could travel (figuratively and literally) far beyond the Southern Eden of their forebears, while remembering, always, the distinctiveness of the special place they called home.

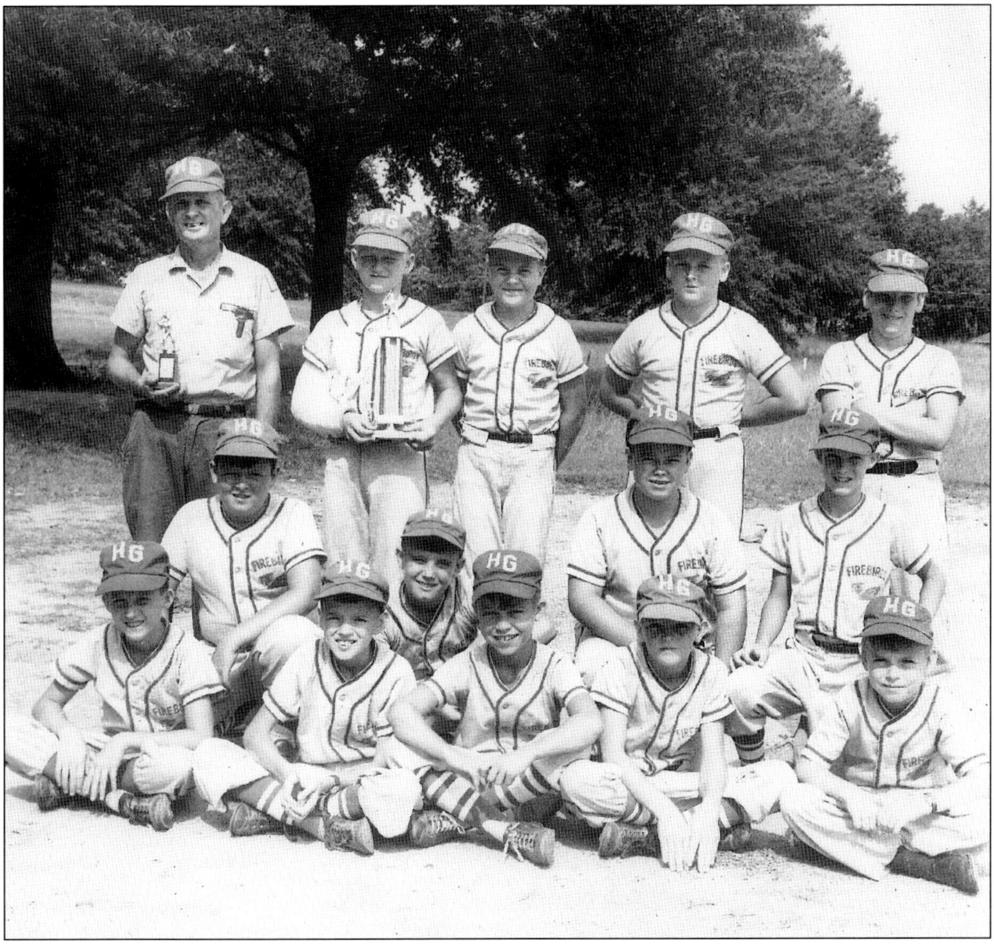

Coached by Madison Estes in 1968, the Hickory Grove Firebirds were the town's first little league baseball team. During the twentieth century, there were many clubs, both recreational and civic, throughout the county to involve men, women, and children in social activities.

7. God's Country

The independent spirit displayed time and time again by the Revolution's heroes was born in the early churches of Western York County. Scots-Irish Presbyterians like Hill, Bratton, Watson, Moffet, Lacey, and others hailed from a long line of dissenters. The Scots-Irish were, by nature, a quarrelsome lot. Their proclivity to question authority had caused them to be exiled in the 1500s from Scotland to North Ireland. Still, they refused to blindly support monarchs. Arriving in America in five waves, commencing in 1717 and concluding in the late 1700s, they came just in time to stand in the front lines for the cause of liberty.

In Western York County, four Presbyterian congregations were formed in the mid and late 1760s; the earliest was Bethel, which was organized in 1764, a few miles east of the present-day town of Clover. Among the members buried in the historic cemetery is Revolutionary War hero William Hill and a number of veterans of the Civil War.

Shortly after Bethel was organized, three other Presbyterian churches were established in Western York County—Beersheba, Bethesda, and Bullock's Creek. Beersheba and Bullock's Creek (originally called Dan) were organized just one week apart. Because the pastors of all four of these churches openly preached liberty and resistance to the British Crown, they became known as the "Four B's in King George's Bonnet."

Sometime just before the Revolution, a small congregation of New Light Baptists appeared on the east bank of Turkey Creek about 5 miles from the Presbyterian congregation of Bullock's Creek. This church, sometimes known as Fowler's or Flat Rock Baptist Church, was pastored by Reverend James Fowler up until 1803, when he died. The congregation was never strong in numbers, and after Fowler's death, the members united with Skull Shoals Baptist Church across the Broad River in Union County. When they disbanded, Western York County returned to being a Presbyterian stronghold.

Another Baptist congregation was located on Buffalo Creek in what is now Cherokee County. Reverend Joseph Camp, an Anabaptist dissenter, organized the church in 1772 and was closely associated with Reverend Fowler of Turkey Creek and Reverend Philip Mulkey of Fairforest in Union County. During the

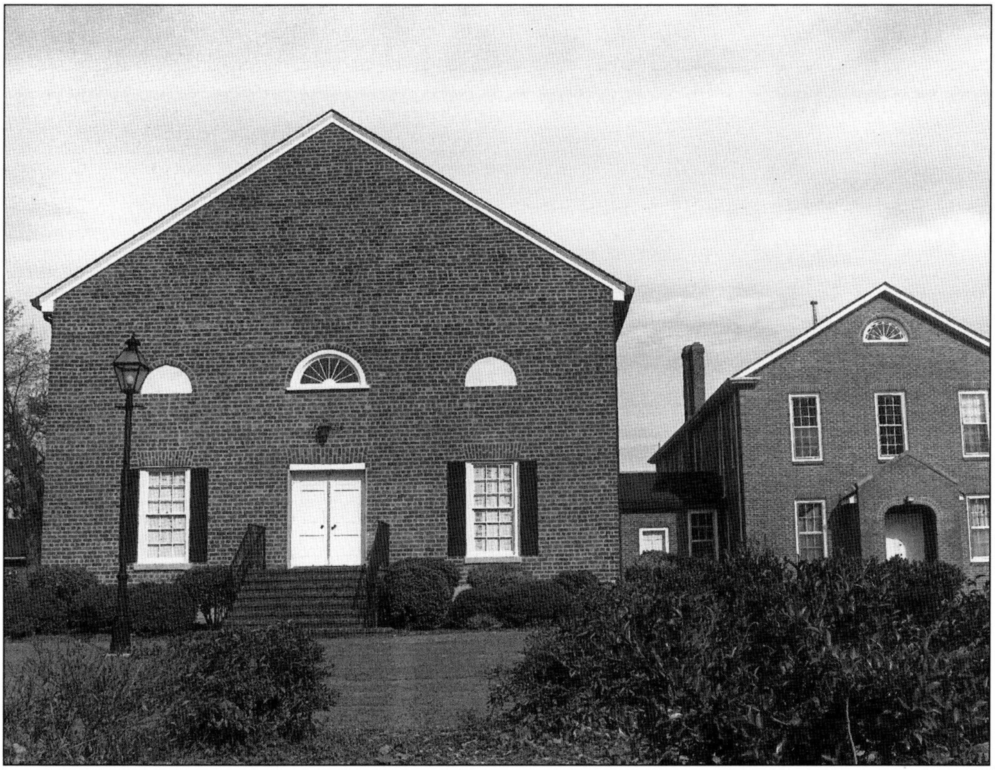

Bethesda Presbyterian Church, located near McConnells, is one of the oldest churches in York County.

Revolution, Camp (as well as Fowler and Mulkey) urged his congregation to remain neutral. In 1781, as Cornwallis was marching out of South Carolina, he had Camp arrested and questioned him about the whereabouts of Daniel Morgan. Buffalo Baptist Church remained, and still is, a strong congregation.

Less than 20 years after the Revolution, a division began to develop within the local Presbyterian church over the introduction of hymns. In the 1790s, Watt's Hymns were introduced into the churches that had traditionally sung only Biblical psalms. Reverend Joseph Alexander, the old Revolutionary fire-eater, sanctioned them for his several churches as well as Reverend William C. Davies of the area. The inclusion of hymns into public worship created no small fervor. A humorous account is given of the division at one of Reverend Davis's church. It is said that upon announcing the singing of a hymn, one of the elders rose from his pew and stomped out of the church. Just as he was leaving, Reverend Davis called out the first line of the hymn, "Cast out the Devil and all his minions."

The division finally erupted into a full blown schism in 1797, when a number of members from Bullock's Creek and Beersheba left to unite with the Associate Reformed Presbyterian Church. These "Seceders," as they would be called,

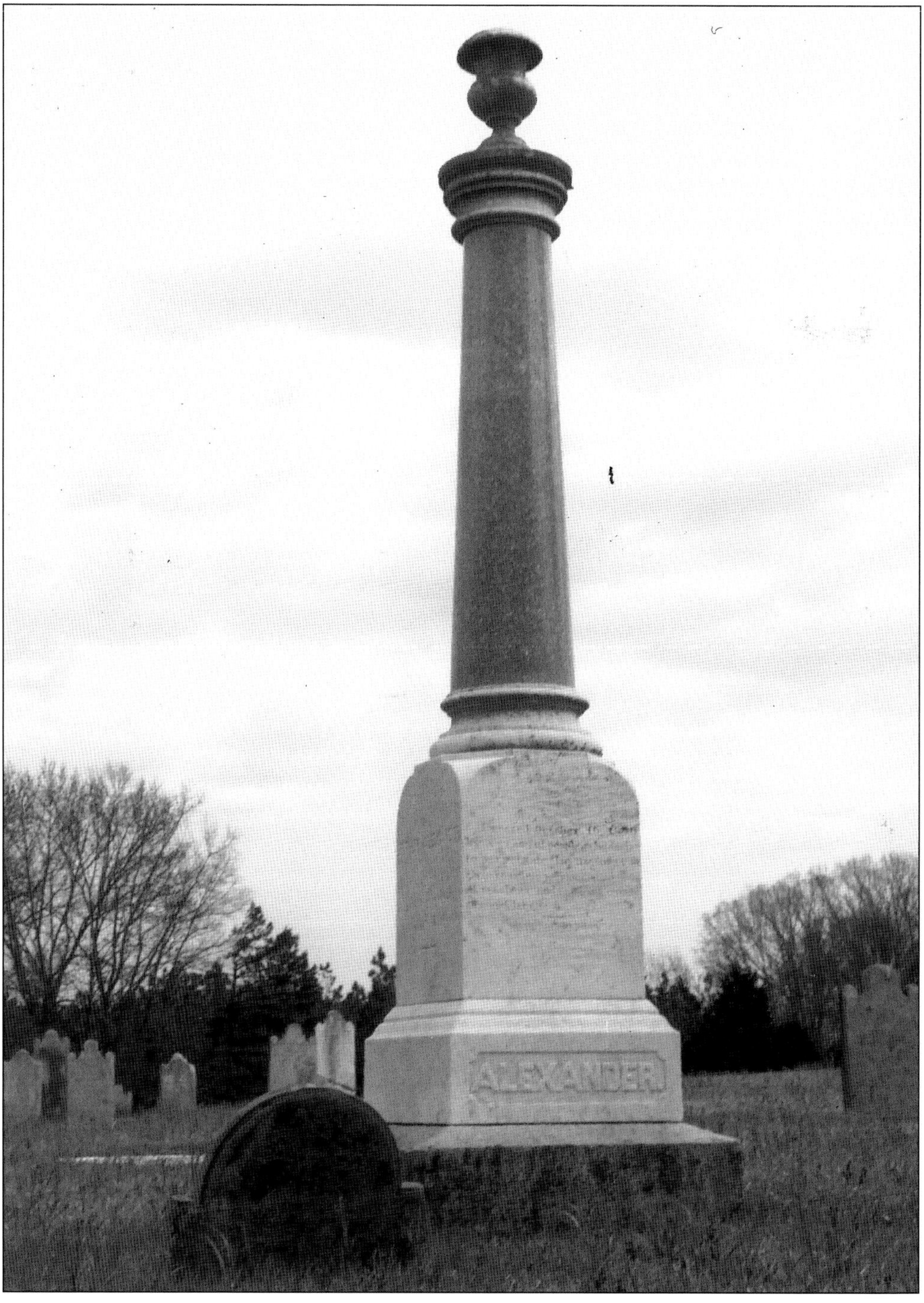

This marker for Reverend Joseph Alexander (1735–1809) honors and remembers the first pastor of Bullock's Creek Presbyterian Church. The monument was erected on October 16, 1890, "by a grateful people, who desire to perpetuate the memory of this fearless patriot, distinguished teacher and faithful minister of Christ."

established the centrally located Sharon Associate Reformed Presbyterian Church, between the two Presbyterian churches, later giving its name to the town in 1889. When the population increased in the extreme portion of Western York County, the Smyrna Associate Reformed Presbyterian (ARP) Church was established in 1843, which had served as a preaching point for several years.

An Associate Reformed Presbyterian Church was not established in Hickory Grove until the town was chartered by the state in December 1888. The 29 charter members (24 from Smyrna Associate Reformed Presbyterian) immediately began constructing their church on Wylie Avenue, holding its first worship service on March 23, 1890. The Hickory Grove Orphanage was established by this congregation in 1897. After eight successful years, it was consolidated with the Dunlap Orphanage in Memphis, Tennessee.

Although Methodist Bishop Francis Asbury visited the area in 1812, that denomination did not establish a church in Western York County until 1841, when Prospect Methodist Church was organized. This church was established several miles southwest of the present site of Hickory Grove, a short distance from the agricultural community of Hopewell. Before Prospect was organized, it may have been that those of the Methodist persuasion heard circuit-riding preachers at the old Unity Baptist Church, which was organized about 1820 and used by various denominations. In 1880, the congregation moved to the present town of Hickory Grove and established themselves under the name Mount Vernon, and they remain a strong congregation today.

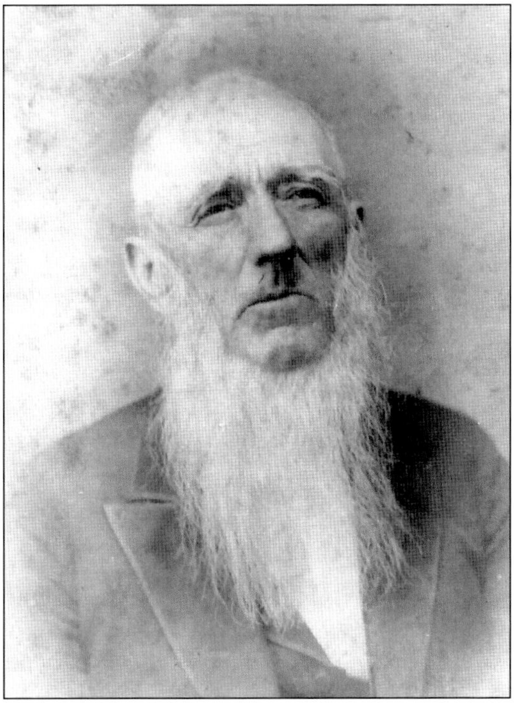

For 50 years, Reverend Dr. Robert Armstrong Ross served as the pastor of the Sharon Associate Reformed Presbyterian Church.

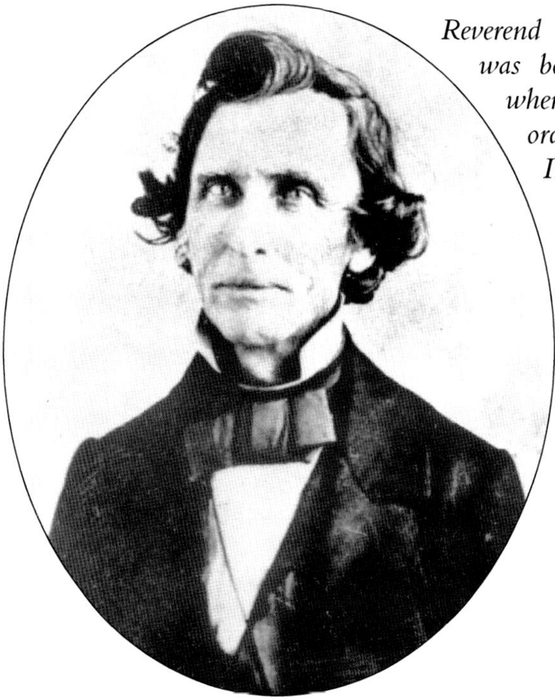

Reverend Robert Young Russell (1800–1866) was born in Ireland, arriving in America when he was one year old. Russell was ordained on April 22, 1826, in the Independent Presbyterian Church, and he helped in establishing a union between the Independent and Orthodox Presbyterian Churches in the area.

It appears that "Old Prospect" had two sites prior to the congregation's move into Hickory Grove. The oldest site is on Beaver Dam Road near the Hopewell community and the second site about a quarter of a mile farther east. When the church moved into a newer log building, about 1860, the older structure was sold to Salem Presbyterian Church for use of free blacks and a few slaves. Renamed Salem-Howell, the church was governed by white elders of the Salem church, but must have had black men as deacons. The pastor of this church probably was Reverend Robert Y. Russell, who was preaching at both Bullock's Creek and Salem. This effort came on the heels of movement by the Presbyterian Church to "Christianize" the slave population.

About 10 miles west of Hickory Grove, another Methodist church was organized sometime before the middle of the nineteenth century. The earliest records referring to the Canaan Congregation is in the Fourth Quarter Conference of 1841, which assembled at the Unity (now Baptist) Church near Hickory Grove. Other Western York County Methodist congregations mentioned in that report were Feemster's (Shady Grove), Prospect, Zion, and Walnut Grove.

About the same time that the "Old Prospect" congregation moved to Hickory Grove in 1880, another Methodist church was organized near the York–Chester County line. On a site located about 5 miles east of the Bullock's Creek Presbyterian Church and 1 mile south of the old site of Fowler's Church, the Bethany congregation built their meeting house. Bethany became defunct about 1910, leaving only a small cemetery to mark its presence.

Also in that same vicinity, nearer to the York–Chester County boundary, is the site of the New Bethel Baptist Church. Only an overgrown cemetery marks the site where this church was established in the late 1800s near the now-defunct town of Sandersville.

Near the western Chester County community of Wilkesburg, a Brushy Fork Baptist Church was organized about 1812 (some say 1822). The church, formerly known as the "Old Shaw Church," continued to be one of the oldest and strongest in the area. In 1870, a new meeting house was built with a seating capacity of 200.

In York County, one of the oldest continuing Baptist congregations exists near the town of Hickory Grove. Unity Baptist Church and the Unity Academy is a very real example of the riddle, "which came first, the chicken or the egg?" The exact organizational year of the church is unknown. Folklore has it that a group of fox hunters (some say deer hunters), recognizing the need for a meeting house in the area, agreed to build one which could be used by all denominations—thus, the name, Unity. While the records of the York Baptist Association gives the year of its organization as 1833, there is a persistent tradition that it existed at least ten years before.

At that time, in 1823, Reverend Aaron Williams of the Presbyterian Church established the Unity Academy, which appears to have been the earliest school

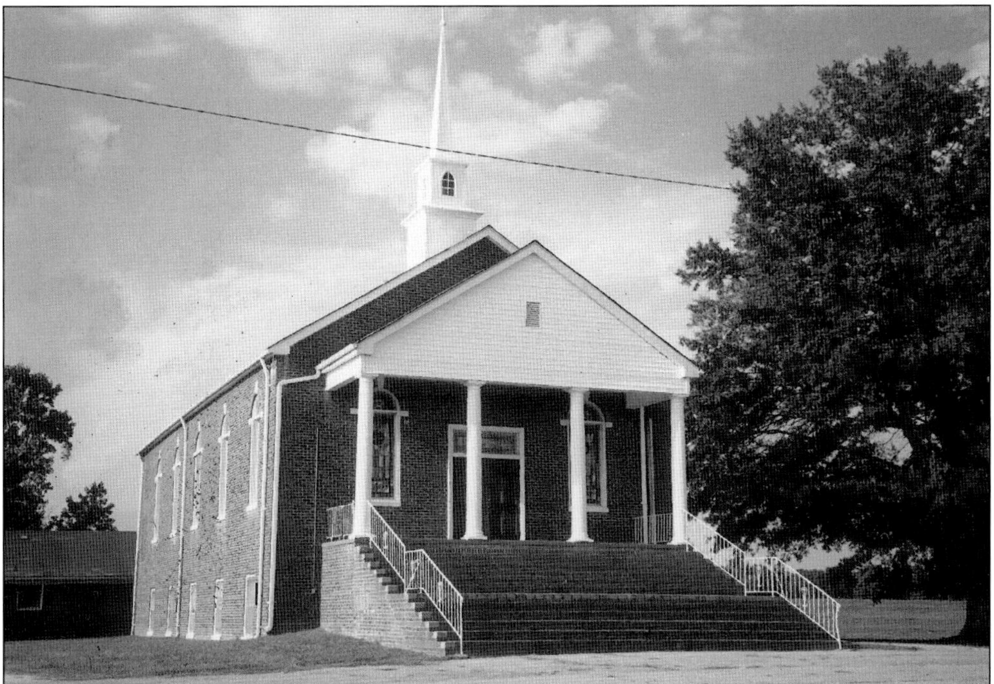

Unity Baptist Church of Hickory Grove is the town's oldest church. Its name is derived from the fact that it was originally used by several denominations.

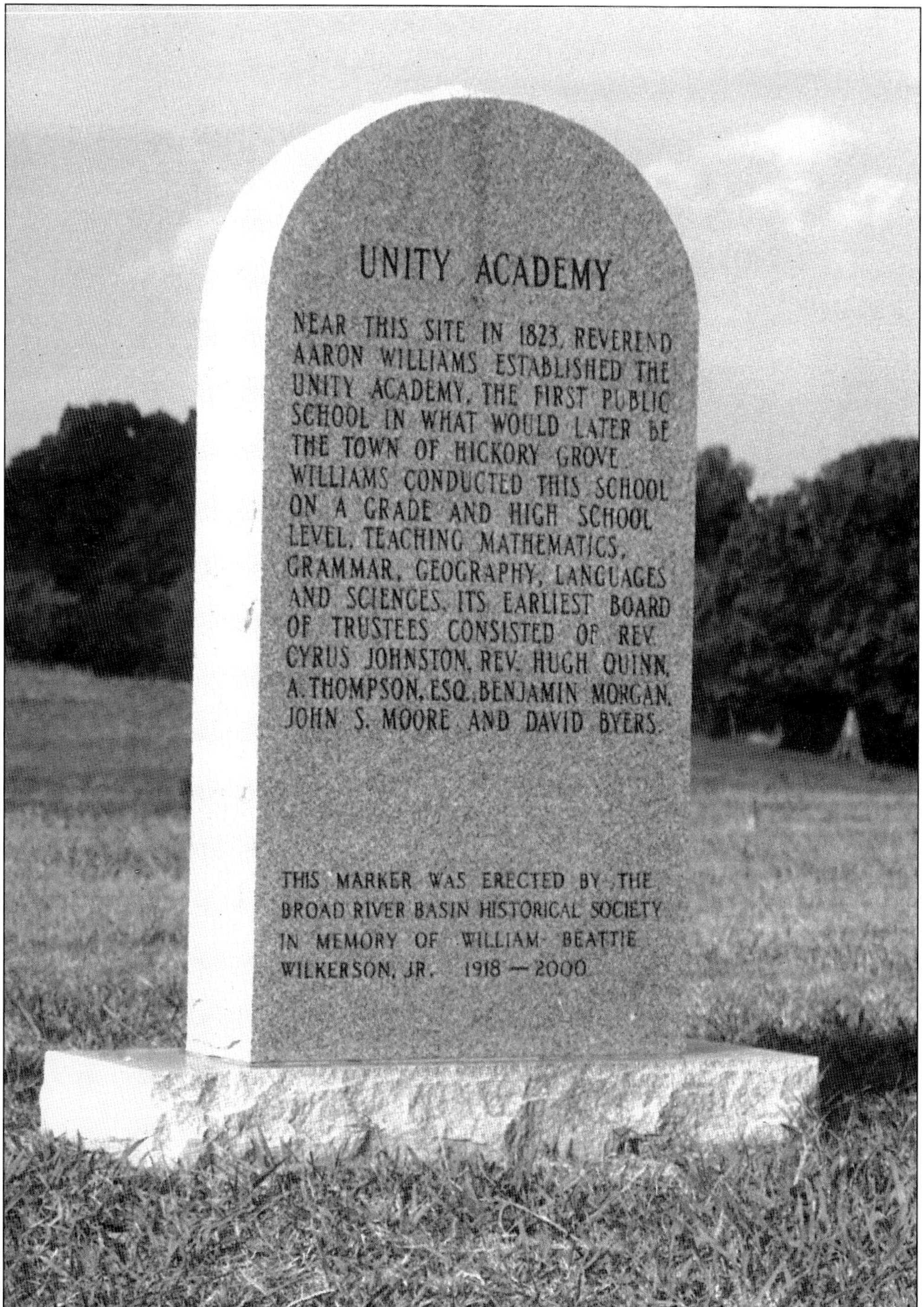

Unity Academy was established in 1823 by Presbyterian minister Reverend Aaron Williams and was one of the area's earliest schools. This historic marker was erected in 2000 by the Broad River Basin Historical Society in memory of W.B. Wilkerson Jr.

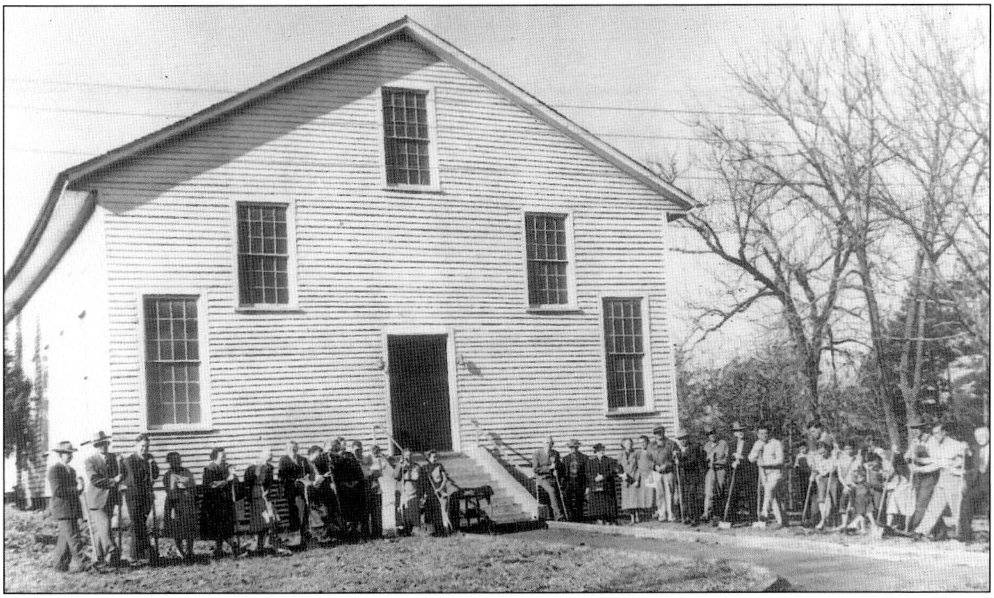

The congregation of Bullock's Creek Presbyterian Church is seen here in 1950 breaking ground for a new church, which was completed within a year. The 1860 sanctuary stands behind the assembled congregation.

in the Hickory Grove area. The question lingers, which came first, the school or the church? Was the schoolhouse used as a meeting house when preaching was available, or was the meeting house used during the week as a school?

W.S. Wilkerson in 1921 recalled that the church came about through a discussion among several deer hunters (not fox hunters)—one of which was Abe Smith. They all lamented that there was no church in the immediate area and agreed to build a meeting house that could be used by any preacher that might pass through. Wilkerson specifically mentioned that there was "only one Methodist preacher in the whole of York County" and that he came only about twice a year to conduct services. Wilkerson also told that it was Smith who gave the land and timber for the meeting house while others supplied the nails and labor.

Reverend William Cummings, pastor of Bullock's Creek Presbyterian Church in 1810, became the catalyst for a major church division. Described by his antagonists as "a brilliant man given to metaphysical speculation," a Mr. Davis and part of the congregation separated from the orthodox church and established the Bullock's Creek Independent Church and the Bullock's Creek Presbytery. Several other area churches splintered off the mainline denomination to become a part of the movement that lasted for nearly 60 years.

Approximately 15 churches were organized into the Independent Church across Western York County and in North Carolina on the state boundary. In the early years, the organization showed much vitality; however, several of the churches lost large numbers in the westward movement of the 1830s. The Independent Church suffered from a lack of ministers, and combined with the death of their founder, morale was weakened and growth was hindered. By the late 1850s, a move to reunite with the orthodox church was being spearheaded by the Independent's most outstanding minister. The union was finally initiated in 1860, and the Independent Presbyterian Church became part of the area's history.

One of the oldest African-American churches in Western York County is Blue Branch Presbyterian Church, located 3 miles east of the Bullock's Creek Presbyterian congregation. This church was founded shortly after the Civil War and gave birth to several other local Presbyterian, Baptist, and Methodist churches. Reverend Baker Russell, formerly a slave of Reverend Robert Young Russell, was installed as the congregation's first pastor. Prior to emancipation, Baker Russell was taught to read, write, and interpret the Scriptures by his master.

The people of Western York County have always taken their religion seriously. The early Presbyterian churches, the Associate Reformed Presbyterians, and the other Protestants who organized congregations in the region give credence to the importance of religion to the people of the area. Ministers were routinely "pounded" or welcomed when they arrived at their assigned churches with gifts of hams, breads, homemade jellies, various staples, and sometimes feed for the family cow. Outstanding male members with a reasonable level of education stepped forward to teach Sunday school and to serve as elders and deacons. Originally, women served in lesser capacities, organizing luncheons, and social functions of the church. After the Civil War, they began heading fund-raising drives, teaching small children, and serving on auxiliary committees. Gradually, they rose to the highest positions in the local church, other than in the more orthodox denominations which held steadfast to male-only church officers.

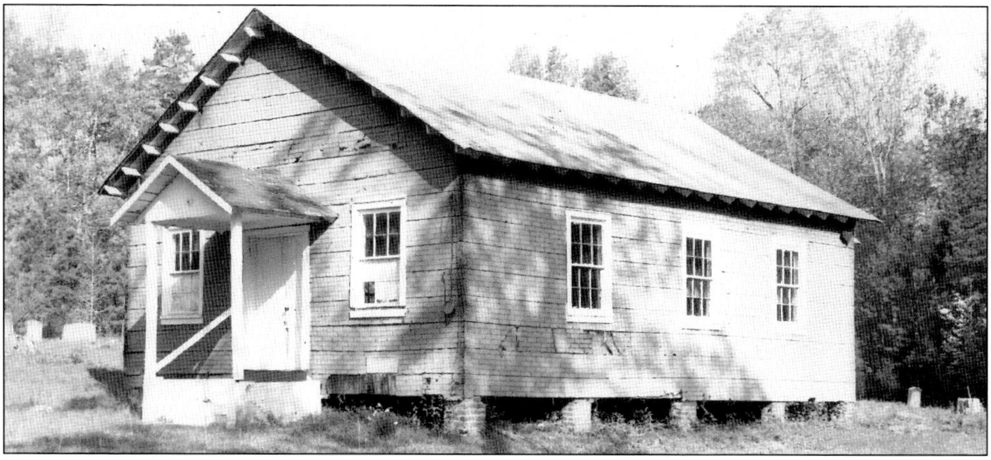

Blue Branch Presbyterian Church was organized in the early 1870s and was one of the first African-American churches in the Bullock's Creek area. Reverend Baker Russell, who had been educated by his former master, Reverend R.Y. Russell, became the church's first pastor.

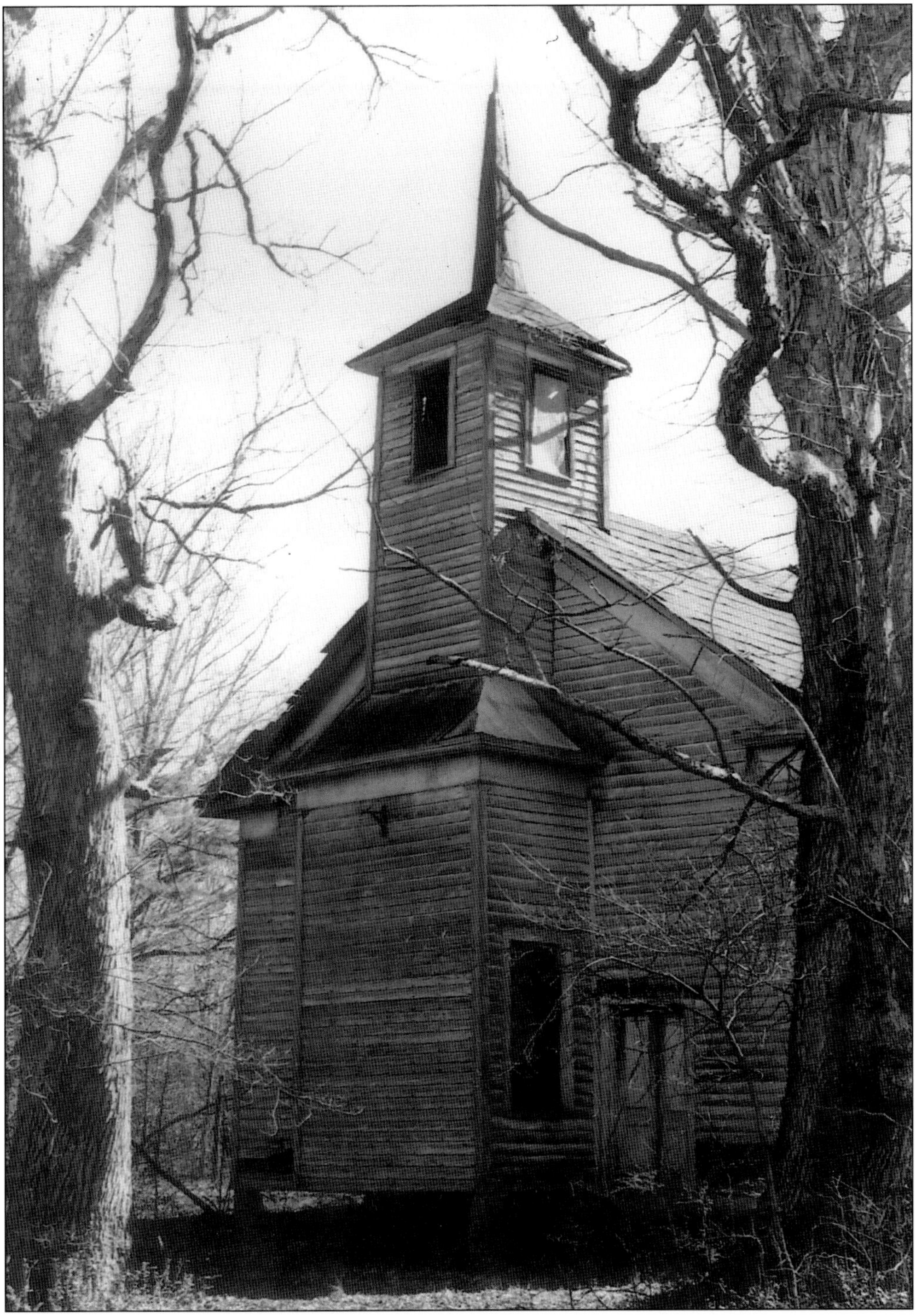

This rear view of the Hickory Grove Baptist Church reveals its unusual architecture. The extension provided the building's pulpit area, with the belfry and steeple directly overhead. Before the structure's collapse, the old church was used as a hay barn for the Pratt farm.

8. A Time of Transition

The Civil War, followed by the tumult of Reconstruction and the Ku Klux Klan activities, climaxed with the 1876 gubernatorial election in South Carolina, which resulted in the state being "redeemed" by former Confederate General Wade Hampton. York County, like most of South Carolina, supported Hampton, and by early 1877, Reconstruction had ended. Western York County turned its attention to rebuilding its shattered economy and adjusting to the political and social changes caused by the war and occupation by Union troops. The Ku Klux Klan went into a period of dormancy, but there was a whirlwind of activity on the horizon.

The *Yorkville Enquirer* reported that a tornado struck Western York County on Wednesday afternoon, May 27, 1885. It was a repeat of a tornado that fell sometime the year before, and followed the same track, but caused less damage. The tornado of 1885 first struck the plantation of S.C. Chambers on Bullock's Creek, 8 miles west of York, where it damaged trees and fences. Moving west to east, it struck the plantation of R.M. Whitesides at Meeks Hill, blowing down fences and twisting off large trees. Next in its path was J.T. Summerford's farm, where several small buildings were unroofed. J.M. Smith, who lived on the west of York, received a visit. Next in line was William Dickson, Joseph Neal, A.E. Carroll, Hugh B. Wallace, and William Carson. Trees were twisted, buildings damaged, fences demolished, and crops were badly damaged. Wallace's kitchen and Carson's home were unroofed. The violent storm then struck J. Harvey Dickson, who lived 3 miles north of York and next door to William Carson. Here, eight buildings were damaged, part of his chimney was toppled, and his orchard was ruined. The tornado then fell upon William B. Thomasson, J. Butler Thomasson, Thomas N. Wood, and James G. Thomasson. The upper story of Wood's home was blown off and a buggy and wagon were blown from a shed and carried 80 feet away. His nearly completed new home was damaged as well. After a small house was flattened at J. Butler Thomasson's property, the tornado advanced northward into Mecklenburg County, North Carolina.

That following June 24, rain fell in torrents for nearly an hour. The paper reported that Doolittle Creek was 15 deep and 125 yards wide, "sweeping everything before it." The creek at Elijah Hawkins's farm was 500 yards wide and

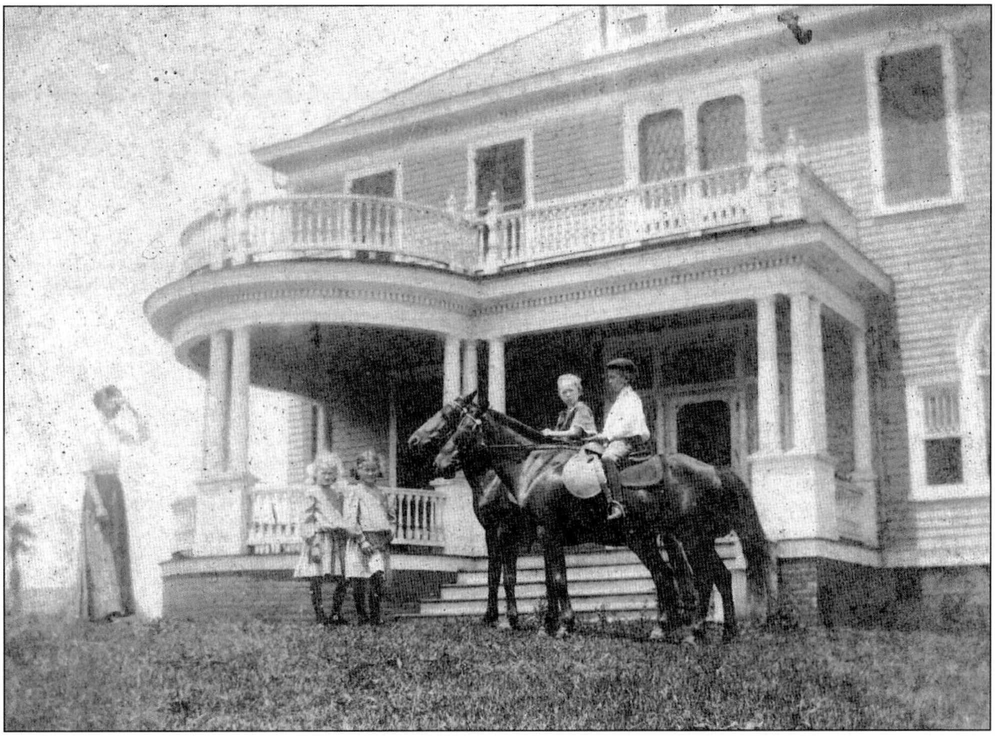

York and the communities of Western York County, like much of the South, struggled through diverse storms of violent weather, unpredictable economy, and a changing society. This scene recalls a quieter moment in these years of dramatic transformation.

was the greatest freshet ever on that creek. The dam at Ira Hawkins's gristmill was carried away and H.M. Moor lost 200 chocks of wheat. The greatest toll was taken on those who lived on Kings Creek and in the Antioch section. Gill Hambright, Drewry Neal, Elijah Hardin, James Dillingham, E.J. Downey, M.M. Tate, Lewis H. McSwain, and Mark Wells all suffered heavy losses. Three mills in Spartanburg County were destroyed—Madison Surratt, Lewis Clary, and P.O. Lemons. Those that lived on Kings Creek and suffered from the flooding were Reverend L.H. McSwain, O.P. Morgan, M.M. Tate, E.J. Drewry, E. Hardin, William Borders, J.M. Hambright, A.F. Hambright, A.C. Hambright, D.R. Hambright, and J.S. Wells.

Three J's Robinson recalled the following of the 1886 winter, when the Broad River froze over a solid 11 inches thick:

> February 1886 was the coldest spell of weather I mind anything about. That was the year that the bluebirds were all killed. . . . There were lots of bluebirds in this country then. They were almost as plentiful during the winter as English Sparrows are now at all times . . . it was several years after that winter before I again saw a bluebird.

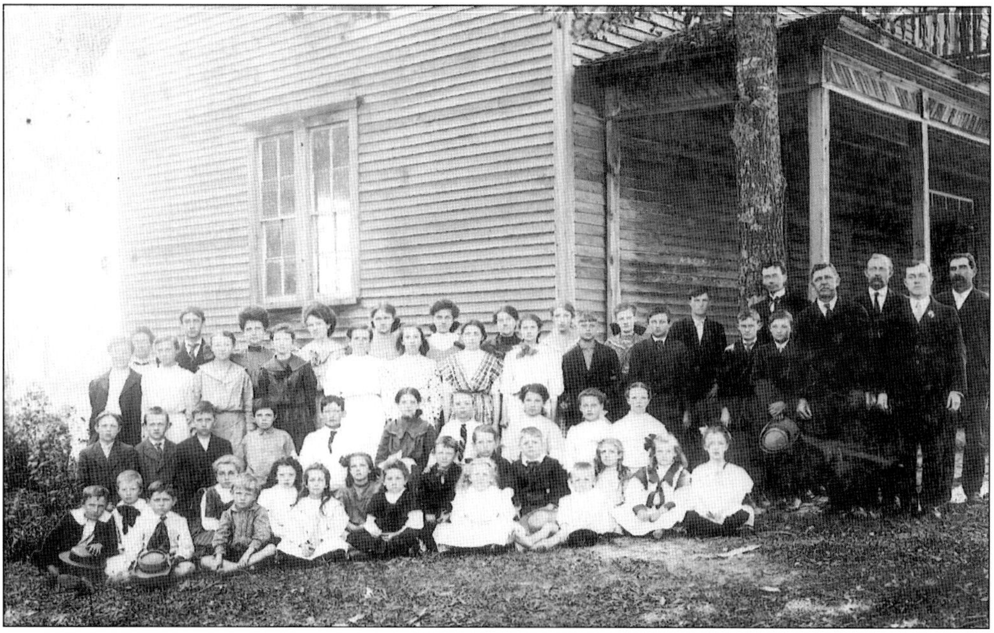

These students and faculty from Hickory Grove School pose for a class portrait in the early part of the twentieth century.

> Well, it was dreadfully cold from the middle of January as I recollect, on into March, and there was but little to do for the greater part of the time except to stay about the house and look to the firewood. Also we had to draw water for the stock, for the springs and branches were all frozen.
>
> The river froze from bank to bank and the ice got thicker and thicker. Bateaux went out of use and people who had business on the opposite side of the river went across on the ice. Just anybody walked across, and while I did not see it, I understood that a Negro rode across on a mule.
>
> When the breakup came, an ice gang was familiar in a bend a short distance below our house and the river was banked up for nearly a mile. The ice was piled up like a little mountain. People came from all about to look at it. When the ice began to break, it made a noise like the falling of forest pines and the like. Just how thick the ice was at the thickest I do not know, but after the breakup, I measured . . . eleven inches thick.

South Carolina in the last decade of the nineteenth century was going through an identity crisis. The Confederate heroes, like Wade Hampton, who had "redeemed" the state from the carpetbaggers and scalawags of Reconstruction, had aged. Now Hampton was seen as a Bourbon aristocrat, too linked to the industrial cities of Charleston, Columbia, and the politically powerful of Washington, D.C. to appeal to farmers.

Thus, the Bourbons would be challenged in 1890 by pugnacious men like Edgefield County's Benjamin Ryan Tillman. The Tillmanites, who had tremendous appeal among the dirt-under-the-fingernails people of Western York County, shouted, "The sun doesn't rise and set in Charleston." The University of South Carolina, located in Columbia, should be closed; Charleston's Citadel was a dude ranch, the Tillman farmers' army suggested. The Farmer's Alliance was immensely popular in Western York County. Tillman spoke fluently the language of cotton and corn. The efforts to found colleges for the sons of farmers (Clemson) and the daughters (Winthrop) were clear demonstrations of his affinity for the land.

The turn of the century saw Tillman in the United States Senate, with the blessing of York County voters, and the farmers believing, for a moment, that their future, like their past, would spring forth from the red land of Bullock's Creek. The twentieth century would be a period of stress on the farm but not before Tillman routed the urban Bourbons and gave the farmers a sense of triumph during this time of transition.

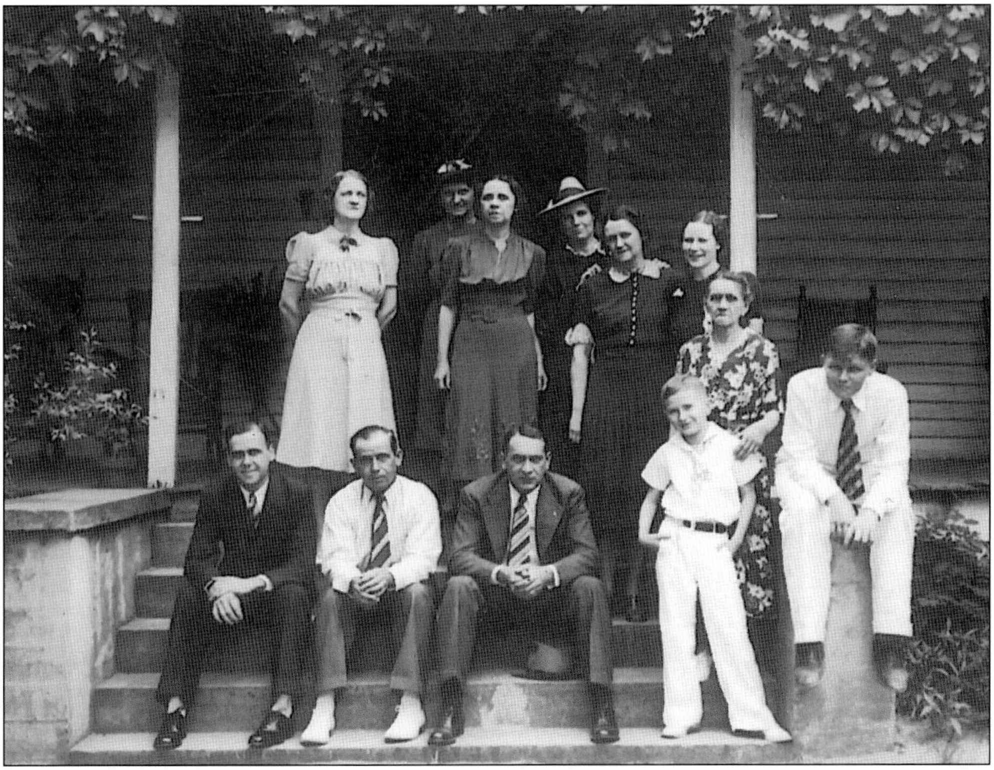

After church and a long, Sunday dinner, Western York County families, as did many families across the South, retired to vine-covered porches for a relaxing afternoon since air conditioning was still several years away for many families. This photograph captures the Mendenhall family of McConnells in 1939.

9. The Village of Yorkville

In 1785, York County and 33 other counties in South Carolina were established with York, Chester, Lancaster, and 4 other counties making up the Camden Judicial District. The act establishing these counties stipulated that each of the counties should erect courthouses and public buildings in the most convenient part of each county, with a tax to be levied to cover the cost of 'building the courthouses, prisons, pillories, whipping posts and stocks."

A commission was appointed to select a county seat and to build a courthouse at some suitable point. Maps of James Cook and Henry Mouzon, made in 1771 and 1775, respectively, show the road from Charles Town to Rutherford Town crossed the Road from Charlotteburg to Augusta at a place called Fergus Crossroads. Being near the center of the county, this place was chosen as the county seat, streets and lots were laid out for a planned town, and the community was named Yorkville.

The 1785 Act also provided for seven country court justices, or justices of the peace, for each county. Colonel William Hill was one of the first seven. Five of the other six were John Moffett, David Leech, Francis Adams, James Wilson, and John Drennan. Any combination of three was authorized to hold county court.

The April 1786 term of court appointed three commissioners: Captain Alexander Love, William Fergus Sr., Esq., and John Currence. Their instructions were to acquire 2 acres of land and to build a courthouse and jail. The court also directed the commission that the courthouse be 30 feet long and 22 feet wide. It was to be one and one-half stories high and to be built of square logs and dovetailed. The jail on the other side of Congress Street was to be 22 feet long and 16 feet wide. The same term of court instructed York County's first sheriff, Lieutenant Colonel James Hawthorn, who had commanded local troops in the Battle of Kings Mountain, to have built a pair of stocks and a whipping post. Both were used liberally.

Yorkville's existence has been documented during the Federal period in American history. The first authentic record that can be located referring to the town of York is dated October 21, 1790, and reads as follows:

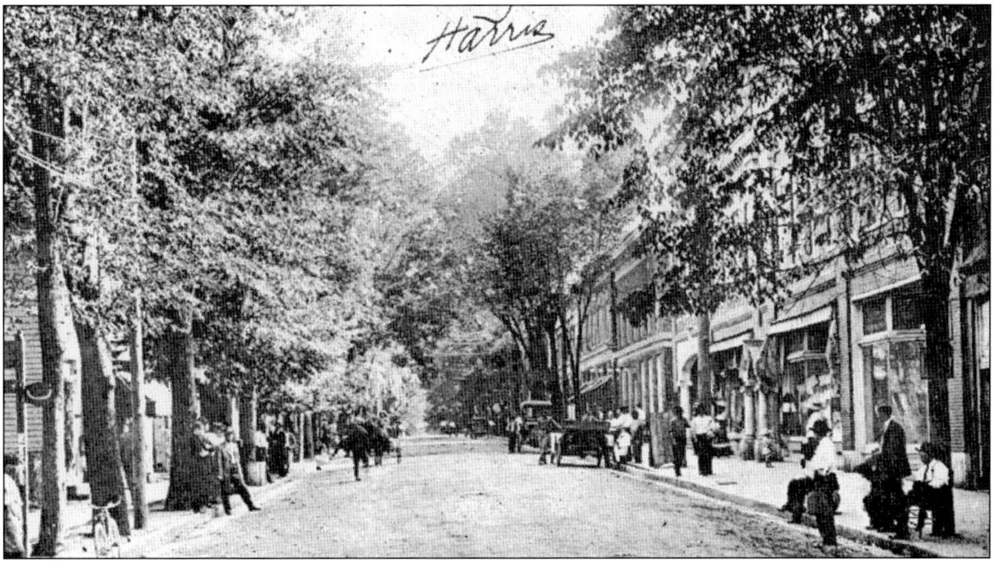

This early-twentieth-century image of downtown Yorkville illustrates the tranquil beauty of Fergus Crossroads.

> In consideration of the sum of One Hundred Pounds to them, the said William and John Fergus, in hand paid by the said William Hill, Jr., Two hundred acres of land in York County, South Carolina, including Yorkville, being a part of a tract of land granted by patent to John Miller from His Majesty's office in North Carolina and being dated the 25th day of April, 1767 and from him conveyed to William and John Fergus.

The tract was described as "Beginning at a hickory tree near the road from Yorkville to Caleb Powers plantation and running N70 W240 poles to a post oak at Alex Ramsey's near John Caraghan's; thence N40 E270 poles to a blackjack [oak] on one side of the glade; thence S40 E270 poles to the beginning, including Yorkville."

The first house in Yorkville was built at 10 West Liberty Street, where the First Presbyterian Church now stands, and was built by Robert Smith. The second house was located on the northeast corner of Congress and Liberty Streets and was built by Alec Love. According to Dr. Maurice Moore's *Reminiscences of York*, the third was a large two-story log building erected by David McColl, and he conducted the first "house of entertainment." Within a few years McColl sold the establishment to his brother, John, who, for many years, conducted the only tavern in the village.

Court week in Yorkville soon became a social occasion. It became the custom for women to accompany their husbands, and families to bring their children. Peddlers found court week provided a ready market among the crowds and sales days often coincided with court schedules. In 1930, Dr. Joseph H. Saye of

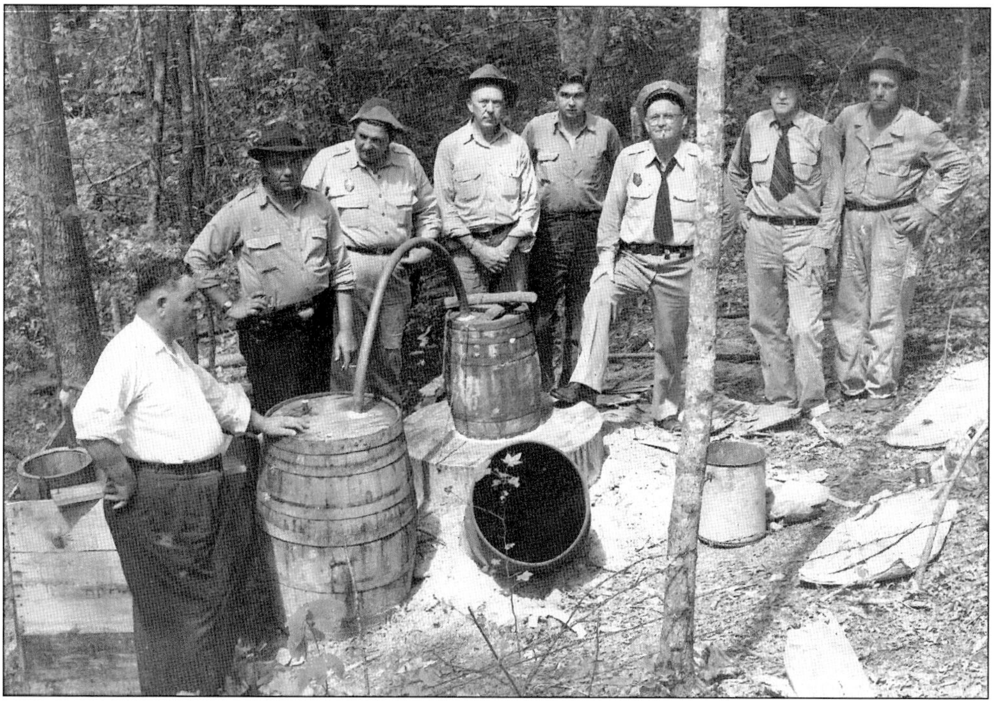

County police and sheriff's deputies pose in front of a typical Western York County liquor still. Since the boisterous days of court week in Yorkville, York and Western York County have seen days of carousing and bootlegging.

Sharon recalled attending sales day in Yorkville as early as 1885, saying horse and mule traders mainly attended it with a lot of carousing and drinking. He recalled the following:

> The first time I ever came to Yorkville on sales day was about 1885, and after that between each September and February I was usually in town for sales day. I would go up in Rufe Parish's lot and get a place to sit down out of the way and watch the horse traders. It was more fun than a circus to see the traders at their game. They would bring old horses and mules that were so poor that they could hardly stand up and they would trade around with those old plugs all day long.
>
> Those fellows were good comrades. Sometimes one of their old plugs would fall down and the traders would gather around to help it up and after the horse would stand for a little bit to steady itself they would help the owner up on its back and off he would go again.

People with business in Yorkville also found entertainment and accommodation of a makeshift variety in the "portable hotel," operated by Michael Moore and Jimmy McNeil. During court week these two men arrived in Yorkville in a wagon loaded with bedding and cooking utensils. They rented a house and set up their business. At the end of the week, as the court prepared to move to the next county, usually Chester, they packed up their "hotel" and moved along.

The first permanent store in Yorkville was operated by Michael Moore. When James Latta first came to the area, he would bring his goods every court week and display them. Eventually he decided to establish a permanent store in Yorkville. Lot No. 4, across from the courthouse, was sold to him in 1805, and was spoken of as the lot "where James Latta keeps his store." From this beginning resulted his large store with branches in Camden, Chester, Columbia, and elsewhere. John McColl sold a lot to James Latta for his residence, presently occupied by the York Funeral Home.

After Michael Moore's mobile hotel, Yorkville developed more refined accommodations, and by the mid-1800s, the town contained several hotels offering various amenities. One of the finer establishments was Rose's Hotel, which was built in 1852 by Doctors Rufus Bratton and E.A. Crenshaw, and completed by Edward Rose. This public house was one of the most modern hotels in the South Carolina Upcountry, hosting a restaurant and shuttle service to the local railroad depot. In 1865, when the Confederate cabinet was fleeing southward

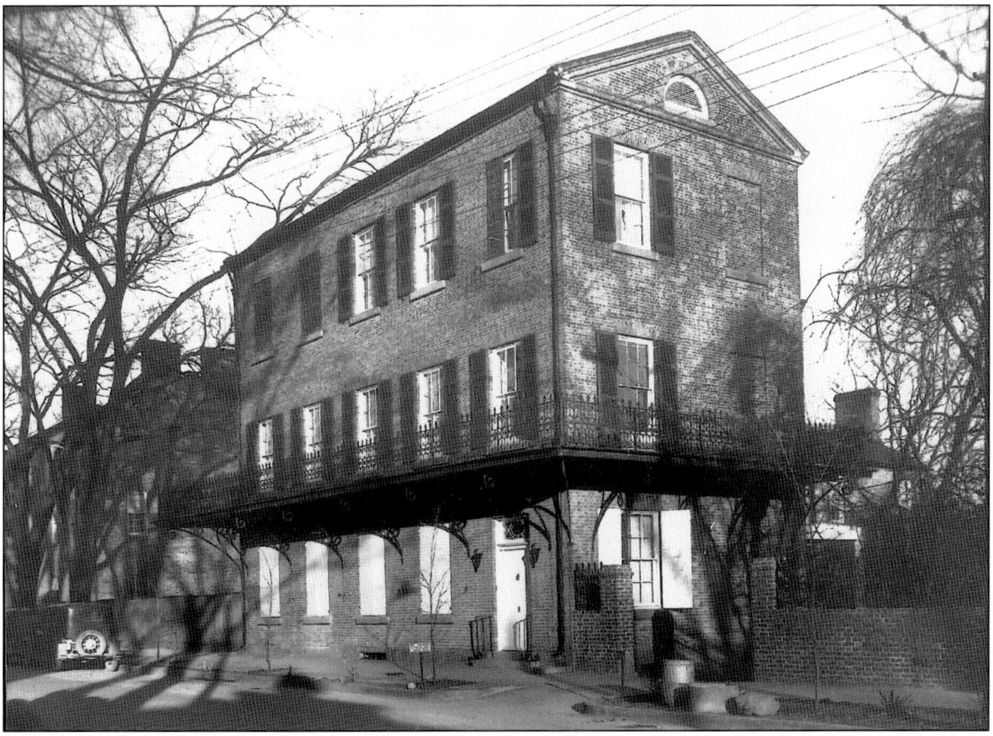

Seen here in the 1930s, the Latta House in York was built in 1827 by merchant Robert Latta as a dry goods store and residence. (Courtesy Winthrop University Archives.)

with President Jefferson Davis, members of the cabinet stayed overnight in the imposing structure, while the president stayed next door with Doctor Bratton. The following morning, as the entourage was about to leave, Secretary of War General John Breckenridge made a speech from the second-floor balcony, encouraging the people of Yorkville to "keep the faith."

Rose's Hotel underwent renovations in 1867 to include a barbershop, billiard room, and bar. Within a few years, during Reconstruction, it was occupied by Federal troops and Radical Republicans. Colonel Lewis Merrill, the federally appointed officer to investigate Ku Klux Klan activities in York County, located his office within the hotel. After the turbulent Reconstruction era passed, Rose's Hotel continued to satisfactorily serve the area and it visitors.

Interestingly enough, Yorkville did not have an organized house of worship for the first 35 years of its existence. The Independent Presbyterians, of the Bullock's Creek Presbytery, established a preaching point in the town about 1810 and organized Yorkville's first church on November 18, 1821. Eight years later, under the direction of Reverend Robert M. Davis, the congregation built a large frame meeting house on East Liberty Street at the site where the Confederate monument now stands in front of Rose Hill Cemetery.

The Methodists arrived in 1824, building a small-frame sanctuary on Jefferson Street where College Street now intersects. Although the Presbyterians were the first to establish themselves in Yorkville, it was the Methodists who became the oldest continuing congregation with a meeting house.

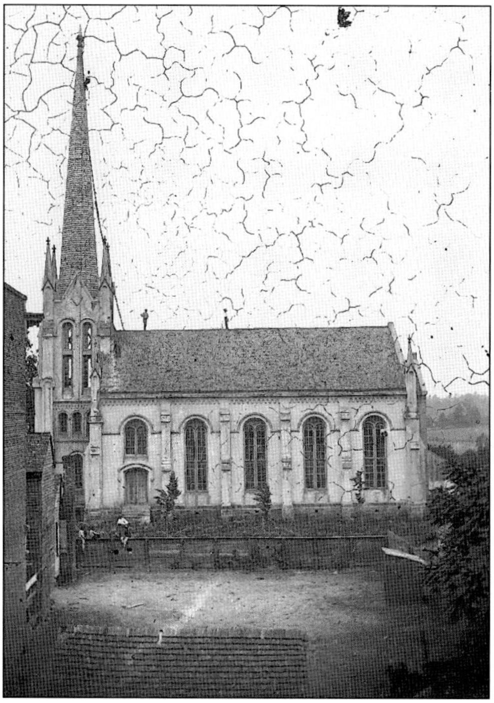

The First Presbyterian Church in York was organized in 1842. This church building was constructed on West Liberty Street in 1860–1861. (Courtesy Winthrop University Archives.)

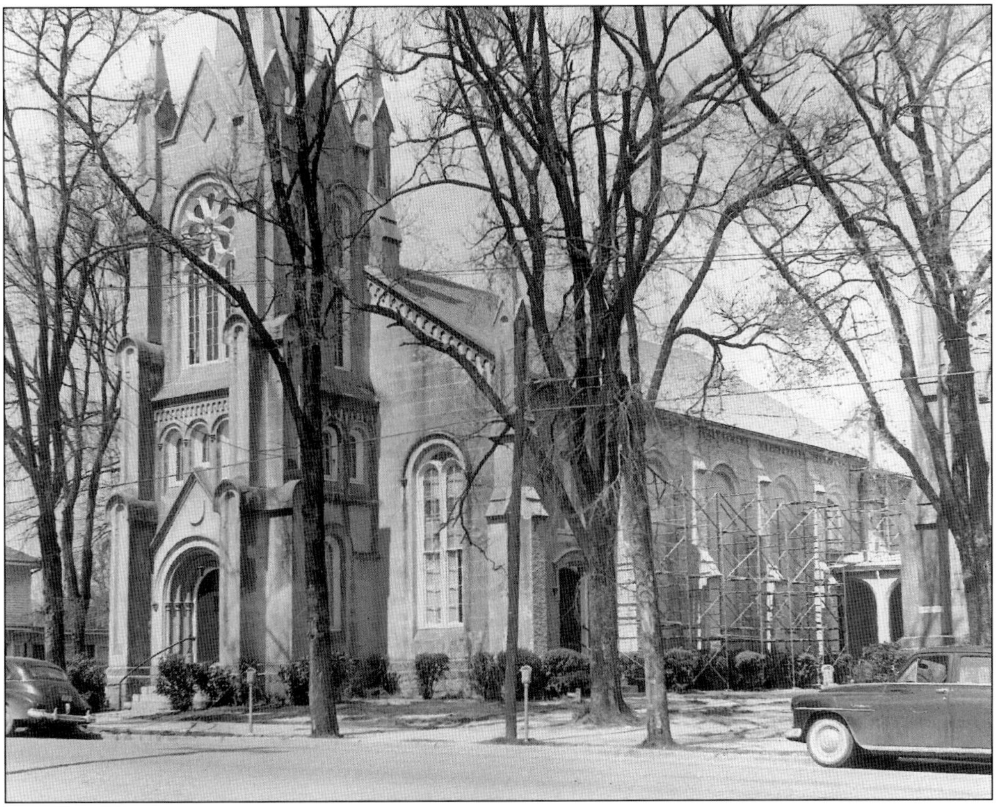

This is a c. 1950s view of York's First Presbyterian Church, organized in 1842.

Independent Presbyterian minister Reverend William Cummings Davis was instrumental in bringing a publishing house to Yorkville. Sometime around 1820, Patrick "Paddy" Carey came to Yorkville to print the several books of theological writings of Reverend Davis. Carey soon provided the area with its first newspaper, the *Pioneer*. In 1833, John E. Grist of Spartanburg County came to York and began publishing the *Patriot*, a political newspaper espousing nullification—the newspaper died with nullification. On June 1, 1840, Grist published the first issue of the *Yorkville Compiler*. It also had a short life, ending July 1843. Grist's next newspaper was more successful. The first issue of the *Yorkville Miscellany* appeared in August 1843 and continued under the direction of Grist and his son, Lewis, until 1851, at which time, John sold his interest to his son. Lewis Grist increased the size of the paper and changed the name to the *Yorkville Enquirer*. The *Enquirer* continues today as the oldest weekly newspaper in South Carolina.

The 10 or 15 years prior to the Civil War were prosperous years for South Carolina. The style of living in Yorkville changed drastically during this period, allowing the town to be known as the "Charleston of the Upcountry." In 1861, the per capita income in York was the second highest in the state, and during that same time, South Carolina became the third wealthiest state in the Union.

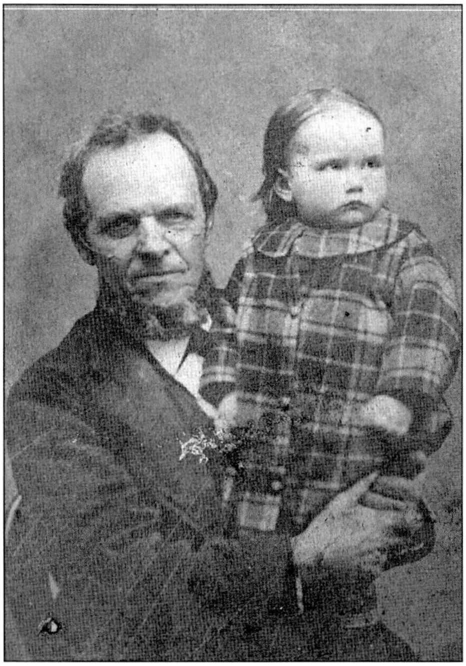

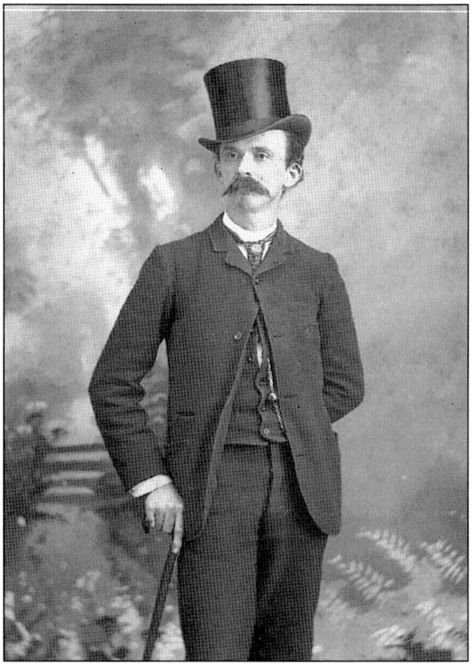

Left: John R. Schorb, famed Yorkville photographer, poses with his daughter Mary for this c. 1874 portrait. (Courtesy Winthrop University Archives.)
Right: This unidentified gentleman posed for Schorb at his studio in the 1880s. (Courtesy Winthrop University Archives.)

In 1852, the Kings Mountain Railroad Company was formed and York became a terminal, connecting with a main line in Chester. The railroad was a boom to the economy of the town, which soon became a strong market for King Cotton.

The original log courthouse was replaced in 1823 by one designed by Robert Mills of South Carolina and the nation's first federal architect. This building was partly destroyed by fire in 1890 and rebuilt with notable design changes. Finally, in 1914 an imposing structure of sandstone was built and is still presently used to house much of the county's business.

After a period of private schools, the Yorkville graded school system was inaugurated in 1888 and was the second public school system in the state. The high quality of institutions in York attracted a number of excellent teachers, among them was John R. Schorb, who taught music and chemistry at the Yorkville Female College. He was a German immigrant who had studied at Hamlin College in New York. His chemistry teacher there had learned Daguerre's photography methods and was able to teach young Schorb, his assistant, firsthand techniques of the process. In 1842, Schorb became one of the country's first traveling photographers. He was an expert in photography by the time he arrived in York, and in addition to teaching, he operated a photography studio.

For many years, people living in the most northwestern corner of the county and across the Broad River suffered the hardship of having to travel 30 miles or more to conduct legal business. By 1895, all the lands of York County that laid west of the Broad River and Cherokee Township had petitioned for a new county. At the same time portions of Union and Spartanburg Counties petitioned the General Assembly to form a new county with portions of all three counties. Finally, in 1897, Cherokee Township and all lands on the west side of Broad River seceded from York County and formed Cherokee County.

Just more than a year before the extreme western portion of York County was given in the creation of Cherokee County, a murder took place in Blacksburg, urged "by the charms of a dangerously handsome and fascinating woman." During the dead of night on February 6, 1896, a good-looking, 30-year-old Charles T. Williams was shot down on a residential street in the little railroad town.

The first clue that all was not as it appeared was the fact that Williams had registered at the Merchant's Hotel as Jerry H. Williams of Atlanta, Georgia. A letter found on the body revealed his true name and that an affair was in progress with a beautiful milliner by the name Ellen Anderson. The letter spoke of her undying love for Williams, pledging she would be with him as she had been before—but not just now. She bewailed her condition to her lover saying she had lost the respect of everybody, and herself, gently telling him he was the blame for her troubles. She replied to his desire to come to be with her at Blacksburg, imploring him not to come.

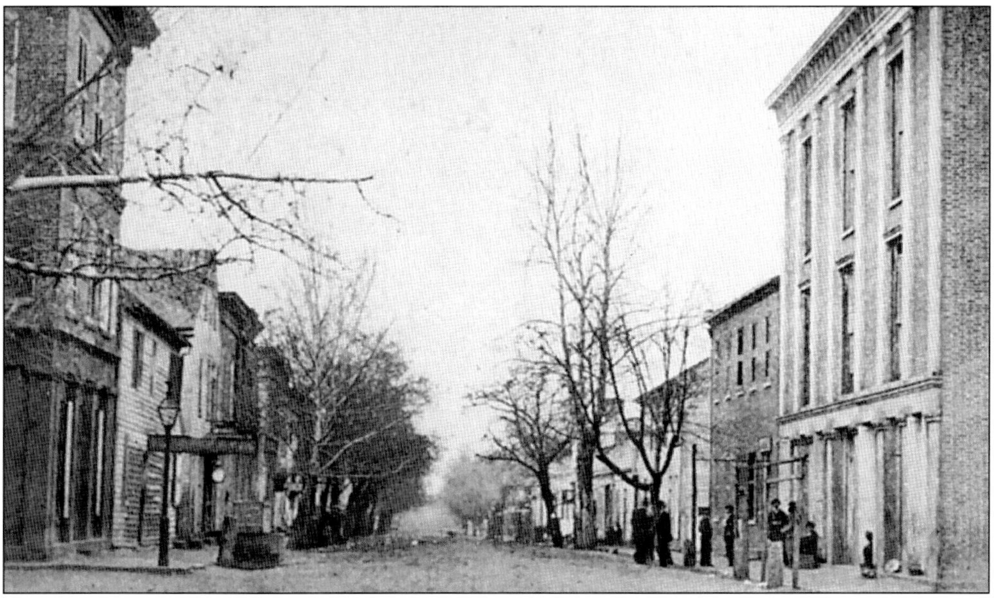

The Merchant's Hotel is visible on the left in this early-twentieth-century image of Blacksburg's business district.

The jury at an inquest held several days concluded that real estate broker Marion R. Reese was the murderer and that Ellen Anderson and her brother, Daniel F. Luckie, were accessories. When warrants were taken for the three, Reese could not be found—at the November trial he claimed that when he saw the tide of opinion was against him he fled over the mountain to the home of A.J. Goforth, where his mother was living. Shortly before the June term of the Court of General Sessions, Reese surrendered to the sheriff of Marion, North Carolina, and the trial was set for the following November.

When the York courtroom opened for the trial, there was a mad rush for seats; within two minutes every seat was taken and the court was packed with spectators. Everyone expected a sensation when Robert A. Anderson, the husband of Ellen Anderson, was called to the stand. Examination proved that he and Ellen had been married twice. The first ended in divorce on her complaint of drunkenness, cruelty, adultery, and threatening her with a pistol. Supposedly, they remarried for the sake of the children, but the marriage lasted only a few days and he left for Mexico, New Mexico, California, and Arizona, where he had been for the last two years. The witness was described as living "a life of a libertine and despoiler of virtue" and was a fugitive of the courts, wanted for whitecapping. He denied the charges that he had hanged a woman and whipped his wife with a horsewhip.

For the remainder of the day, letters written by Ellen Anderson to Charles Williams confirmed that their love affair had continued for four years, covering

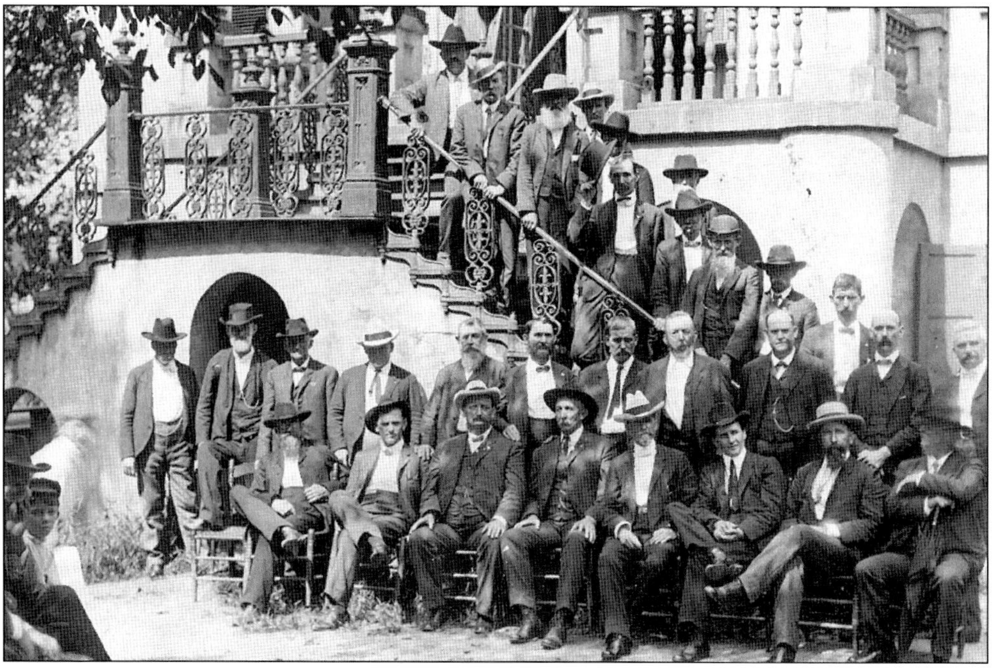

Draping the courthouse entrance, c. 1901, these town fathers demonstrate the prominence of the York County Courthouse.

the time she was living with her husband. Anderson said she despised her husband and was living with him only because of money, that she hated Reese, and that she was deeply in love with Williams. She said she did not like the people of Blacksburg, and that the only reason she came was to make money. The subjects of the letters were so filthy that the judge emptied the courtroom of everyone 17 and under.

When the court reconvened Monday morning, another mad rush was made to capture a seat. Some had come by train to catch some of the courtroom excitement. Defense attorney Leroy F. Youmans requested that the jury retire and bring in an acquittal in the case of Mrs. Anderson so that she could testify in defense of Luckie and Reese without incriminating herself. But the prosecutor would not agree. The judge, however, agreed with Youmans, but he would proceed with the trial, and that at the proper time he might give such an instruction to the jury.

When Ellen Anderson was called, an intense stillness fell upon the courtroom. Youmans questioned her concerning her birth, parents, and marriage. She testified that at the time of the shooting she was in her room, ready for bed. She said that while her brother, Daniel Luckie, was out to fill his lamp, she heard a slight noise at the window and saw that the blinds had been opened by someone. That person went around to the front steps, came up on the piazza, opened the door, and walked into her room—it was Charles Williams.

"I told you not to come in here," she said and grabbed a revolver and pointed it at her lover, telling him to leave. He backed out of the room. She followed him out of the house and into the street and fired a shot. She pulled off another shot and then two more. She claimed she did not mean to kill him, only to scare him. She claimed that the only reason she was telling about the incident was became "the feeling, prejudice and suspicion against Reese and her brother was so strong she knew they would not get a fair trial and that she had rather go to the gallows." The state subjected her to severe a cross examination and sought to discredit her testimony.

Marion Reese said Ellen told him the next day that she had shot Williams and was worried over the future of her little girls if she went to jail. Reese said he was willing to cover for her until she and her brother started "trying to saddle it on me." The trial continued for a least two weeks. Later in November, Mollie Hope, of Sharon, wrote in her journal, "Oh my, what a time of reading and conjecture and talking and asking questions as there has been for the last two weeks . . . and oh my, my! The lies that have been told on the stand at that court house."

W.B. DeLoach, state prosecutor, took nearly three hours for his closing remarks. He contended that all three—Luckie, Reese, and Anderson—were guilty. DeLoach reviewed the whole trial beginning by reminding the jury how each of the defendants pled "not guilty" upon arraignment, how the state had piled up damaging evidence, how the pistol shots had been heard and the flashes seen, and how Reese and Luckie had been no more than 14 feet away from Williams when he was shot. "Did you ever hear of such a thing, gentlemen? Do you believe it? You cannot believe such an absurd story. No gentlemen, she did not do it. This man, Charles T. Williams, was murdered by M.R. Reese, with the assistance of Daniel Luckie, and not by the woman."

Defense attorney Thomas F. McDow, representing Reese and Luckie, painted Williams to be a serpent coiling himself around the cords of this poor woman's heart, and after robbing her of her reputation and virtue, continued to pursue her under threat of publishing information that would rob her of her child. He told how she had tried to break off with him, how he came to Blacksburg in disguise, avoiding her brother, and forcing himself into the room of a defenseless woman. McDow pointed out how impossible it was that anyone other than Mrs. Anderson could have fired the shots that killed Williams.

Solicitor Henry rose and proceeded as follows:

> Here is the house in which a woman, fair and fascinating, but with the wiles of the serpent. Here is this man, Charles T. Williams. He tried to see her. After writing again and again, at last, he goes to her house, the lascivious Reese and his willing tool, Daniel Luckie, the partners of his sister's shame, have been lying in wait for him. They came upon him suddenly. He flees up the street. They follow. A bullet goes crashing through his spine. This is not only wreck; it is ruin. Ruin pained with a brush dipped in the blackest pigments to be dredged from the lowest depths of hell. Ruin without hope!
>
> Gentlemen of the jury, I stand on the bank of a turbid stream. I have known all along that the water was muddy. It is unpleasant to cross. As I have come close to it, I find it filled with driftwood, trash and filth. There are also floating down beautiful flowers, pearls and diamonds that have been placed there by the learned council to confuse my path. But, gentlemen, I see on the opposite bank a shining light. That light is duty. You and I have sworn to go to it. It devolves upon me to lead and you to follow. I am responsible only for myself, and not for you. Gentlemen, I am going to yonder light!

In the evening, just as the clock in the courthouse tower struck nine, the jury announced they had reached upon a verdict. Within ten minutes, the judge, council, sheriff, and about 100 people gathered in the courtroom and heard the clerk read, "Guilty!" Guilty with recommendation of mercy to Reese and Luckie and "not guilty" to Ellen Anderson. Attorney Youmans immediately gave notice of a motion for a new trial.

Deputy R.L. Scoggins led Reese out of the courtroom first, followed by his brother, Frank Scoggins, with Luckie in tow. Reese broke from the deputy and made a dash for freedom. Scoggins shouted. "Stop," and not getting a response, raised his firearm and fired—Reese staggered and fell into a gutter.

Reese was carried to Dr. Miles Walker, who, with Doctors Andrel Bratton and W.G. White, probed into Reese's skull for two hours before extracting half of the bullet in three pieces. When the projectile struck Reese's skull, it shattered and scattered; the physicians believed the remaining bits were lodged somewhere in the neck muscles. After they had finished, Reese was led off to jail. On the way he spoke to Scoggins, "I wanted to die, and not desiring to take my own life, I ran in the hope that you would kill me. I wish you had killed me. I know I did wrong, and I do not blame you, for you only did your duty."

Although she was freed, Ellen Anderson's troubles were not over. Her estranged husband sued for custody of their six-year-old daughter. On Saturday, November 21, a large group of spectators crowded into the courtroom to here the case of *Anderson v. Anderson*. Robert Anderson alleged that the state had proven Ellen was an unfit mother, that she lived in a house belonging to Reese and in adultery with him. Ellen denied everything. Judge Watts ruled that he had no jurisdiction over the child since she was in the custody of the chancery court of Georgia, and that she must remain in the custody of her mother.

In the meantime, another case was spawned by the murder. J.H. Riddle, administrator of the estate of Charles Williams, sued Reese for $10,000 in damages on behalf of Williams's widow. The case was brought under the "Lord Campbell Act," which provided support for the dependents of the slain at the expense of the slayer.

The following Monday, after Ellen Anderson won custody of her daughter, Judge Watts heard the appeal for a new trial for Reese and Luckie. Between 50 to 100 people filled the courtroom and gave their attention to the four hours of

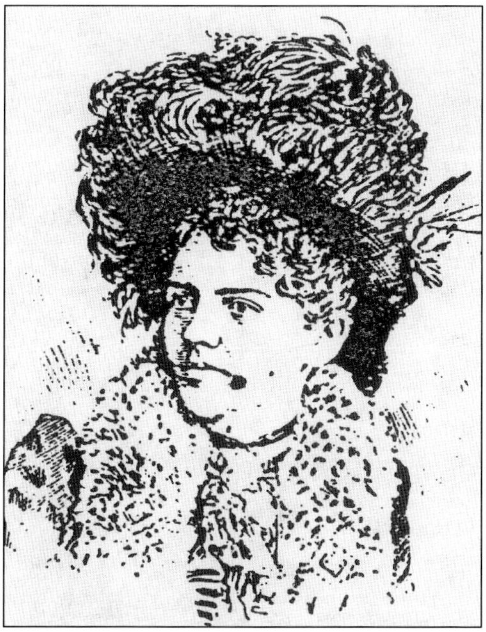

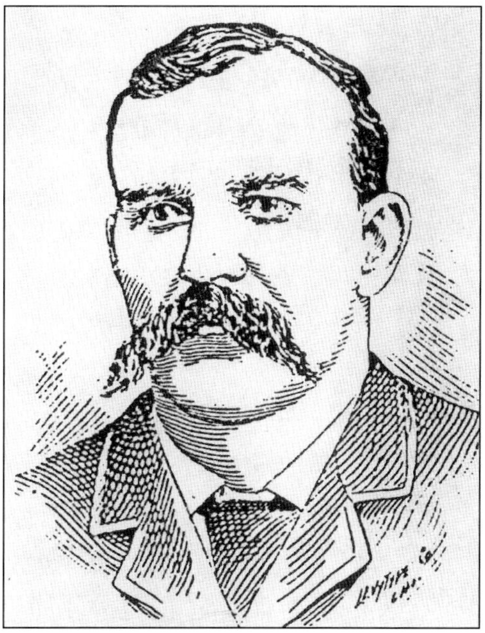

Ellen Anderson (right) and M.R. Reese (left) were both involved in the infamous murder trial of Charles T. Williams.

proceedings. Although Colonel Youmans alleged the court was guilty of several errors, the judge declared none of them were serious enough to warrant a new trial and ordered the prisoners to be brought for sentencing.

Standing before the court, Judge Watt spoke as follows to the two men:

> I am always sorry for anyone in your condition. You have been tried for the murder of Charles T. Williams. The jury said that you are guilty, and in my opinion the verdict is sustained by the facts. Your two are the murderers. You, Marion Reese, have led an irregular and vicious life, and you are now reaping as you have sown. You, Daniel Luckie, I regard as the weaker vessel. The testimony satisfies me that you have only been a servile tool of the strong mind of M.R. Reese. There is no doubt in my mind that Mrs. Anderson is morally responsible for the death of Charles T. Williams, although I do not believe that he came to his death, as she says, at her hands. It was at the hands of you, Marion Reese, and you, Daniel Luckie, but to my mind the woman is responsible for your present condition—the sacrifice of your liberty for the balance of your days. But I do not wish to be unnecessarily cruel in my remarks. They can be of no benefit to you now. The sentence of the court is that you Marion R. Reese, and you, Daniel F. Luckie, shall be confined in the state penitentiary, at hard labor, for the balance of your natural lives.

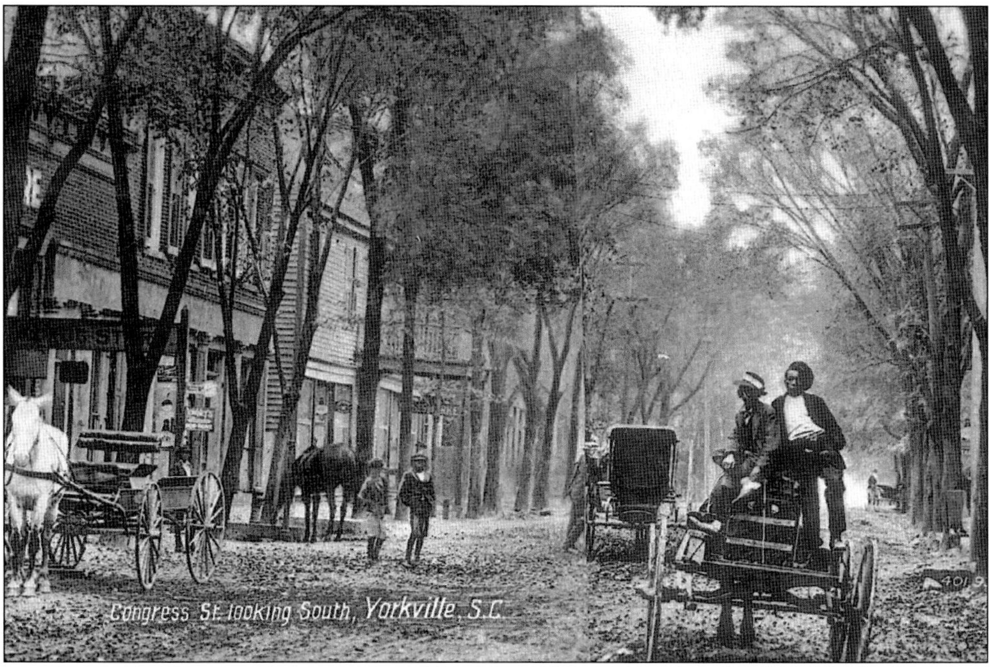

This c. *1890 postcard captures an early scene of Congress Street looking south.*

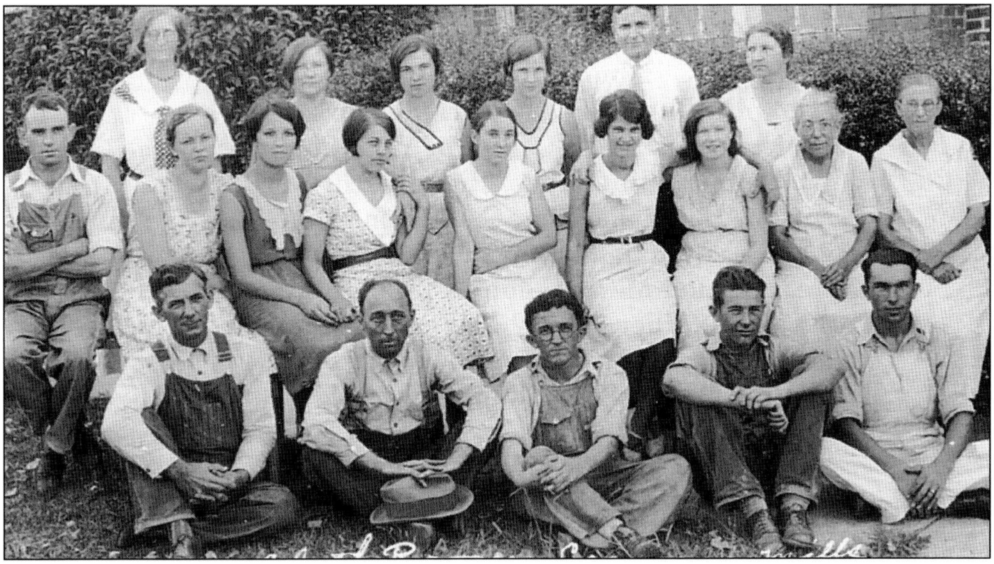

Cloth room employees pose for this portrait at York's Cannon Mills.

A variety of enterprises were being carried on in Yorkville in the late 1880s. The Carolina Buggy Company was thriving under the ownership of M.C. Willis. A great deal of lumber was being cut and shipped to various points in the nation. G.H. O'Leary was manufacturing almost all the saddles and many of the harnesses sold in Yorkville.

York's textile industry had its beginning in the early 1890s when the York Cotton Mill was established. A few years later the Neely, Lockmore and Sutro (later known as the Travora) were built. W.B. Moore was one of the more prominent names in the textile industry, as he served as president of the Neely, Travora and Lockmore.

York's major industry continued to be textile related for many years, but now has been replaced by more diversified industries. Presently the leading industries are Ovako-Ajax and Meritor, heavy equipment parts suppliers; Republic Textile Equipment, a textile machinery and equipment dealer; Austin International, manufacturing knit goods; Moldan Corporation, producing non-woven textile batting; Sediver, Inc., makers of high-voltage insulators; Champion Laboratories, making automotive filters; and American Eagle Wheel, producing custom auto wheels.

In 1929, Barnett Brothers Circus located its winter quarters in York and remained until 1944. On a quiet day, the elephant's trumpeting and the lion's roar could be heard throughout the town. York had the distinction of having Santa Claus arrive riding on an elephant in the annual Christmas parade. Each year, before putting the circus on tour, Barnett Brothers would introduce the season's show to a local audience. To boost attendance, circus managers would showcase popular film stars for the tour.

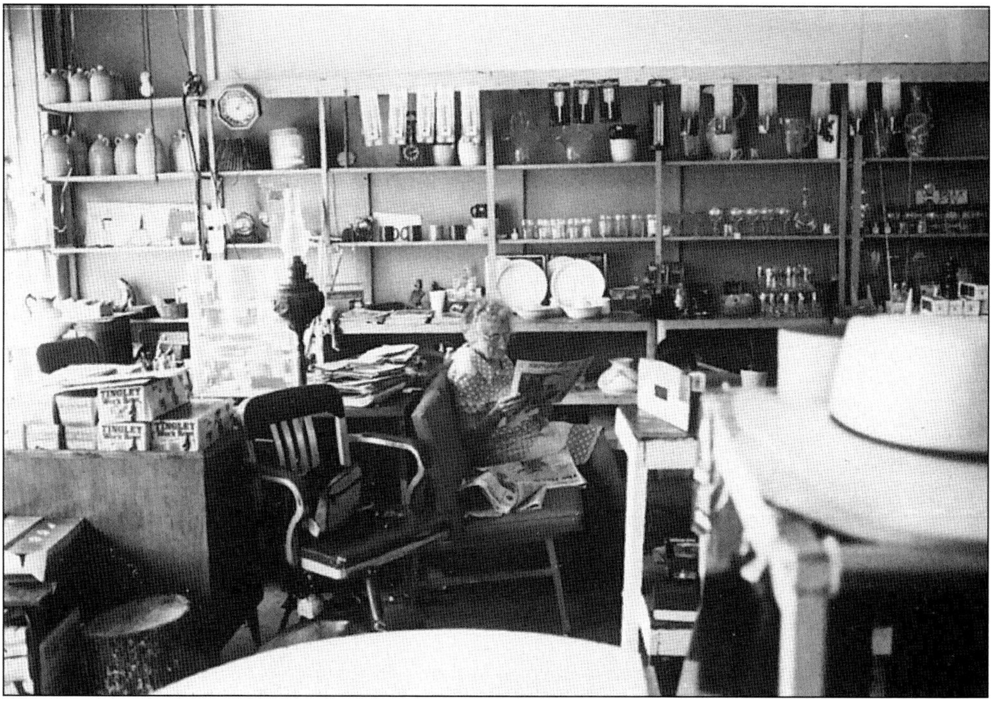

Coleman's Trading Post has been a fixture on York's main thoroughfare for a century.

While Yorkville discarded the "ville" in 1915 (just as McConnellsville had done), the community clung to traditions that had been nurtured in the previous century. The county seat, with its imposing courthouse, resisted efforts by Rock Hill, the county's largest city, to siphon off government offices and establish itself as the political center. York was, like Sharon and Hickory Grove, a town built on ancient ground, sprinkled with farms and railroad depots that contrasted sharply with the textile industries of Rock Hill and the classrooms of Winthrop University.

York's streets were named for cherished heroes like Washington, Jefferson, Madison, and Roosevelt and sacred institutions like Congress. Congress Street intersected, symbolically, with Liberty Street and the city's residents savored this connection. The business district, until radical economic change occurred in the 1980s, featured establishments such as Neely's Drug Store, J.R. Barnwell's hardware store, a candy kitchen staffed by Greek immigrants, and the Sylvia Theater. The latter business drew huge crowds in the 1950s as viewers watched, for 25¢ a ticket, movies such as *From Here to Eternity* and *Ben Hur*. At the Sylvia, however, customers sat in a segregated movie house. African Americans watched the screen from the balcony while whites congregated on the main floor.

The city's general stores, Ferguson and Youngblood and Coleman's Trading Post, were popular meeting places. Patrons purchased farm tools, dry goods, groceries, and fresh produce and exchanged news. When time allowed, citizens ventured down Congress Street to York Drug Store or Neely's Drugs, where they had their prescriptions filled and sampled ice cream.

Education in York, until 1970, was segregated. Blacks attended Jefferson High School while whites learned their lessons at York High School, located on Jefferson Street. The schools were nearby and within sight of each other, but in the segregated climate of the 1940s and 1950s, they were worlds apart.

Change was in the air. Politicians like Lewis Wallace spoke of the justice of integration and helped break down racial barriers. Wallace, a state senator, helped Rock Hill's Winthrop University become co-educational and helped his hometown, York, grasp the fact that a color line sapped the creativity of both races. Wallace would pay a political price for his bold progressivism, but later in life, he recovered his political clout and returned to prominence in the late 1970s as mayor of York.

By the 1980s, York's historic business district began to see itself squeezed by new shopping malls in Rock Hill, Charlotte, and Gastonia. Stores, like the pharmacies and Belk Department Store, struggled amid the competition and then closed. Still, Coleman's Trading Post, with its unusual items such as straw hats and cast-iron baking pans, resisted the shifted economy. Ferguson and Youngblood, with its roasted peanuts and bottled soft drinks, also stayed open.

The people of York, like their relatives in Sharon and Hickory Grove, have withstood calamities like the 1886 Charleston earthquake, which created cracks in some of York's buildings, and have adapted to a massive Wal-Mart, which opened

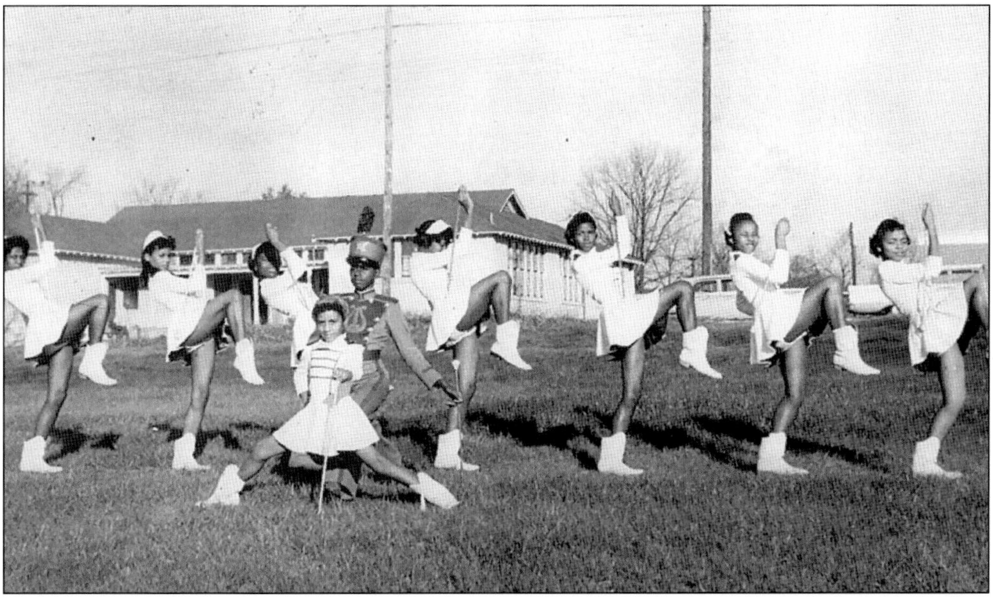

York's Jefferson High School majorettes pose for this photograph in 1958. At this time, York's schools were segregated, with black students attending Jefferson and white students attending York High School.

its doors in 1998. The courthouse remains, despite Rock Hill's best efforts, on the ancient site of Fergus Crossroads. The pews at York's churches remain full on Sundays with the descendents who first came, as chosen people, to Western York County.

Until 1952, York covered an area about the same size as when originally chartered as a town, a circle of 1 mile radius or 3.14 square miles. In 1952, York began annexing adjoining areas and currently includes and area of 6.52 square miles. In 1976, as part of the National Bicentennial, the inner city of York was designated a Historic District on the National Register of Historic Places, having one of the largest historic districts in the state. The district contains 340 acres and over 180 historic structures and landmarks.

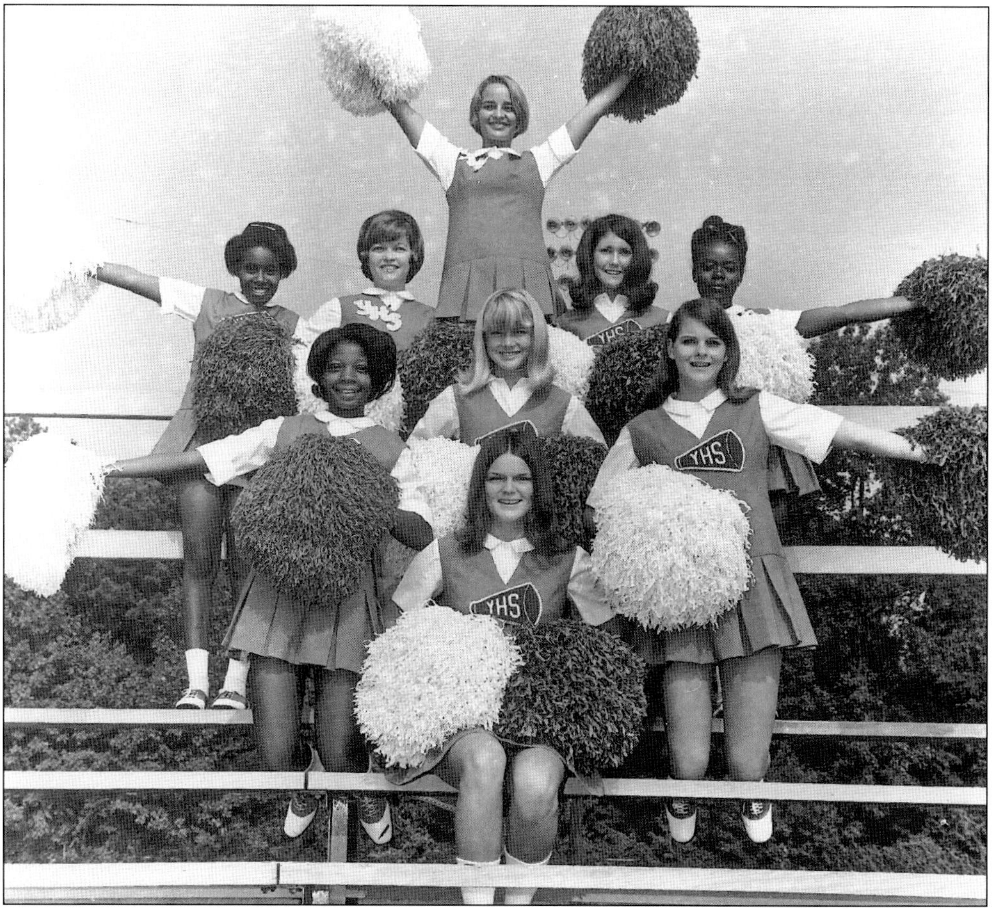

York High School's cheerleaders pose for this shot in 1971. By this time, the students from Jefferson High had integrated York High School. (Courtesy Winthrop University Archives.)

10. The Sharon Tragedy

Western York County has not escaped the horrors of the modern era. Since the Revolution, patriots from Bullock's Creek and Hickory Grove have put aside their plows and left their families to serve the cause of liberty. The twentieth century, however, brought with it more deadly forms of carnage and took citizens far away from the communities they loved so much.

Hickory Grove's Forrest T. Buice, stationed in France at the time of the Armistice, wrote this letter to the *Yorkville Enquirer* in late 1918 to "carry a message to those many friends we have left within the circulation of your paper":

> France, October 23, 1918
>
> . . . There are a number of York County boys in our regiment, and as far as I know they are all well and doing fine. I am, and so are you, proud of them. They have made good in every respect. Many of them are now wearing "bars." Everyone that I know within our regiment is a noncommissioned officer, being either a "sergeant" or "corporal." Any one who knows anything about the army will know that this speaks well of them. Some are my friends and I have paid special attention, though not to criticize, to their manner of doing things. They are always awake to duty, and I feel sure that those whom they have in charge have perfect confidence in them.
>
> There is no need for me to say that we all think often of home and the friends left there. But we are here for a purpose, and do not wish to return until we have accomplished it. The most of us think the crisis has about arrived. Of course we don't know.
>
> France is a beautiful country. In fact, I think it is more beautiful than any I have yet seen. The greater part of France is hilly. These hills are covered with a beautiful coat of grass and clover, which is used for grazing. The cattle are of the finest breed. You never see a "cross breed" over here. This, of course, accounts for their fine qualities. The cattle and sheep are all watched by the French maids. They bring them in before sundown and milk them. The milk is carried to the

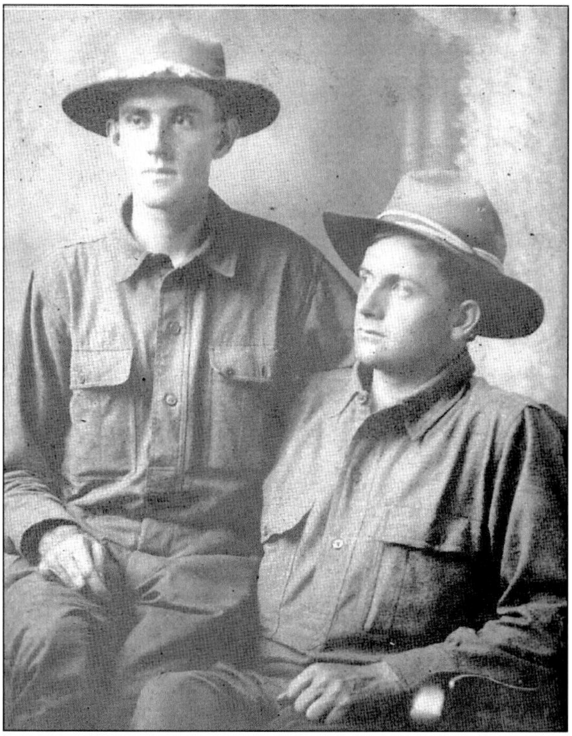

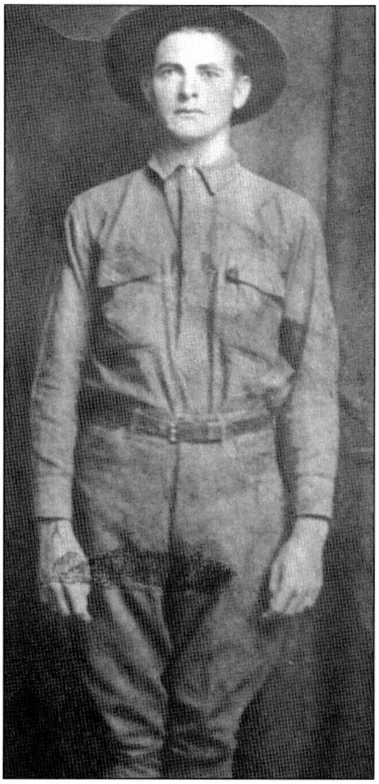

Left: Like many patriotic York County men, Paul Mendenhall joined the armed services in World War I. In this photograph, Paul (left) poses with a World War I buddy.
Right: Edgar Norris of Blairsville was one of many young men called from the farms to serve their country during World War I.

creamery to make cheese. This cheese goes to the government to feed soldiers.

I am still with the 318 F.A. Band. We have a grand organization. It is led by a man who is ably fitted for the position. Mr. O.K. Wilson of Orangeburg, S.C. This band is composed mostly of South Carolinians. There are now forty pieces. Officially this band is considered one of the best in the service. We were told at the port of embarkation before leaving the United States that ours was the best band that had embarked there. "Self praise" is void, therefore I shall not say more about this, for I hope some day we all may be able to play with your hearing.

To the many friends who have sons over here: You may feel assured that Uncle Sam is treating his soldiers well. We have plenty to eat and wear, and a sufficient amount of sleep. With best regards and trusting that we may see you before long, I am,

Very truly yours,
Forrest T. Buice

Not all the challenges facing the area's people were confined to foreign shores. The Great Depression, with its empty bank vaults, wrecked stock market, unemployment lines, and parched fields, came in a stark way early to South Carolina. By 1920, the cotton economy, which had been so reliable, was collapsing amid the weight of a tiny insect, the boll weevil. This long bug, originally from Mexico, stripped the cotton plant's boll, shredding it and gnawing its way across York County, and compounding the arrival of the boll weevil was the drought and the loss of overseas markets.

In 1922, South Carolina farmers produced fewer than one third the number of bales (500,000) grown in 1920. And prices for food, much of it imported, skyrocketed. As a refrain of the period lamented, "Ten cent cotton and forty cent meat. How in hell can a poor man eat?" A diet of pork, cornbread, and molasses robbed farmers of their vitality and caused an outbreak of pellagra. Historian Ben Robertson explains the situation facing South Carolina's rural people this way: "Those were the draining years on the cotton farms. Nearly all of the strongest tenant families left the cotton fields. Only the old and the young and the determined stayed on."

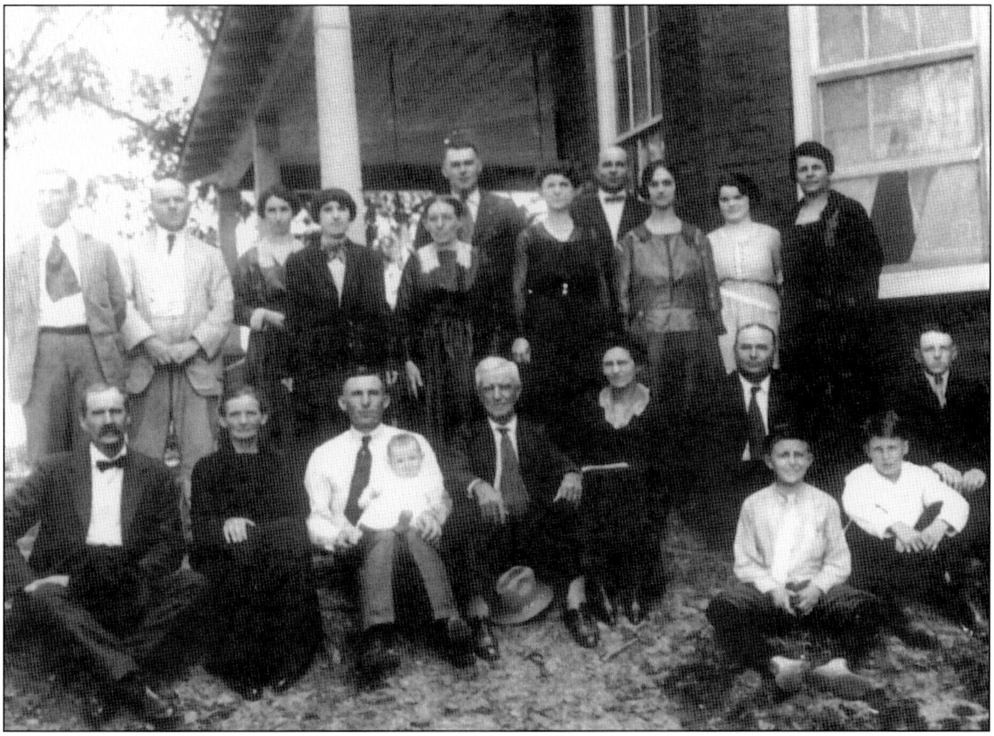

The Castle-Whisonant family poses for this photograph at a reunion in Smyrna c. *1920. With World War I having ended, the citizens of York County turned their attention back to their homes and farms, but were to be met by many challenges, from a new insect to a changing market place.*

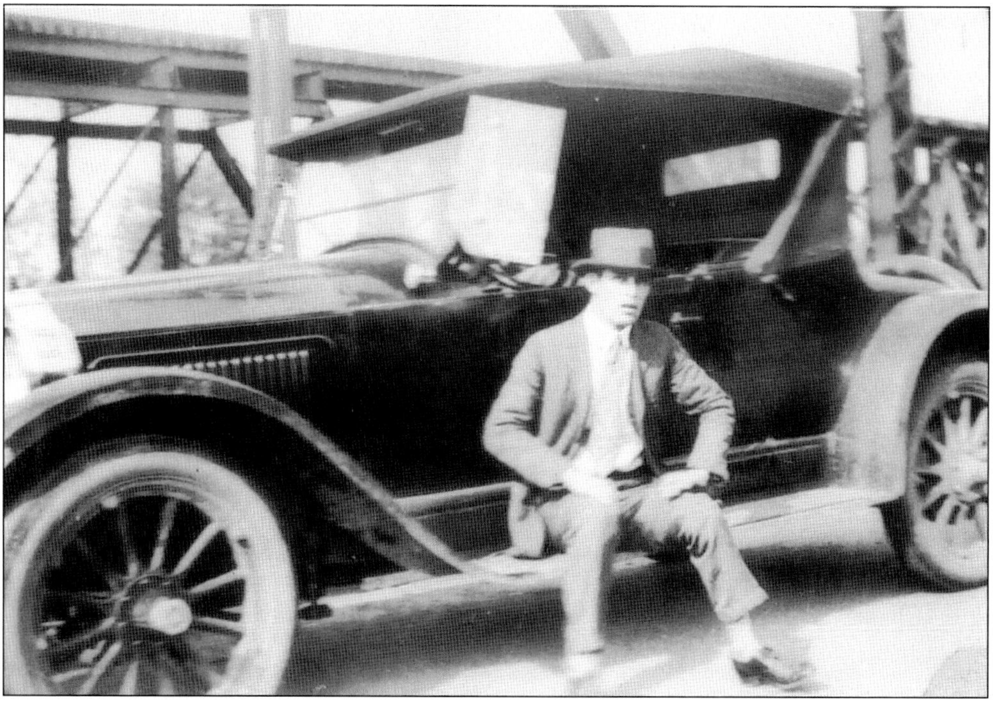

The new 1925 Bullock's Creek Bridge between Sharon and Hickory Grove became a favorite site for a Sunday afternoon trip. Behind a youthful Paul Ferguson can be seen the trestle of the Southern Railway.

And the Great Depression settled in, like an oppressive summer heat spell, with no relief in sight. This economic catastrophe, caused by overproduction of durable goods, a one-crop agricultural economy, the default of Germany's reparation payment, an unregulated stock market, and reckless banking practices, continued on a grand scale until the outbreak of World War II—despite the best efforts of Franklin D. Roosevelt and his "braintrust" in the 1930s to solve the multitude of problems facing the nation—and especially apparent in the cotton kingdom.

Thus, Western York County's citizens had much time on their hands and little prospect of economic recovery any time soon. In the summer of 1929, with Herbert Hoover in the White House, a murder occurred in Western York County that would, even with the collapse that October of the stock market, take center stage in the region.

On July 1, 1929, a trial began in the Chester County Courthouse involving the heinous murder of a young French teacher, Faye Wilson King. The murder took place in Western York County on January 25, 1929, and time has proven it to be the most famous and sensational in the history of York County and most particularly, the small town of Sharon. Still, in this small Western York County town, it remains among the sensational events and is mentioned over and over again. *True Detective Mysteries*, a magazine with national circulation, carried Sheriff Fred E. Quinn's account of the murder, and in May 1952, the *Herald*, in its Centennial Edition, reprinted the story.

On that fateful day in January, Faye King left her home on Sharon's Woodlawn Street. Amid the cold drizzle of rain, she hurried to Sharon High School, where she was to teach two French classes at noon. Her husband, Rafe, was ill that day and remained in bed. Sometime around 7:30 p.m., Rafe King went to the home of S.T. Ferguson, a farmer, and inquired of his wife, "Faye—my wife—is she here?" Ferguson's wife and daughter went out to see if they could find Faye. Mr. Ferguson, who was sick himself, kept King there while they went to find Mrs. King.

King was extremely nervous and began to pace the Ferguson home. He told his friend that she had given him two sleeping pills about 10 o'clock that morning. She then kissed him good-bye and went next door for some milk. He said he woke up about 2 p.m.; the fire was out in the fireplace and he called out to her, but got no answer. He said that all afternoon he kept listening for her. Sometime, in the afternoon, Rafe called to a boy in the street, asking him to tell Dr. C.O. Burruss to come to him. About 3:45, Dr. Burruss arrived. He examined King and finding his pulse and temperature near normal, gave him 30 drops of laudanum to help him sleep. But the dose did not work and King continued to be anxious

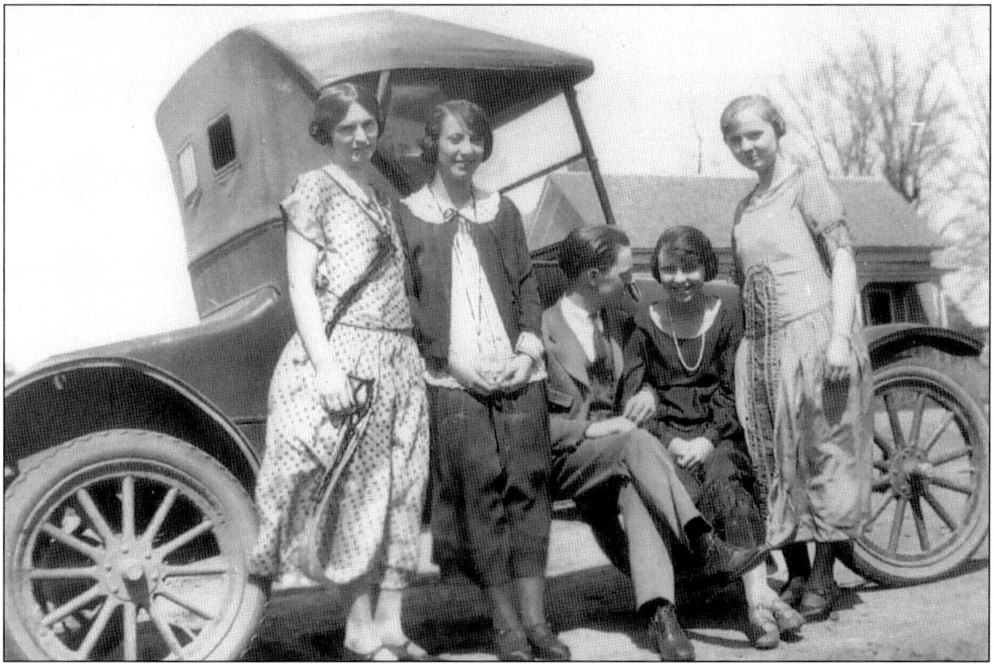

These young people clearly illustrate America's romance with the automobile. This new invention soon captured the hearts of those living in Western York County and its emergence as an economical mode of transportation initiated a new era in American society.

about his wife. King became greatly alarmed when it got dark and that is when he went over to the Ferguson home.

While Ferguson rested, King slipped out of the house; nearing the home of Reverend C.W. McCully, he met the preacher, who had been told of Faye's disappearance by the searching Mrs. Ferguson. Reverend McCully took him home and placed him in bed. He left Rafe and went to several homes in the community to inquire of Faye King, without success.

Reverend McCully searched the house for some evidence or a note that might explain her absence. Under the direction of King, the preacher called her sister in Charlotte and her parents in Shelby to see if they knew anything about her. Reverend McCully left the house to make the calls. Returning to the King home with R.L. Plexico, he was met by his daughter, Frances McCully, who cried out, "Papa, we've found her!" The men were led to the smokehouse at the rear of the home. There the young teacher, lying on her back, was splattered with blood. A closer examination revealed a small triangular wound on her forehead and a few inches from her hand was an empty 2-ounce bottle with a skull and cross bones on the label. Her lips showed a whitish burn—a burn that might have been made with acid. Several of the men wrapped the body in a quilt and brought it into the house.

The news spread like wild-fire over the community and a crowd began to gather around the King's home. The town was shocked over the murder of the young woman who had grown up near Sharon. Just a little over two years before,

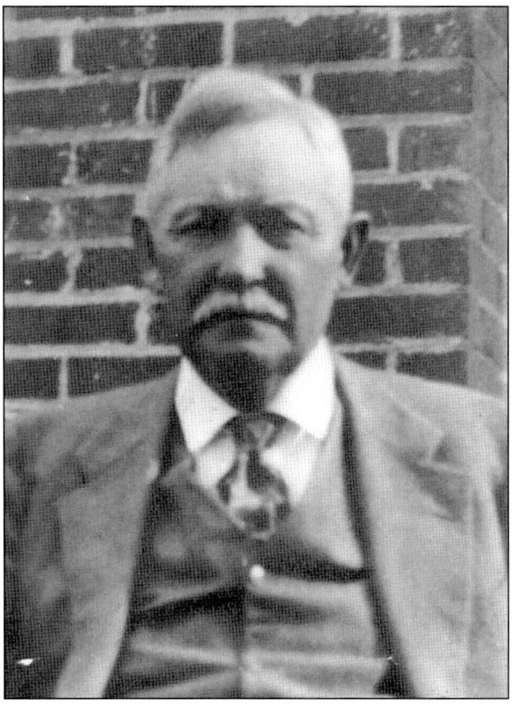

Dr. Joseph Saye, physician, banker, and legislator, conducted the autopsy on Faye King.

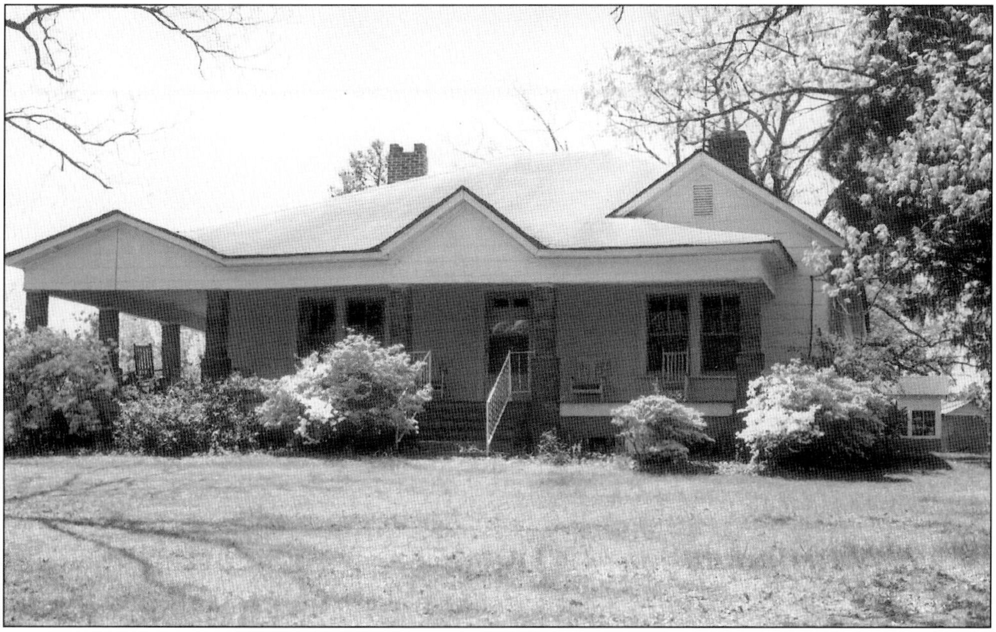

The site of the 1929 murder of Faye Wilson King was rented by Charles McGluckin that year, and he conducted tours of the scene for 25¢.

she had married Rafe King on Thanksgiving Day, 1927. About a year later they came back to Sharon to live.

Among those that came to comfort Rafe was Doctor J.H. Saye, one of the town's first doctors and president of the Bank of Sharon, and Reverend E.B. Hunter, who was a resident of Sharon for 20 years. Reverend Hunter stayed by King's bedside, trying to comfort the sick and bereaved man.

Responding to a call, Doctor Burruss came that evening about 8:45 and gave him a hypodermic containing half a gram of morphine. Although the dose was larger than he normally administered, it had no effect on the distraught husband. Meanwhile, Dr. Saye was examining the body and found the membrane inside her lip was burned as well as her tongue and back of the throat. He was shown the little bottle found by her body. One of the women nearby questioned, "Why do you suppose she would want to kill herself?" Doctor Saye walked back into King's bedroom and asked, "Had Faye ever threatened to take her life?"

"Yes," he replied, "She had been threatening to kill herself for three or four months. About a month ago she talked a lot about it. She said then that she would drink poison and kill herself but she had heard that it would turn her black." King paused nervously and continued, "Last night she came to me and suggested that we both drink poison and go away together!" Dr. Saye questioned her reasoning, to which King replied, "She told me she had found she was going to have a baby; she learned some time ago that she had some trouble that would make it dangerous. She told me she just couldn't go through with it."

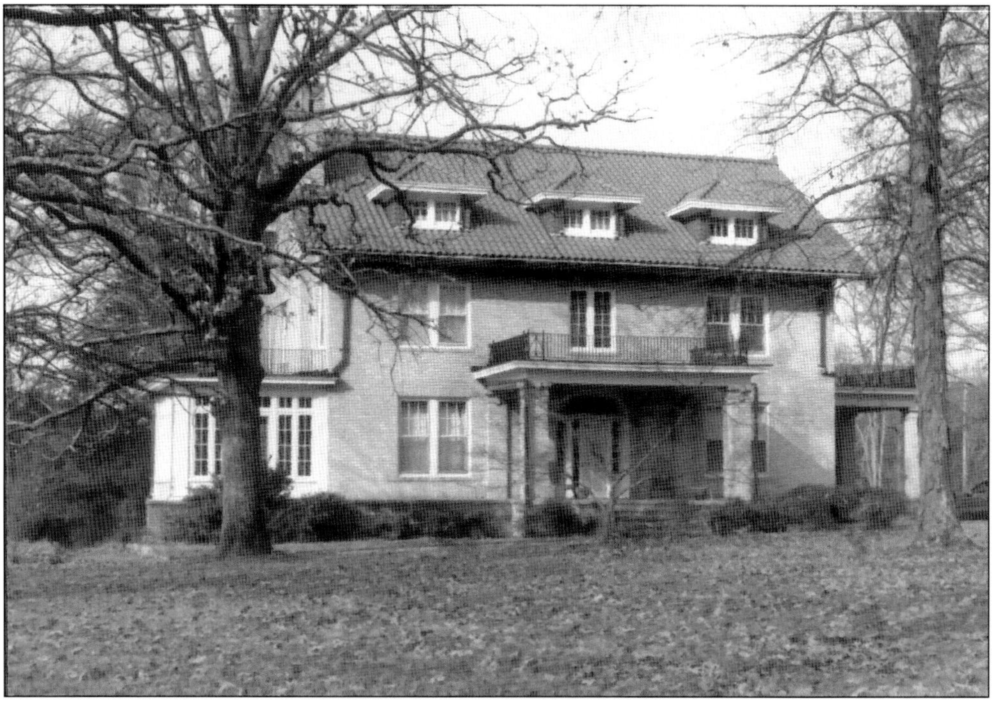

In stark contrast to the murder scene, the stately home of Sharon entrepreneur William Lawrence Hill was erected in 1929.

Doctor Saye left the bedside and returned into the room where the body lay on a cot. A second examination convinced him that she had taken a disinfectant, and not carbolic acid as he first believed. The little bottle found near her body was marked "Nomoppin." About this time, Doctor Saye's daughter, Mrs. Charles Bankhead, went into the kitchen to press a kimono in which the women had chosen to dress the body. She found the electric iron and a cord hanging nearby. Plugging it in, she waited a few minutes, but something was wrong, it was not heating. She then sent over to the Ferguson home for an old flatiron. All was progressing as usual. Reverend Hunter helped the ladies with carrying in water and heating it on the oil stove. Taking the flatiron from Mrs. Bankhead, he placed it on the stove and told her to go do whatever she needed to, and he would take care of things there. Then, through a common incident, assumption of suicide turned to suspicion of murder. Moving near the fireplace, Reverend Hunter leaned in and spat out a mouthful of tobacco juice. As the spittle sank into the ashes a sizzle sound came forth—but King had said the fire had been out all day! The preacher reached out and could feel warmth on his chilled hands. At that time, he then noticed that the wood floor in the kitchen was damp in spots as if someone had scrubbed the floor. He assumed that water might have been spilled. He went into the room where the body had been placed and noticed that the neck was bruised.

Shortly before midnight, Thomas Fulton, an undertaker from Kings Mountain, North Carolina, Mrs. King's former home, came and removed the body. The next morning, Reverend Hunter helped King dress (he was no longer complaining about his back); he had been persuaded to go with his sister, Mrs. Ione Moss, to his father's home in Shelby, North Carolina. Soon after his departure, the sheriff arrived, accompanied by the coroner who impaneled a jury of the six men who had seen the body. At that time, Reverend Hunter privately voiced his suspicions to the sheriff. This conversation resulted in Doctors Saye and Burruss going to Kings Mountain and conducting an autopsy in the Thomas Fulton Funeral Home. They found a coal-tar preparation in her stomach and concluded her death was by suicide. But the sheriff and minister were not satisfied—as well as many of the local citizens.

An inquest was to have been held on Wednesday, January 30, but because Solicitor J.L. Glenn could not attend, it was rescheduled for the following Monday, February 4. Early in the morning of the January 30th, Sheriff Quinn, Reverend Hunter, Reverend McCully, Doctor Saye, and J.A. Jackson, of the rural police, went to the King home for a more thorough investigation. The sheriff found two discolorations in the kitchen floor. Stains were found on a strip of carpet leading to the back porch, on the oil cloth on the kitchen table, on newspaper that covered another table, and on the door leading from the kitchen to a pantry. In the plunder room, several spots were on the floor and on the door leading from the kitchen to the dining room and from the dining room to the back porch. Reverend Hunter could no longer contain his suspicion, "I believe Faye King was killed, and I believe that the murderer moved about this house with her blood on his hands.!" But Sheriff Quinn held his peace, not wanting to leap to a premature conclusion. Going through an old trunk in the plunder room, the two ministers came across a union suit which bore a red stain on one leg.

On February 4th, Corner McCorkle held the inquest in the schoolhouse in Sharon. While the inquest was in progress, Rafe King called Sheriff Quinn outside, and he told the sheriff that he was not being given a fair chance. Also, Rafe wanted to talk to the newspapers. When the sheriff told King that they had found a lot of blood in the house, King suggested, "To tell you the truth, Sheriff, I'm positive she was killed and that she didn't die where she was found out in that little house. I remember the dog barking a lot that day. There were always Negroes prowling about the place. Do you suppose one of them?" About that time, Solicitor Glenn walked up; King made the same suggestion to him.

The coroner's jury brought forth the verdict that Faye Wilson King had come to her death from poison administered by an unknown hand. Immediately, Solicitor Glenn sat down and wrote out a warrant for the arrest of Rafe King, charging, "On the 29th day of January, in York County, Rafe King did willfully, maliciously and feloniously kill and murder Faye Wilson King, by administering poison to her, and by striking her on the head with some iron instrument, contrary to the form of the statue in such cases made and provided and against the peace and dignity of the State." It was sworn to by John M. Davidson, policeman.

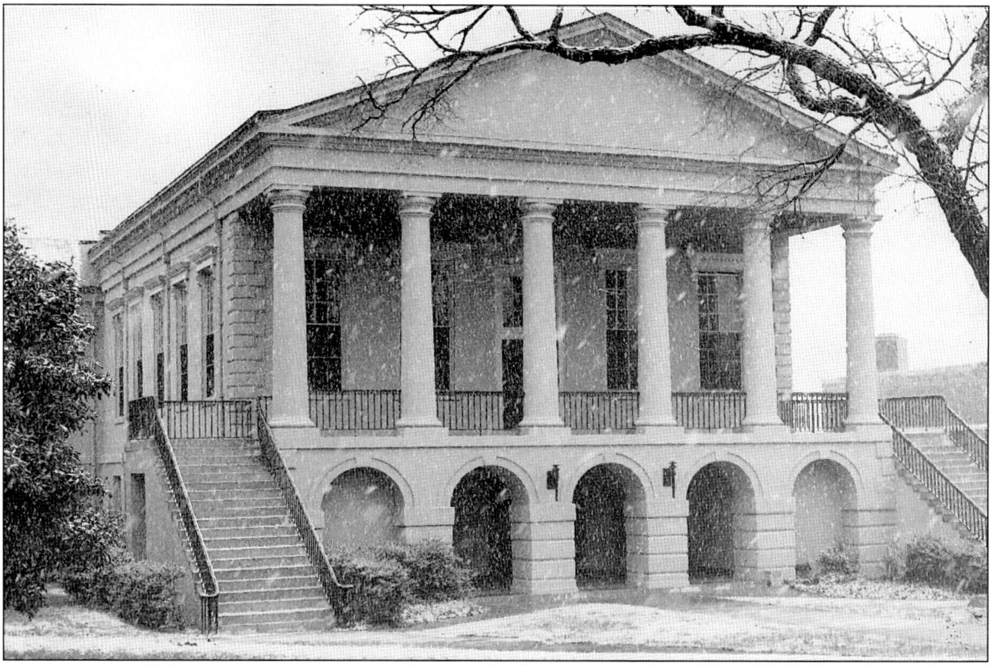

The Chester County Courthouse, originally built in 1852, served as the site for the famous King Murder Trial. (Courtesy Winthrop University Archives.)

The warrant was handed directly to the sheriff who served it on King, who was hustled into an automobile with policeman J.A. Jackson and Davidson. All the way to the York jail, King kept up a running conversation that he was sure a Negro had killed his wife. Even in the jail, he continued this line of thinking like a mad man.

A second autopsy was ordered and the body was exhumed and examined by a group of physicians and surgeons. The local people were ablaze with excitement when King was arrested and the news of the autopsy fanned the blaze to a roar. The autopsy showed that Faye did not die of poison and that the wound on her head was superficial. The examiners found that she had been strangled to death—and that she was not pregnant! Sheriff Quinn went to the house and took four electric cords as evidence—one was to the iron that Mrs. Bankhead found was inoperable.

King was released from jail on a $3,000 bond and went to his father's home in Shelby, North Carolina. On the afternoon of the 20th, the sheriff, along with W.A. Faris (a carpenter), and Chief J. Frank Faulkner of the York County Police went to the scene of the murder. The sheriff directed Faris to cut out the stained places in the woodwork. Chief Faulkner made a careful search under the house but found nothing. The sheriff opened a closet door; looking to the ceiling, he found an opening into the loft of the house. He called Chief Faulkner, who climbed into the opening. Peering into the darkness, he clicked on his flashlight;

the place was thick with dust and crisscrossed with cobwebs. The chief, shining his light along the joists, noticed a trail in the dust as though something had been dragged across the old joists. He followed the trail to the edge of the roof to over the porch; shining his light into the opening, something caught his eye. He thrust his arm into the opening and retrieved a bundle of clothing. He stood up on the joists and found a dark, three-piece suit tied up in a white-striped shirt. Unrolling the shirt, he found it stained with scarlet! Dropping them down to the sheriff, daylight revealed blood stains on the lapel of the coat and on one leg of the trousers. The label on the inside of the coat bore the initials, "R.F.K." and on the pocket of the trousers, printed in ink was, "King." In one of the coat pockets was a small, unlabeled bottle, half full of a reddish fluid.

The curiosity seekers kept coming. Charles E. McGuckin, seeing a money-making opportunity, rented the house, and for 25¢ allowed the curious into the King home. As many as 2,000 poured in on Sundays from the Carolinas, Virginia, Maryland, and as far away as New Jersey. Many came from Shelby, North Carolina, the former home of King and from Kings Mountain, North Carolina, where Faye had lived with her parents.

On July 1, 1929, the King Murder Trial began in Chester County. It was moved to the adjoining county since the feeling was that King would not get a fair trial in his home county. The majority of the spectators were from the Broad River and Bullock's Creek Townships, as well as many from York and the Bethesda areas. The defense attorneys described a man who had suffered many wrongs and was now being hounded by speculators. But the prosecution scorched and seared King, branding him as a heartless killer and a despoiler of women; they declared that the red-handed murderer deserved nothing short of the electric chair.

The defense contended that Mrs. King had committed suicide, but the prosecution said he strangled her to death by use of "his hands and arms, and with cords, wires, ropes and belts placed upon, about and around [her] neck and throat."

The King Murder Trial produced the most plain and frank testimony about sexual facts ever heard in a local courtroom. It seems that King had contracted a social disease before his marriage and had infected his wife. In fact, this was the reason for her resignation as a teacher in 1928 in Shelby, North Carolina. A total number of 38 witnesses testified at the trial; but it was W.C. Reagan, Faye King's brother-in-law, who gave the motive for her murder. Reagan told that he had been the administrator for the estate of Mrs. King's mother, and held a mortgage for $1,000, signed by both Rafe King and his wife. He told the jury that King had approached him with a proposition to borrow $3,000 on a new mortgage. He would pay off the old note and keep $2,000 for himself. But Faye King refused to agree to King's plan.

Reagan quoted King as saying, "I want to move to the farm; Faye says she ain't going. I'm going to move; I don't give a d—n where Faye goes." He also attested that on Christmas Day, 1928, Faye said at the dinner table that she was worth more dead than alive "Why, Faye," someone asked, "you got lots of insurance?" "I have between six and seven thousand dollars; Rafe's next wife would have a good time off that money."

It was shown that on several occasions, King had remarked that he had never been in worse need of money in his life. At the age of 38, King was convicted of first-degree murder and his death in the electric chair was slated for September 20, 1929.

He appealed his conviction and a second trial began in adjoining Lancaster County on May 4, 1931. The new state solicitor at the time was W. Gist Finley, who was assisted by Arthur S. Gaston, Hamilton MacCauley, and the law firm of Sapp & Sapp of Columbia, South Carolina. When the verdict was returned about 7:30 in the evening of May 7th, at least 700 rushed into the Lancaster County Courthouse, which had a seating capacity of 350. Again, King had not taken the stand. With no new evidence entered, the guilty verdict stood, but this time with a recommendation of mercy. He drew a life sentence and died in prison about two years later.

James Goodlet Johnson, who has been described as a "one-man band," wrote several songs, including, "Papa, Please Buy Me an Airship" and "The Sharon Tragedy," which were recorded for Columbia Records. Johnson's daughter, Nell J. Ramsey, has provided the lyrics here of "The Sharon Tragedy" and her father's ballad entitled "Depression."

The Sharon Tragedy

In a town named Sharon in the State of SC,
Lived a schoolteacher, She was sweet as could be.
She taught in the week time, On Sunday she'd sing.
The name of this teacher was Faye Wilson King.
One day she was murdered, in Nineteen-twenty-nine.
Rafe King, her husband, was accused of the Crime.

McCorkle, the Coroner, Held the inquest.
Fred Quinn, the Sheriff, made the arrest.
They brought him to York and placed him in jail.
Three thousand dollars was the amount of the bail.

King has seven lawyers; for him they made plea,
To find him not guilty and let him go free.
King claimed he was ailing all day in his bed;
But in an old outhouse, they found his wife dead.

Just how it all happened, God only knows.
King must have been guilty by the blood on his clothes.
Judge Henry of Chester was the Judge at the trial.
When the jury said guilty, King sat there and smiled.

In the courthouse at Chester, in the month of July,
Judge Henry told Rafe King, For this crime he must die.
He was placed in the death house, stayed there awhile,
Supreme Court granted a new trial.

He was tried in Lancaster for killing his wife,
King was committed and sentenced for life.
Just like all our criminals, King, He looked proud
They dressed him in overalls, and clipped off his hair.
Kings number now is 28758,
Beginning his life term to work for the State.

DEPRESSION

This whole wide world's in Trouble, and don't know what to do.
The depressions on—We are all in debt, and don't know who is who.

Ten million people out of work in the good ole USA;
But the Good Book says we should not faint, but always watch and pray.

Chorus
Good bye to the Ole Depression, when we all change our way.
Get on our knees, ask God to help us and to guide us each day.
Be ye kind to one another, love thy neighbor as thyself,
That's the only way that God will ever help us, and put the depression on the shelf.

The South of 1929 was beginning to reel under the burden of drought, financial catastrophe, social deterioration, and infestation of the boll weevil. Many would see their farms wither, their livelihood wilt, and in their helplessness they welcomed anything that might break the monotony and take their mind off their immediate problems. The murder of Faye Wilson King by her husband, Rafe, played out before the people of Western York like a grand theatrical production. It seemed as though the whole countryside had become a stage and the tragedy that swirled over it caught up every spectator and made them an important player. It was a perfect classic tragedy involving symbols of innocent beauty and villainous arrogance, and for a time it allowed the people a brief escape from the events that made them feel so helpless. Rafe King became a symbol for all that was out of control in the world, of dark forces that engulf and destroy innocent people. The murder of Faye Wilson King explained a lot of things to the people of Western York County.

11. The Road from Tokyo to the Horizon

War again began engulfing much of the world in the late 1930s and, for the United States, December 7, 1941, was "a date that will live in infamy." Swept away were discussions about President Franklin D. Roosevelt's decision to seek a third term, the struggling cotton crops, and the new buildings that had been constructed under F.D.R.'s New Deal programs. Now, the nation mobilized for the great crusade of World War II. Western York County's people enlisted in the cause and served honorably in uniform and on the homefront.

World War II became what General Dwight Eisenhower called "a great crusade." Some of the warriors paid the ultimate price in defense of freedom. In York, Marine Joe Keever was listed as missing in action during the summer of 1942. The *Yorkville Enquirer* published the sad news in its July 23 edition, with a photograph of the young marine, and a large above-the-fold sketch of Uncle Sam pointing at the reader proclaiming "York's number one has paid the price! What are you doing for Joe's sacrifice? Buy U.S. Bonds and stamps today!"

The men of Western York County, like their forebears of the Revolutionary era, enlisted to take Joe Keever's place. On the homefront, men who did not serve overseas often enlisted in the South Carolina Defense Force, a regiment of home guards. Women sold war bonds, prepared supplies for their loved ones in the Pacific and European Theaters, filled in the vacant positions in local textile mills, kept the farms of Hickory Grove producing Victory Gardens, and actively attempted to contribute to "the great crusade"—even while living with ration coupons.

The local newspaper, the *Yorkville Enquirer*, cheered on the men in uniform, publishing photographs of sailors, airmen, and soldiers stationed in places far away from Smyrna and Sharon. And when the missing, like Joe Keever, were declared dead, the *Enquirer* announced the demise of these heroes who had courageously fallen in America's struggle with dictators like Hitler and Tojo.

By early 1945, it became apparent that the tide of war was shifting in America's favor. Families eagerly awaited news and feared telegrams that announced the missing servicemen. James J. Hill, son of Mr. and Mrs. W.L. Hill Sr. of Sharon, served in the United States Navy during World War II and was on the

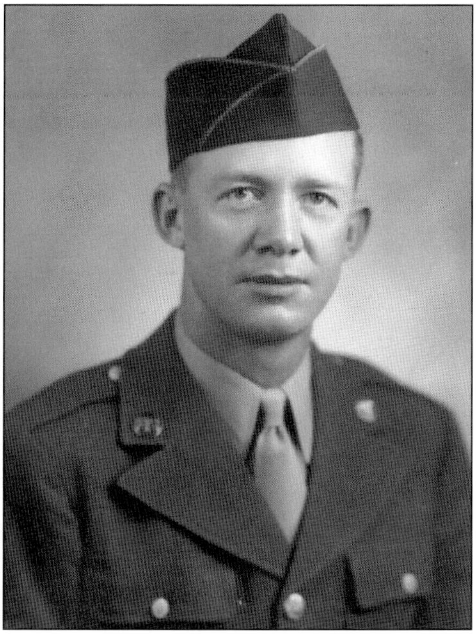 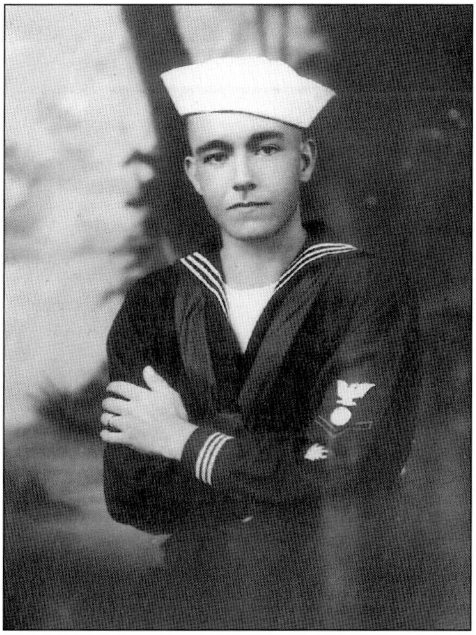

Many men in Western York County answered their country's call for service in World War II, such as Thomas Jackson Caldwell (at left) and Lee Plexico, of the Hoodtown community (at right).

USS *Missoula*, which took part in the invasion of Japan's strongholds in Eniwetok and Siapan. On March 24, 1945, he wrote the following from aboard the *Missoula*:

> Dear Folks: It has been awhile since I have had a chance to write—I have been so busy. I have been to Eniwetok and Siapan and was in the invasion of Iwo Jima the 19th of February. As you probably know from reading the papers it was the 2nd largest operation of it kind in the Pacific. It is a small but strategic island, five by three miles approximately and only about 100 miles from Tokyo. It was a furious battle event though our planes bombed it for 70 days in succession before D-Day. During the first two days of the invasions the battleships alone expended 8,000 tons of shells. We had beautiful weather the day of the landing. We couldn't have hoped for any better because the water there is usually rough. Our casualties in the end ran high. We had more than 4,000 dead and three times that number injured.
>
> Our battleships pounded away day and night. We were close to the beach and could see the Marines, tanks, and other equipment moving. Our planes were constantly bombing and firing rockets on the Jap positions but it didn't seem to do much good. The Japs continued to fire. You can say one thing for the Japs—they will not give up no matter how great the forces are against them. The noise of the bombing, the

rockets, and battleships was at time terrific. The one thing that will stop the Japs is the flame thrower.

On D plus 4 the Marines we brought over raised our flag, which came from the *Missoula*, on Mount Suribachi the highest point on the island, top of the volcano.

Two casualties that had been sent back to the ship for treatment mingled with a boat load of other Marines going to the beach and slipped back ashore. I suppose they wanted to stay with their units.

For several days we did not have regular meals, just coffee and sandwiches whenever we could get them.

They have a good radio system out here. They make it as much like home as possible—lots of music, war news and news of the states. The station at Guam announces itself—"This is station AEP at Guam, on the road to Tokyo."

Sometimes I listen to the Tokyo radio. Of course they have their special propaganda program for us. "Tokyo Rose" is their star. She has a very pleasing voice, talks convincingly and plays the latest American records for us. Before the invasion she said in one of her programs that the 5th Marines would never land on Iwo.

I am sending you a few news write ups from "Yank" about Iwo Jima. Maybe you will find them interesting.

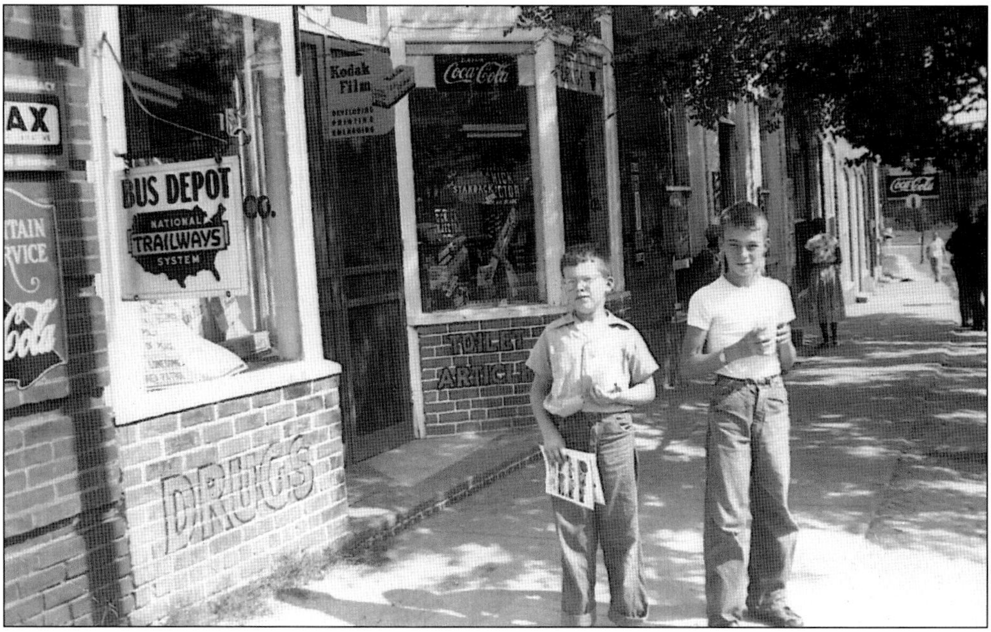

When Sharon had shady, tree-lined streets, Sim's Drugstore was a favorite stop for a comic book or fountain coke. In 1952, Hugh Sherer and Henry "Sonny" Sharp made one of those fun stops.

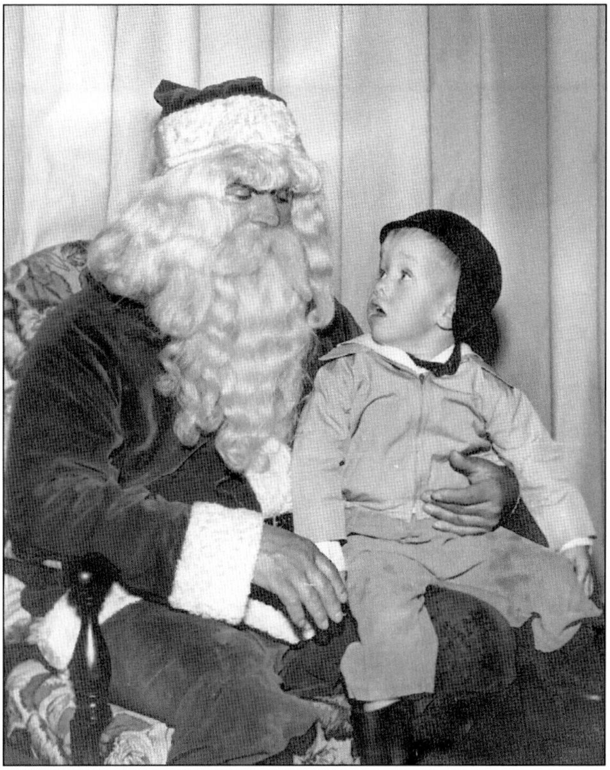

York's Bill Caldwell sizes up Santa Claus in this 1948 photograph.

> Our mail gets slightly jazzed up now and then. But considering the moving about we do I guess the mail service is pretty good. Air mail reaches us in 8 to 10 days sometimes. Regular mail is slow, especially newspapers. I am now reading December and January *Yorkville Enquirers*.
>
> For quite awhile I stood supervisor mid-watches (midnight to 4 a.m.) when the ship was underway. The Navigator and Executive Officer took the other night hours, but now the Jr. officers have learned enough to take over by themselves and it is certainly a relief and I have more time to give to my other duties. This is all for now. Love, Jas. J.

The returning veterans brought with them a wider view of the world. They had ventured far from the waterways of Western York County to the Rhine and they had glimpsed the horrors of Adolph Hitler's death camps. America's triumphant warriors, black and white, helped guide Western York County past the tumult of social and political change.

Women, who had assumed their husbands' places in York's textile mills or in Blairsville's fields, now raised young families, instilling in a new generation the same values which had caused so many people to make sacrifices in the battlefields of France and the seas of the South Pacific.

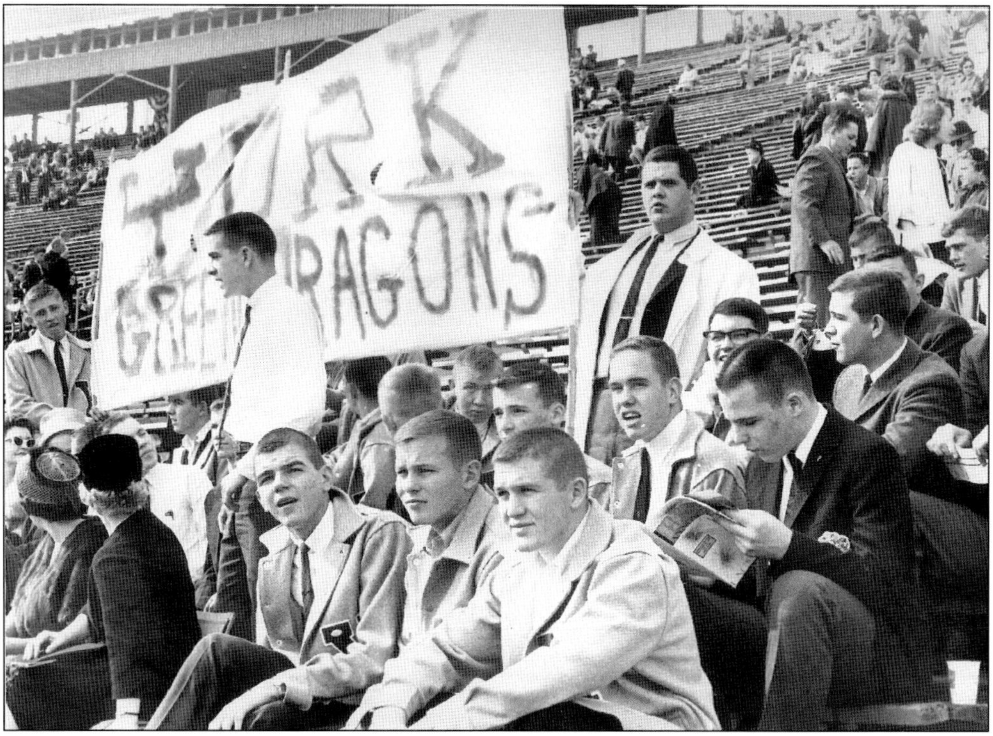

These York High School athletes are pictured at the Gator Bowl in 1964.

The post-war years brought change to Western York County. Schools were consolidated in the late 1950s and integrated during the 1960s. Black and white children who had always played together now learned together in the same classrooms. Disappearing were the "White Only" and "Colored" signs that had drawn a color line across the South for so many years. There would be, however, racial tensions. When the schools were consolidated, it was decided to keep the old school's colors to appease old community loyalties. The basketball team was known as the Blue Devils, for the all-black Jefferson School; the baseball team was the Cardinals for Sharon–Hickory Grove; and the football team was the Green Dragons, York's old colors. Rather than appeasement, inter-school rivalries were created by old loyalties. When the decision was made to discard the old school colors of all three schools for an entirely new set of colors, allegiance to the old mascots and colors generated heated discussions among the adults and fights among the youth.

The chaos of the 1960s and 1970s, with the unpopular war in Southeast Asia and radically different relationships between the sexes and races, did not alter the basic tranquillity of Western York County. While school integration did produce tension between black and white students in the early 1970s, the pupils and their parents accepted the end of segregation and a diverse educational system that has become noted for its excellence.

By 1980, the silver-and-black cougar mascot was widely accepted and the various communities were attempting to resolve racial problems that had lingered from slavery. African Americans such as state representative Juanita Goggins, a former York teacher, won a legislative seat in 1976 for a portion of Western York County. Other black leaders gained positions on local councils and boards.

At the height of the Women's Movement, Sharon displayed its progressive thinking when, in 1975, the people elected their first female mayor, Sarah Latham Harris. In 1978, Nancy Scronce was elected to a seat on the town council, serving under Mayor Harris. After seven years on the council, she was elected mayor in 1985 and served eight consecutive terms. In nearby Hickory Grove, Leila Thomas Moss became the first woman to sit on that town's council in 1991. She completed the term left by the death of her husband.

Politics in Western York County have always been hard fought and sometimes brutal. As we have seen, some citizens spoke out against secession on the eve of the Civil War. And, during the Reconstruction era, Democrats and Republicans battled over power—even when Union troops were stationed at York's Rose

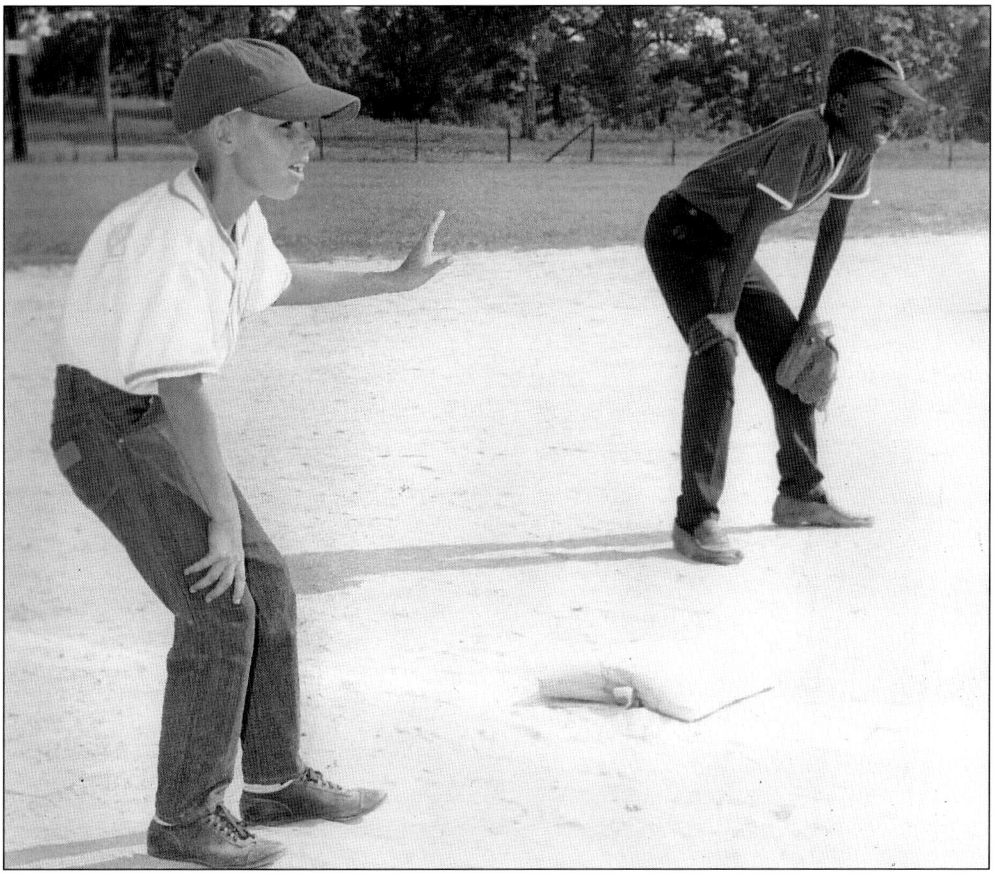

By the 1970s, integrated athletic teams competed across Western York County.

Hotel to maintain order and to subdue the Ku Klux Klan. After Wade Hampton "redeemed" the state for the Democrats in 1876, Republicans clung to the coattails of their national patronage system, seeking appointments to postmasterships and other offices.

In the 1930s, when Republicans were attempting to make a comeback in York County, the few party members were led by Carl Hambright and they were known as "Hambrighters." It was, however, nearly 50 years before the county and the state became known as a Republican stronghold. Beginning in the late 1970s, and believing that the Democratic Party had deserted its conservative moorings and that the Republican Party had lost its radicalism, many formerly Democrat families switched over to the Republican Party. Often times, these new party members would agree that had their parents and grandparents known of their political leanings, "they would turn over in their graves."

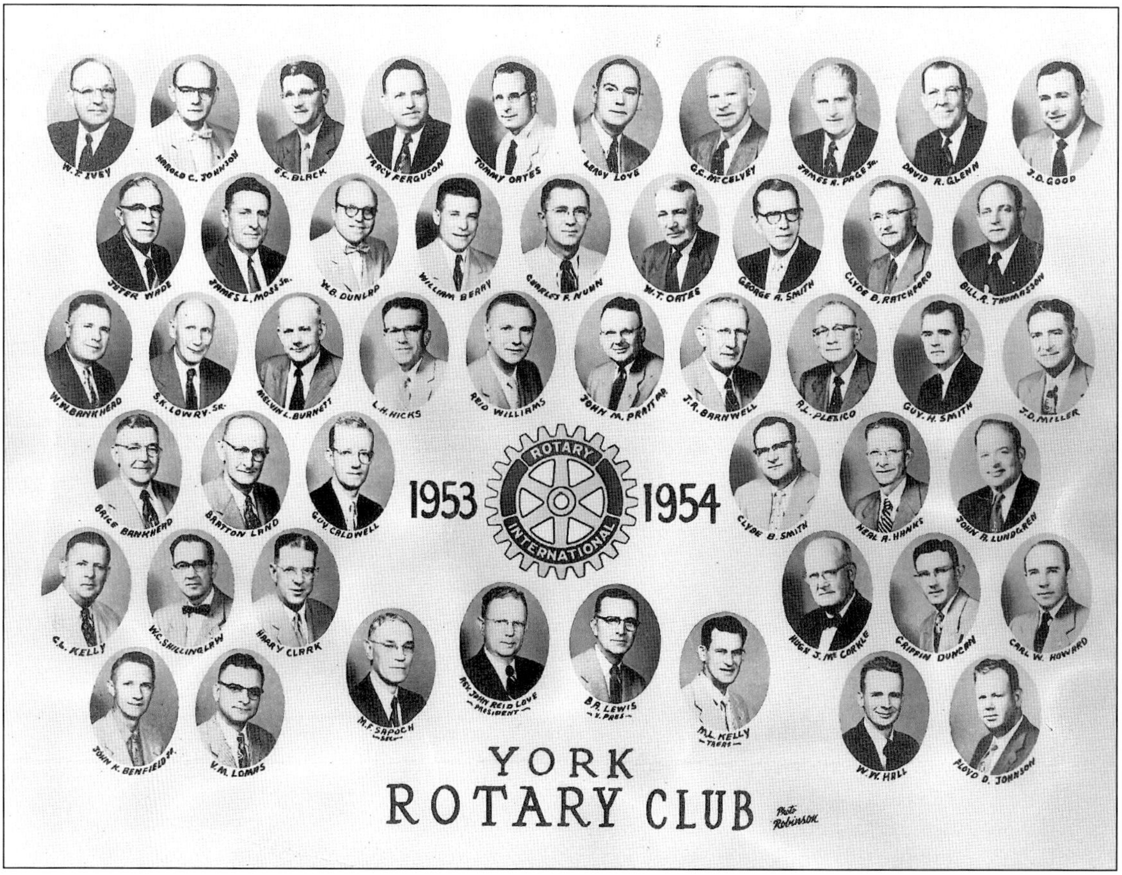

As in many towns across America, the Rotary Club serves an assembly of business, educational, and civic leaders. A decade after its founding, the 1953–1954 York Rotary Club included some of Western York County's most prominent citizens.

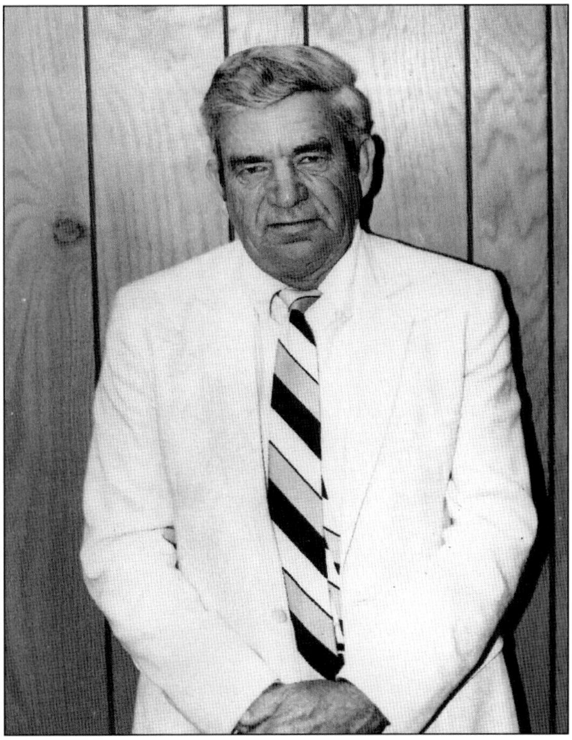

York County Councilman J.B. Comer was a favorite representative among his constituents and an intricate part of the family's political service to Western York County.

But in the former days, Democrats remained potent in Western York County—even when civil rights and the Vietnam War damaged their national reputation. The Democrats would often fight among themselves, but they rarely had serious Republican opposition for Western York County's seat in the county governing board. For example, in 1980, J.B. Comer of Hickory Grove ousted E.C. Black from the county commission. Both men were Democrats. Comer won reelection in 1986 over Harold Dickson and in 1988 over two other challengers. All of these contests were among Democrats. When Comer died in November 1990, shortly after winning another term on the York County Council, Republican Governor Carroll Campbell appointed one of Comer's daughters, Jane C. Gilfillan, to the office. Her appointment was secured on the agreement that she could not run in the next election. Gilfillan served until the election in 1992, when Harold Dickson of York was elected. Gilfillan returned to the campaign trail in 1994, defeating Dickson and write-in candidate Richard Bolin of Sharon. Bolin again challenged incumbent Gilfillan as a Republican in 1996, but she defeated her challenger substantially. She was unopposed in 1998, but in 2000, Bolin resumed his bid for District 3 as a Democrat in the primary. Again, defeating Bolin, she was then challenged by Tommy Robbins, a write-in from Hickory Grove. Gilfillan's resilience as a viable candidate in the county's political scene has been proven over the years.

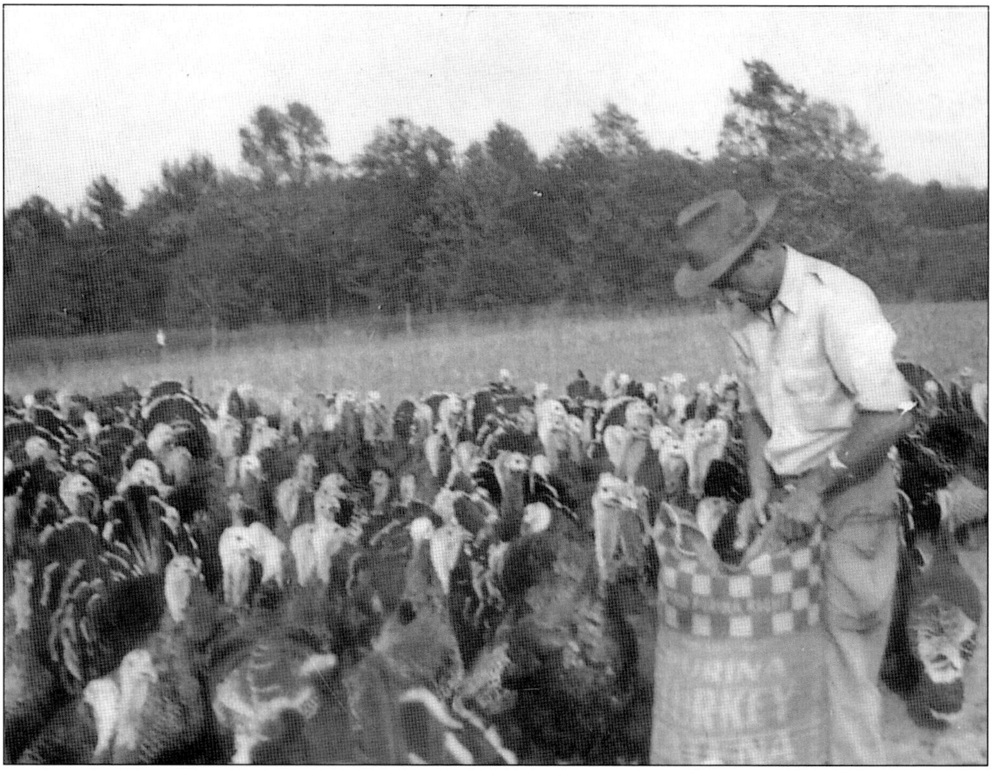

Turkey farms were prevalent in York County in the last half of the 1940s. On his Blairsville farm in 1948, Frank Duncan raised a hundred bronze turkeys for the growing market.

The Comer family of Western York County has successfully built a family tradition in the field of politics. Their political history began in the county elections of November 1938, when Fred A. Comer (Jane C. Gilfillan's grandfather) defeated L.T. Dowdle for Bullock's Creek Township commissioner. In January of the following year, Commissioner Comer proved his honesty and integrity when he reported that a truck dealer had offered him a kick-back if he would buy a vehicle from him for the township. Comer told the *Yorkville Enquirer*, "I turned him down . . . I am signing no voucher or pay warrants against York County or Bullock's Creek Township for anybody or anything until I have inquired into the merits of that claim . . . We only have about $3,400 from ordinary funds and I am going to honestly try to make it go as far as it will on roads . . . As a commissioner, I propose to inquire into the merits of claims having to do not only with Bullock's Creek Township, but all of York County."

Elected in 1949 to the office of magistrate for both Broad River and Bullock's Creek Townships, Fred Comer served the people of the townships until his death in February 1963. At that time, Governor Donald Russell appointed Comer's son, Hugh, to fill his father's seventh term. Hugh Comer served in that capacity until 1992, when he retired from office. Melvin Howell, husband of Dianne Comer

Howell, and son-in-law of Councilman J.B. Comer, was then elected magistrate and has remained unopposed in that capacity ever since. From the time of Fred Comer's election to township commissioner in 1938 to the present day, with Melvin Howell sitting on the magistrate bench and Jane Gilfillan occupying the seat of District 3, the Comer family has served Western York County with dedication for more than 60 years.

While some things in Western York County seem frozen in time (such as battle reenactments at Kings Mountain, favorite family recipes shared at reunions, and love of the church where one grew up), change is visible, on a clear day, just over the horizon. Development is affecting Western York County just like it is encroaching on all such rural paradises. Employment opportunities take citizens along interstate highways leading to Charlotte, North Carolina, Gastonia, North Carolina, and Spartanburg, South Carolina.

York's main thoroughfare, Highway 5, is an ancient road that transverses the county, entering the city as Liberty Street. Now, at the dawn of a new century, Highway 5 is being widened to four lanes from Rock Hill to York. This construction will bring Rock Hill and Interstate 77 closer to York. On the other

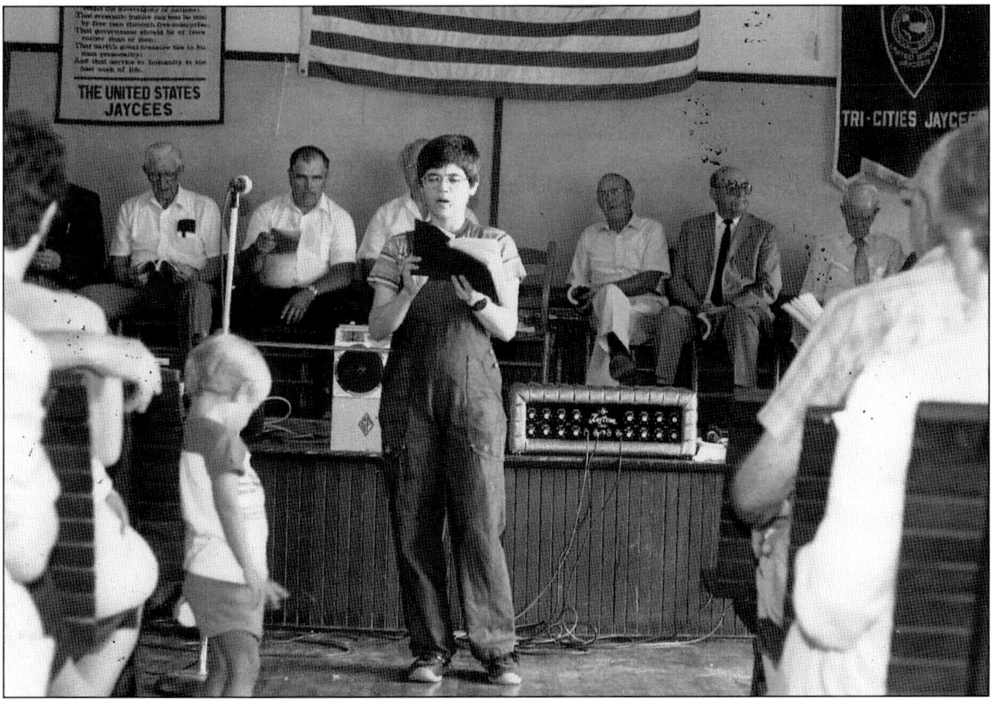

Hopewell's annual singing and beef hash celebration is reported to be over an 80-year-old tradition. August singings and picnics have been held on the site since 1895. "Hopewell Day" evolved out of a singing school that lasted for a week every year and ended with a day-long singing and picnic. While there were other such events across the county, Hopewell Day is the only event that preserves this part of an earlier culture.

side of Western York County, Highway 5 will be widened and will open a new corridor into Sharon, Hickory Grove, and Smyrna. Farms are being left fallow as the sons and daughters of farmers travel to North Carolina cities for employment. Dirt roads, the old farm-to-market transportation system of the 1880s, have virtually become extinct. In their places are highways and modern interstates that carry a new generation to places their parents considered distant and too hard to reach. Jobs and leisure activities are sought for in urban areas like Charlotte, whereas a century ago, they would have been found closer to home and nearer to the land of their birth.

Festivals have come and gone. York's Colonial Days evolved into the Grape Festival of the 1960s and 1970s and now the Summerfest of each August. Students still attend elementary school in Sharon and Hickory Grove but, by middle school, they learn beside their York cousins using the latest technology including the Internet. Customers can shop at Howell's Furniture Store or Smyrna's Whitesides Company or they can venture to York's Super Wal-Mart or the malls of Charlotte. The Cotton Kingdom has been dethroned by a mobile society, prepared, at a moment's notice, to drive across state and county lines to shop, to be entertained, and to work.

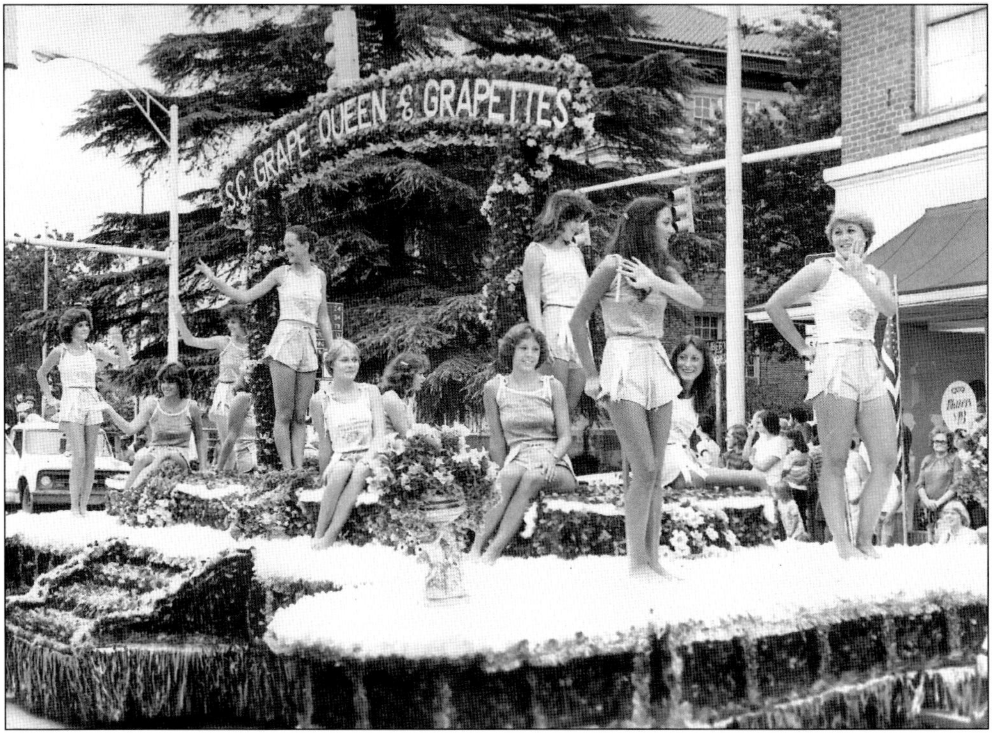

During the 1960s heyday of grape production in York County, the town of York instituted the Grape Festival. When grape production fell to the wayside, Summerfest replaced the Grape Festival and has become one of the state's highest-attended events of the year.

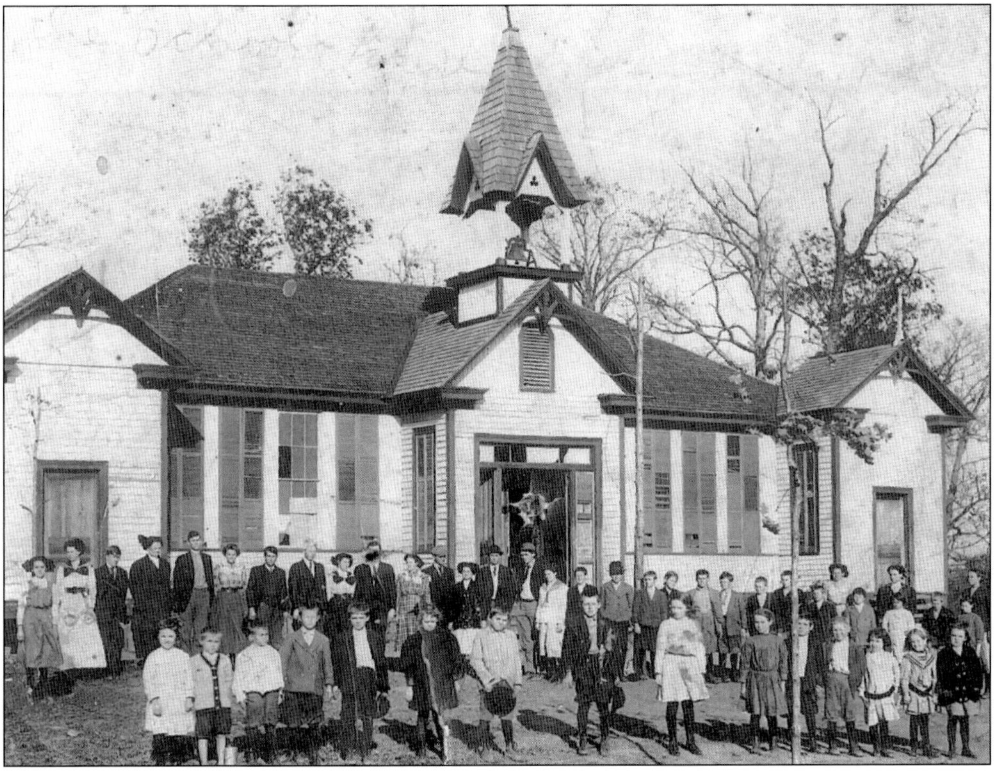

These students pose for a photograph in front of McConnellsville School c. *1910.*

Still, there is about Western York County the intangible attraction which, in 1941, brought Hollywood's Tallulah Bankhead "home" to Bullock's Creek. This Southern Eden was built by men and women of hardy stock with a sturdy genetic composition. They knew the meaning of hard work and did not shy away from it. Thus, their descendants know, instinctively, the nature of this special place and they speak of the beauty often—even as change awaits just over the horizon.

Change is inevitable—even in this Southern Eden of Western York County. The communities of York, Hickory Grove, Smyrna, Sharon, and McConnells are about to be changed in ways that the early settlers, their Catawba neighbors, or even residents 15 years ago could never have imagined. Take McConnells, for instance. The town was incorporated as "McConnellsville" in 1906. The "ville" was deleted in 1915. For several decades, social life revolved around churches such as Olivet Presbyterian, or the general stores run by Harshaws and Williams. The pace was leisurely, slow, and friendly. Neighbors helped neighbors and families more or less remained in place, never moving away from the red soil of their ancestors.

Now, the residents of McConnells have become more mobile, speeding each morning to jobs miles away in Rock Hill or Charlotte, returning home to sleep. Its population has become pluralistic and increased from 171 in 1980 to 321 over 20 years later. Now, McConnells is seeing fundamental change. Presently,

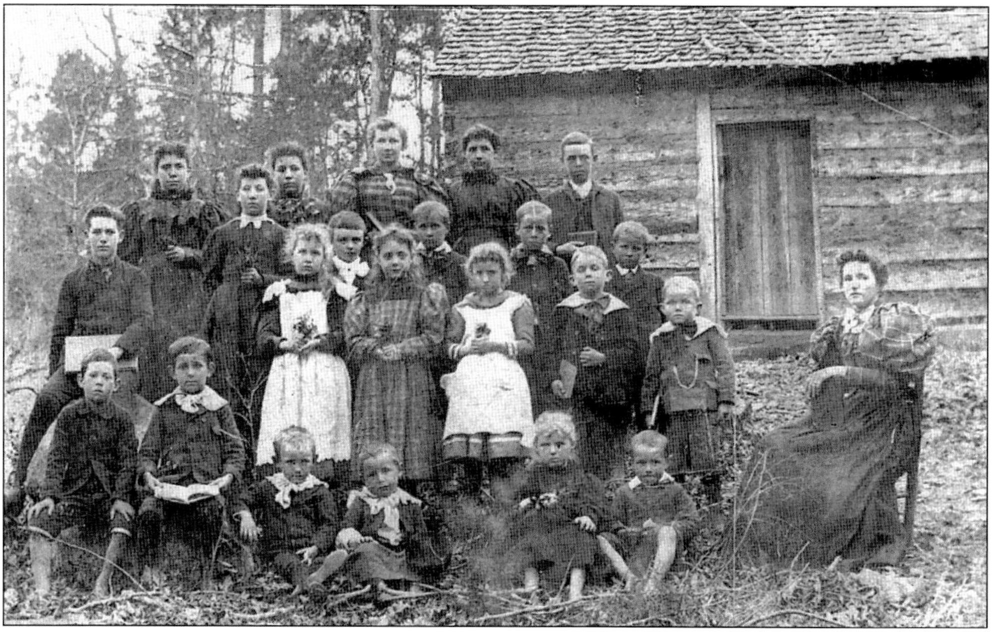

Victoria Sanders and her students gather at Sandersville's one-room schoolhouse in this 1895 photograph. Sandersville, now a defunct community, was located on the York–Chester County line on the Susie Bowl Creek.

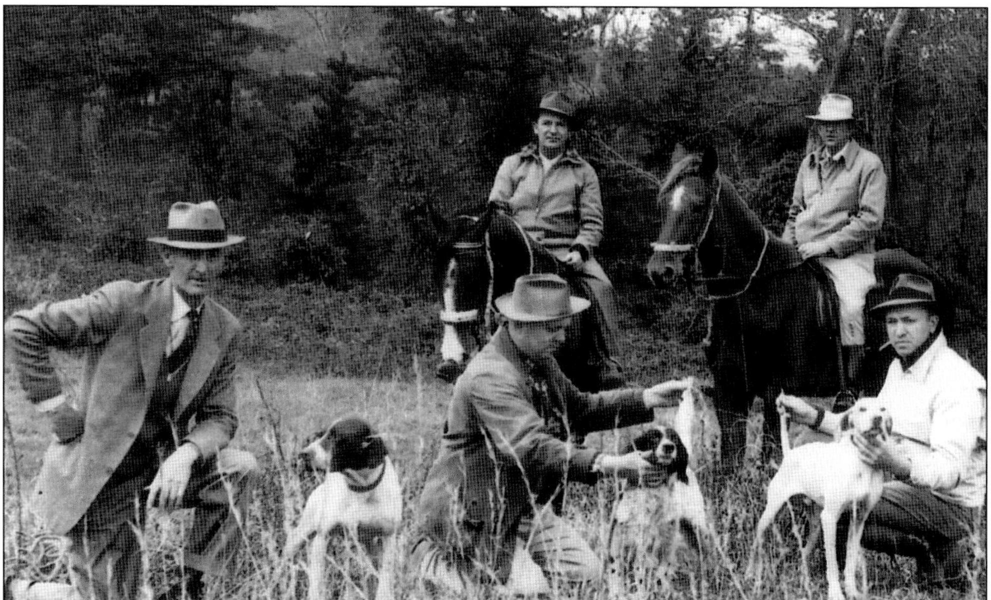

Field trials during the mid-1900s were a favorite pastime for outdoorsmen of Western York County. Images like these remind today's readers of the pastoral beauty and rural nature of Western York County.

a 30-lot subdivision is being developed within the limits of the tiny town. There "new county" is joining with "old county" in the church pews, ball games, and the two convenience stores, bringing new ideas and talents which will transform communities like McConnells and Hickory Grove forever.

In nearby York, the population is similarly on the rise. Highway projects are speeding access to interstate arteries and each morning folks make their way from Liberty Street and Madison Avenue to jobs in Gastonia and Rock Hill. People choose to live in York and Sharon, but they often work elsewhere—they love the land but they are not married to the land. Gradually, the area's farms and open lands are being overrun by industrial parks like the York Industrial Park, which features a number of international companies. And York's population has zoomed from 6,412 residents in 1980 to nearly 9,000 today—more people, more traffic, more challenges, and more opportunities lie just over the horizon.

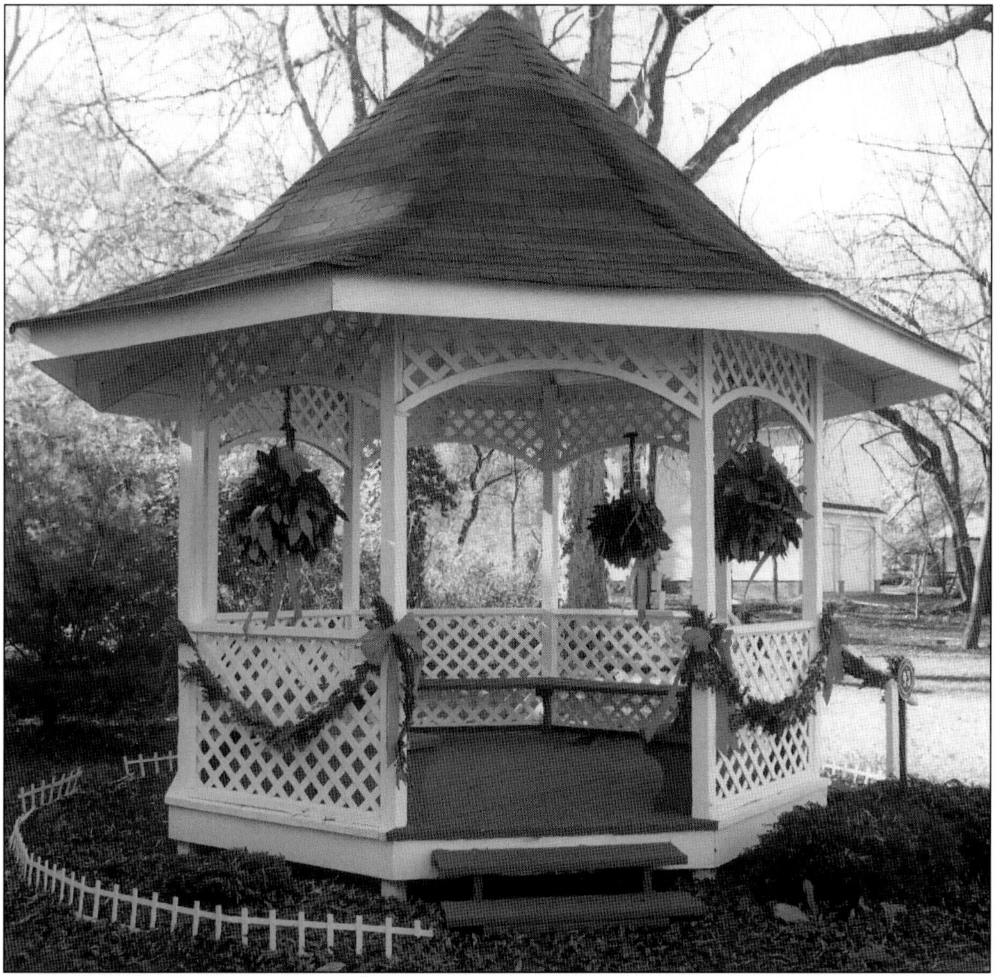

Each Christmas, York's Moore Park and its gazebo are decked out in wreaths and ornaments celebrating the holiday season.

Bibliography Essay

While Western York County is an ancient place, the literature on the area is modest. In our book, we mined the resources of the Historical Center of York County, the White Homestead, the Catawba Indian Nation, and the Winthrop University Archives. Primary sources abound in each of these repositories and we suggest them as starting places for researchers interested in the region.

The Broad River Basin Historical Society and its quarterly publication, the *Broad River Notebook*, regularly document the rich history of Western York County. The *Notebook* has been published for a decade and is edited by Jerry West, the author of *Sharon: The First Fifty Years*. The Society has sponsored a number of other publications including *Settling the Old Account*, *York District 1868 Voters Registration*, *Revolutionary War in the Upcountry of South Carolina*, and *The 1850 Federal Census of Union County, SC*.

For information on the county seat of York, Edward Lee's *Yorkville to York*, an award-winning book published in 1998 by Taylor Publishing Company, is an excellent source as are church histories with the stories of various Presbyterian, Associate Reformed Presbyterian, Methodist, and Baptist churches. One of the best of these books is William White's *First Presbyterian Church of York* (Josten's, 1993).

A word must be said about the *Yorkville Enquirer*, one of South Carolina's oldest newspapers. This publication has, for more than 150 years, reported on Western York County events, including political battles, weddings, funerals, and economic happenings. The *Enquirer* is an invaluable resource, as are the people themselves of the region, many of whom we interviewed for *York and Western York County: The Story of a Southern Eden*.

INDEX